ANTHROPOLOGICAL PAPERS OF
THE UNIVERSITY OF ARIZONA
NUMBER 74

Burnt Corn Pueblo

Conflict and Conflagration in the Galisteo Basin A.D. 1250–1325

James E. Snead and Mark W. Allen,
Editors

CONTRIBUTORS

Elizabeth Baker Brite
Leslie Cohen
Gregory Greene
Genevieve Head
Phillip Leckman
Lori Barkwill Love
Marit K. Munson
Monica Smith
Anthony J. Thibodeau

THE UNIVERSITY OF ARIZONA PRESS
TUCSON
2011

About the Editors

JAMES E. SNEAD was raised in Santa Fe, New Mexico, receiving his BA from Beloit College and Ph.D. from UCLA in 1995. He began archaeological fieldwork in the Southwest in 1989 as an employee of the National Park Service at Bandelier National Monument. The results of his dissertation and several postdoctoral field seasons were published as *Ancestral Pueblo Landscapes* (University of Arizona Press, 2008). He continues to conduct archaeological field research, focusing on the study of cultural landscapes, evident most recently in an edited volume, *Landscapes of Movement; The Anthropology of Roads, Paths, and Trails* (University of Pennsylvania Museum Press, 2009, with Clark Erickson and J. Andrew Darling). Snead's 2001 book *Ruins and Rivals: The Making of Southwest Archaeology* (University of Arizona Press) remains in print. Funding sources for his various projects include the National Science Foundation and the Wenner-Gren Foundation for Anthropological Research. After 11 years at George Mason University in Fairfax, Virginia, he joined the anthropology faculty at California State University–Northridge in August 2011.

MARK W. ALLEN earned his Ph.D. in anthropology at UCLA in 1994. He has taught at UCLA and Pomona College, and is currently Professor of Anthropology at California State Polytechnic University, Pomona. Previous employment includes stints at the Center for American Archeology in Kampsville, Illinois, and the United States Army's National Training Center at Fort Irwin in the Mojave Desert of California. His regional interests include the archaeology of California, the Great Basin, and the Pacific Islands. In particular, he focuses on cultural ecology, political economy, prehistoric warfare, landscape archaeology, and cultural resource management. He is co-editor of *The Archaeology of Warfare: Prehistories of Raiding and Conquest* (with Elizabeth Arkush, University Press of Florida, 2006) and has authored and co-authored numerous articles, chapters, and reports on archaeological research in Kentucky, Illinois, California, Guatemala, New Zealand, Hawaii, and New Mexico. He is past president of the Society for California Archaeology.

THE UNIVERSITY OF ARIZONA PRESS
© 2011 The Arizona Board of Regents
All Rights Reserved

www.uapress.arizona.edu

Library of Congress Cataloging-in-Publication Data

Burnt corn pueblo : conflict and conflagration in the Galisteo basin, A.D. 1250-1325 / James E. Snead and Mark W. Allen, editors.
    p. cm. — (Anthropological papers of the University of Arizona ; number 74)
    Includes bibliographical references and index.
    ISBN 978-0-8165-2949-0 (pbk. : alk. paper)
1. Pueblo Indians—New Mexico—Galisteo Region—Antiquities. 2. Excavations (Archaeology)—New Mexico—Galisteo Region. 3. Social archaeology—New Mexico—Galisteo Region. 4. Galisteo Region (N.M.)—Antiquities. I. Snead, James E. (James Elliott), 1962- II. Allen, Mark W.
E99.P9B93 2011
972'.01—dc23

2011027780

Manufactured in the United States of America on acid-free, archival-quality paper processed chlorine free.

17 16 15 14 13 12 11   6 5 4 3 2 1

Contributors:

Elizabeth Baker Brite
    Department of Anthropology
    University of California, Los Angeles

Leslie Cohen
    Maxwell Museum of Anthropology
    University of New Mexico

Gregory Greene
    Department of Forest Sciences
    University of British Columbia
    Vancouver, Canada

Genevieve Head
    Cabezon Consulting
    Santa Fe, New Mexico

Phillip Leckman
    School of Anthropology
    University of Arizona, Tucson

Lori Barkwill Love
    Department of Anthropology
    University of Texas, San Antonio

Marit K. Munson
    Department of Anthropology
    Trent University
    Peterborough, Ontario, Canada

Monica L. Smith
    Department of Anthropology
    University of California, Los Angeles

Anthony J. Thibodeau
    Museum of Indian Arts and Cultures/
    Laboratory of Anthropology
    Santa Fe, New Mexico

Cover: The Burnt Corn plaza pueblo (Structure 2) under excavation in 2005. Photograph by James E. Snead.

Contents

FIGURES

TABLES

Preface

The Galisteo Basin of northern New Mexico is one of the most celebrated archaeological districts of the American Southwest. A region only 16 km by 19 km in size contains the remains of several large villages of the late precolumbian era set within an intricate ancestral Pueblo landscape marked by petroglyphs, fields, and farmsteads. Nels Nelson inaugurated archaeological research in the Galisteo Basin in 1912, establishing a widely recognized benchmark for field research. In the century since, the Galisteo Basin has been seen as an ideal place to study issues of central importance to the archaeology of the Pueblo people, in particular migration and conflict.

The prominence of the Galisteo Basin in Southwestern prehistory, however, has not been matched by published discussions of its archaeology. Nelson's report on his research (1914) remains the only full-length study on the subject to appear in print, and information on the region is largely found in the gray literature. Archaeological fieldwork in the region has been sporadic, in part due to the predominance of private land in the basin, and this has limited opportunities for long-range research. Ironically, then, the Galisteo Basin remains poorly understood despite its promise for archaeological study

This volume is designed to bring current fieldwork in the Galisteo Basin to the attention of the Southwestern archaeological community so that new information can be applied to broader concerns in the study of the region's history. The data presented in this monograph were collected during the Tano Origins Project, a multiyear program of survey, excavation, and collections study funded, most recently, by the National Science Foundation. The focus of the project has been Burnt Corn Pueblo, a community founded in the western Galisteo Basin in the late thirteenth century A.D. Burnt Corn Pueblo was one of the principal villages of its time, and investigation of the site now provides an opportunity to look at the region at the critical juncture between the early phase of Pueblo settlement and the dramatic growth of the large, late communities encountered by the Spaniards.

Our work at Burnt Corn Pueblo and nearby sites in the surrounding landscape makes it clear that the end of the thirteenth century A.D. in the Galisteo Basin was marked by significant competition and conflict that we define as a specific crisis bounded in space and time. Burnt Corn Pueblo was destroyed by fire sometime after A.D. 1302, as were farmsteads in the surrounding community and farther afield. Burnt Corn Pueblo was thus established and destroyed within the course of a generation, and this provides a remarkable archaeological opportunity to examine conflict. The contextual information provided by our work here and elsewhere promises both to illuminate the situation in this particular place and time and to supply essential evidence to support theoretical approaches to conflict and population movement that are needed to advance archaeological understanding of the past.

Burnt Corn Pueblo is based on five field seasons of archaeological research in the Western Galisteo Basin beginning in 2000. Our multiscalar effort includes excavation at Burnt Corn Pueblo itself in 2002 and 2005; at Cholla House and Slope House, two farmsteads in the surrounding community, in 2006; and at the Lodestar sites, a dispersed Pueblo community located 11 km west of Burnt Corn Pueblo, in 2005. This approach provided detailed site histories for different aspects of the communities. Unique chronological information has been generated, as have considerable data on architecture, settlement planning, and patterns of occupation. We also collected detailed evidence on the cessation of site occupation, particularly destruction by fire, a process identified in nearly all of the locations we investigated. Our excavated collections from these sites represent a rare body of evidence collected under tightly controlled conditions.

Our excavation data are complemented by considerable data from archaeological survey, with more than 700 ha of land in the Burnt Corn and Petroglyph Hill region surveyed to date. We are thus able to discuss general patterns of land use and landscape organization in the western Galisteo Basin through time, and to provide a detailed evaluation of specific elements of these landscapes. This body of information is presently unique in the Galisteo context.

A program of collections and archival research that has taken advantage of the vast body of unpublished information available for Galisteo Basin archaeology has augmented our fieldwork. Our research on ceramics from Burnt Corn Pueblo and Lodestar, in particular, has been advanced by comparative examination of materials excavated from nearby sites throughout the twentieth century. Additional information from field notes and other documentation of these sites provides important data for further comparison.

This volume is intended to bring new information about the Pueblo history of the Galisteo Basin to the archaeological community in a timely manner. The chapters report on work in progress, presenting overviews of the research and preliminary interpretations for wider review.

Chapter 1, Burnt Corn Pueblo and the Archaeology of the Galisteo Basin, by James E. Snead, addresses the research questions that structure the Tano Origins Project, provides an overview of the project, and establishes a context for the Pueblo history of the Galisteo Basin.

Chapter 2, Dating the Galisteo: Pueblo Settlement in Context, by James E. Snead and Anthony J. Thibodeau, presents an overview of previous tree-ring dating in the region, provides more than a dozen new unpublished tree-ring dates for the Manzanares site, reviews 60 tree-ring dates from Burnt Corn Pueblo, and discusses the region's archaeological chronology.

Chapter 3, Late Coalition Ceramics from the Galisteo Basin: Questions and Contradictions, by Lori Barkwill Love and Leslie Cohen, analyzes potsherds from the Burnt Corn Pueblo, Lodestar, and Cholla House excavations, as well as from collections from elsewhere in the Galisteo Basin, to review arguments about ceramic production and population origins in the Southwest during the thirteenth and fourteenth centuries A.D.

Chapter 4, Construction and Destruction: A Life History of Burnt Corn Pueblo, by James E. Snead, Monica L. Smith and Elizabeth Baker Brite, presents contextual information derived from the 2002 and 2005 excavations at Burnt Corn Pueblo, focusing on the chronology and architecture that shed light on the construction and destruction of the site.

Chapter 5, Archaeological Investigations of Small Sites: Lodestar, Cholla House, and Slope House, by Mark W. Allen, summarizes the excavations conducted at farmstead-size sites in the Burnt Corn community and elsewhere in the region, providing comparative evidence helpful in understanding Burnt Corn Pueblo and similar sites in the Galisteo Basin.

Chapter 6. The Burnt Corn Landscape, by Gregory Greene and Phillip Leckman, documents how archaeological survey within the Burnt Corn community has provided unique evidence about the organization of that landscape. This chapter presents specialized studies about some of the details of this area, including GIS-based analysis of the hundreds of grinding slicks and access patterns throughout the community as a whole.

Chapter 7, Surveying Petroglyph Hill: Cultural Landscapes of the Galisteo Basin, by Marit K. Munson and Genevieve N. Head, summarizes investigations at the site of Petroglyph Hill, immediately west of Burnt Corn Pueblo. Survey at Petroglyph Hill is characterized, and preliminary analysis of the 1,800 petroglyph elements recorded at Petroglyph Hill is presented. Hypotheses about the role this regional shrine played in the Galisteo landscape from the thirteenth century onward are also considered.

Chapter 8, Conflagration and Conflict, by James E. Snead and Mark W. Allen, places our initial conclusions about Burnt Corn Pueblo and the other sites under study within the broader intellectual context of conflict within the Pueblo Southwest and the human past in general.

Acknowledgments

The Tano Origins Project began in 2000 as a three-way effort to study and protect a largely unknown archaeological site in the western Galisteo Basin, Burnt Corn Pueblo (LA 359). The principals were myself, on behalf of George Mason University; Paul Williams, archaeologist in the Taos Field Office of the Bureau of Land Management; and Buck Dant, landowner and steward of Burnt Corn Pueblo. As the project unfolded literally dozens of additional archaeologists, students, volunteers, and local folks were drawn in, making it a remarkably collaborative effort.

Funding for the 2000 Cañada de la Cueva survey was provided by a small grant from the New Mexico Office of Cultural Affairs, Historic Preservation Division (NMHPD, Project No. 35-00-15334.01). At NMHPD, Jan Biella coordinated the grant process, with direct supervision courtesy of Grants Administrator Louise Stiver. Field headquarters in Santa Fe was contributed by Bill and Patty Snead. The field team was composed of the PI and volunteers drawn from several sources. These included Rachel Berry, Patrick Dietz, and Fernand Elbeze, of George Mason University; Monica Smith, of the University of Pittsburgh; Lois Lockhart, of Santa Fe; and several students from Santa Fe Community College, led by Jason Shapiro.

The 2002 excavation season at Burnt Corn Pueblo was sustained by financial support from George Mason University and the BLM. Marit Munson served as field director for the 2002 excavations, with a team that included Monica Smith, Rikki Cohen, Genevieve Head, and numerous volunteers from the local community.

In 2004 primary funding for the Tano Origins Project was obtained from the National Science Foundation, Social and Behavioral Sciences Division, Grant No. 0352702. Processing of the grant and associated logistics comes under the auspices of the Office of Sponsored Programs at George Mason University, with day-to-day liaison service provided by Karen Secrist of the Department of Sociology and Anthropology. Work in the 2004 season focused on the Petroglyph Hill Survey. In addition to the PI, the three permanent staff members of the project in this phase were Genevieve Head, Field Director; Leslie Cohen, Lab Director; and Adam Sullins, Crew Chief. Crew members included George Mason students Lillian Greenawald, Elise Kordis, and Brian Wenham; and numerous local volunteers, including Barbara Chatterjee, Gary Hein, Brent Lambert, Lois Lockwood, Martha Mace, Ruta Marchal, Toni Marks, and Joe Sneed.

The opportunity to conduct the work at Petroglyph Hill was provided by Paul Olafson of the County of Santa Fe's Open Space and Trails Program. Consultation with Design Workshop, which is preparing the management plan for the tract, is ongoing. The best roads leading to the Petroglyph Hill cross Thornton Ranch property currently being developed by the Commonweal Conservancy; Ted Harrison graciously permitted access.

The 2005 season marked a return to excavations and the beginning of a fruitful collaboration between George Mason University and the California Polytechnic University at Pomona. The Cal Poly team, led by Mark Allen, was responsible for work at Lodestar (see below), while the George Mason team worked at Burnt Corn Pueblo. This operation was led by Monica Smith (UCLA), with assistance from Elizabeth Baker (UCLA) and Lab Director Rikki Cohen. Volunteer excavators included Bill Baxter, Barbara Chatterjee, Ondine Frauenglass, Becky Gilbert, Lilly Greenawald, Gary Hein, Jill Heppenheimer, Josh Heppenheimer, Lois Lockwood, R. Marchal, Sal Morreale, L. Schub, Joe Snead, Susan Stephens, Anne Weaver, and Tess Wilkes. Bob Powers and Mike Bremer provided essential assistance at a critical stage of the operation. Visitors in the course of the field season included Kurt Anschuetz, Andy Darling, Sunday Eiselt, Tim Kohler, Steven LeBlanc, Lisa Lucero, Tim Pauketat, Sarah Schlanger, Douglas Schwartz, and the members of several tour groups. The Petroglyph Hill survey continued that summer as well, with continuity of team members from the 2004 field season. Housing was provided for the George Mason team by Hugh Nazor and for the Cal Poly team by Chuck Cambron.

The final field season under NSF sponsorship occurred in 2006. The Cal Poly crew continued excavations, working this time within the Burnt Corn community at Cholla House and Slope House, while George Mason students and local volunteers conducted site survey in the same area. Student participants including Lori Barkwill Love, Todd Brooks, Landon Yarrington, and Lindsey Vos, who in addition kept the records and laboratory in order back at George Mason. Housing for the combined team was arranged at the Santa Fe Indian School, and at the homes of Patty and Bill Snead, and Jim and Georgia Snead.

Several local institutions are close collaborators with the Tano Origins Project. These include the Laboratory of Anthropology of the Museum of Indian Arts and Cultures, which provides laboratory and office resources through its research associate program. Eric Blinman of the Office of Archaeological Studies, Museum of New Mexico (OAS), has promoted the project among his volunteers, and is a frequent consultant on matters of Galisteo archaeology. Other OAS staff who have generously contributed time and effort are Steven Post and Jessica Badner.

James E. Snead
June 2011

This project would not have been possible without the generous and often tireless assistance and contributions of many people. Their roles in the project are gratefully recognized. First and foremost, I would like to thank

Billie Russell for her hospitality during our work on Lodestar Ranch. I would also like to acknowledge the kind assistance of four representatives from the Archaeological Conservancy: Jim Walker, Tamara Stewart, Gordon Wilson, and Steve Koczan. The Conservancy kindly permitted us to undertake the work at Lodestar, and its staff was most helpful in the design of our test excavation approach. The Lodestar Sites will clearly be well cared for.

They key to a successful field project is a good and motivated crew. Fortunately, I could lean on several Cal Poly Pomona undergraduate students during the course of this project: Jose Alvarez, Peter Carey, Claudia Castro, Christopher Duran, Rebecca Gilbert, Gregory Greene, Elizabeth Joerger, and Barry Olson, Jr. We were also joined by several other folks who kindly volunteered their brains and muscles during the fieldwork: Nancy Allen, Rikki Cohen, Mariel Tribby, Lilly Greenawald, and Elizabeth Baker. Steve Post provided invaluable insight, and kindly let us borrow an auger. The field crew at Cholla and Slope Houses consisted of students from both Cal Poly Pomona (Gregory Burns, Laura Cowie, Naoma Staley) and George Mason University (Lorie Barkwill Love, Landon Yarrington, Lindsey Vos, Nichole Newsome, and Todd Brooks). The BLM and local landowners are thanked for access to the sites. Gregory Greene produced the maps for both project areas. Rebecca Gilbert did the majority of the lithics analysis, and Lori Barkwell Love produced the ceramic analysis (see Chapter 3, this volume).

Mark W. Allen
June 2011

CHAPTER ONE

Burnt Corn Pueblo and the Archaeology of the Galisteo Basin

James E. Snead

Burnt Corn Pueblo lies down a long trail in the western Galisteo Basin of New Mexico. Along the way the path crosses open meadows that flower in wet years and passes by skeletal piñon pines that have died in the recent bark beetle infestation promoted by drought. Gravelly slopes and sharply-cut arroyos frame crumbling basalt summits along the near horizon. A wider view from the path takes in a landscape that includes the green uplands of Glorieta Mesa at the eastern limits of the Basin, the grassy lowlands along the Galisteo Creek, and the turquoise-bearing Cerrillos Hills to the west (Fig. 1.1).

Walking through this dramatic landscape is a fitting introduction to Burnt Corn Pueblo and its place in the indigenous history of the northern Rio Grande. Until recently the site was one of the many forgotten pieces of ancient life in a region where precolumbian pueblos of a thousand rooms or more are common and the legacy of archaeological research is deep. The limited archaeological notes about Burnt Corn Pueblo described telltale signs of catastrophe, in particular the charred kernels of corn scattered across the mounds that contain the physical remnants of the village. Evidence of burning is frequently observed at Pueblo sites across the Southwest but at Burnt Corn the destruction appeared notably thorough. Archaeologists in the region are actively pondering the matter of burned pueblos, in particular their relation to conflict, ritual, and warfare, and Burnt Corn—once forgotten—now represents a central case study for these deliberations.

The fact that the ceramics on the surface of Burnt Corn Pueblo date to the late A.D. 1200s is another factor in the newly-recognized significance of the site. The thirteenth century is of interest to scholars working on the Southwestern past because it encompasses the "abandonment" of the traditional Puebloan heartland on the Colorado Plateau at places like Mesa Verde and Sand Canyon, and the subsequent movement of Pueblo people to areas of historic and modern settlement, including the Río Grande, Rio San Jose, Zuni River, and Hopi mesas. It has proven particularly difficult to address the question of "migration" in the Río Grande region, for reasons that include the politics of archaeological research as well as significant empirical challenges. We have been trying to understand this process for more than a hundred years, and new evidence is a welcome addition to the debate

Burnt Corn Pueblo thus offers archaeologists a chance to address two of the central topics of Puebloan history in the Southwest: conflict and migration. When I first came down that path to the site in 1999, in a group that included Paul Williams, the Bureau of Land Management archaeologist responsible for one half of Burnt Corn, and Buck Dant, the landowner who takes care of the rest, the research opportunity was evident. It was also clear that Burnt Corn represented an important node in efforts to preserve a vital cultural landscape. Close to Santa Fe and vulnerable to all of the pressures such proximity implies, the Galisteo Basin sits on a modern social and political fault line where public policy and land use practices sometimes clash. All of these indicators suggested that it was a good time to launch an integrated archaeological effort at Burnt Corn Pueblo.

The research program that emerged from this visit, designated the Tano Origins Project, began in the summer of 2000, and continued with subsequent field seasons in 2002 and 2004–2007. The work initially focused on the Burnt Corn landscape but quickly expanded to include excavation at the pueblo and other archaeological sites in the surrounding area, and additional survey. Our research was integrated with the study of records and artifacts from other Galisteo Basin sites excavated by earlier projects.

Figure 1.1. The Galisteo Basin in the vicinity of Burnt Corn Pueblo. Photograph by James Snead.

The chapters in this volume present results from the six years of fieldwork on the Tano Origins Project. While some of our analyses are still in progress, we think it is important to publish our initial results in order to stimulate discussion.

RESEARCH DESIGN

The Tano Origins Project is designed to explore the relationship between large-scale movement of people and conflict in the Ancestral Pueblo landscape. Both topics have been the subject of scholarly debate for more than a century, although shifting intellectual fashion brings them in and out of vogue.

The movement of peoples is a dominant historical motif in Pueblo tradition (for the Tewa, Naranjo 1995; Ortiz 1979: 280; Parsons 1994: 175, 1996: 215), and early scholars turned to such processes to explain the distribution of archaeological sites across the Southwest

(Bandelier 1892: 27; Fewkes 1900). Attention to the subject was fairly continuous through the 1960s (Dean 1969; Dutton 1964; Ford and others 1972; Haury 1958; McNutt 1969), but faded thereafter in the face of a more processual focus on culture change. Interest in migration revived in the 1990s courtesy of several publications that adopted recent theoretical approaches (Anthony 1990; Burmeister 2000) to Southwestern data (Cameron 1995; Cameron and Tomka 1993; Clark 2001; Duff and Wilshusen 2000; Herr and Clark 1997; Lyons 2003; Roney 1995; Stone 2001). Regional coverage of this issue remains intermittent, however, with a particular need for additional, systematic studies of migration from the "receiving end" (Cordell 1995; Lekson and others 2002).

Historical trends in the archaeology of conflict in the Southwest mirror the topic of population movement in interesting ways. By and large, early anthropologists working in the region perceived conflict exclusively in terms of warfare between Ancestral Pueblo peoples and other cultural groups, such as the Navajo (Kidder 1924: 155). The comparatively limited interest in conflict *within* Pueblo society during much of the twentieth century has been attributed to the dominance of the "Apollonian" model of Pueblo culture promulgated by Ruth Benedict and others, which postulated that Puebloan communities lived in a harmonious balance with each other (Benedict 1934; Fowler 2000: 340; LeBlanc 1999: 22). Dissatisfaction with the Apollonian model ultimately matured in the face of new empirical data on Pueblo conflict and more nuanced theoretical approaches (a debate summarized in Chapter 8). Several recent publications on conflict in Pueblo history indicate that critical perspectives are still evolving (Fowles and others 2007; Kohler and Turner 2006; Lowell 2007; Wilcox and others 2006).

Studies of conflict are at the same juncture as those of population movement in that both need new work to document how processes "on the ground" played out in specific contexts. I am particularly persuaded that an interesting link between the two is emerging. Although we expect that ties of kinship and exchange would have initially shaped patterns of migration, people would have faced an array of negotiations when making such a transition. Economic and social relationships, religious authority, the structure of leadership, and fundamental cultural traditions would all have been challenged by starting over in a new place with new rules (LeBlanc 1999: 279). Linda Cordell (1995: 205) has noted that even though we acknowledge that the migrants would have been organized into small groups, local communities at the receiving end would have been "forced to reorganize in order to accommodate the new population." "Conflict," Jeffery Clark observed, "has the potential of being particularly destructive as every community along the migration route is subjected to internal strife" (Clark 2001: 4). Access to productive resources, in particular, would have been a potentially central source of social and political conflict, as well as a driving factor behind population movement.

Under conditions of migration, therefore, conflict of one form or another would almost seem to have been inevitable. I do not expect that social groups would have been stable as new relationships took hold and new institutions developed in response to the changed conditions. The relationship between conflict and population movement has been acknowledged in specific Southwestern cases (Bernardini 1998, 2005; Chenault and Motsinger

2000; Wallace and Doelle 2001) but demands more detailed exploration. LeBlanc's (1999: 278) discussion of the subject makes it clear that systematic examination of the migration–conflict correlation is requisite to grasping the relationship between conflict and Ancestral Pueblo society, particularly in the Pueblo III–Pueblo IV periods.

I am convinced that a systematic, diachronic examination of the relationship between conflict and migration is needed to provide a critical perspective on the dynamics of ancestral Puebloan society. It is apparent that the northern Rio Grande during the Coalition and Classic periods (congruent with the Pueblo III–Pueblo IV periods elsewhere in the Southwest) is an excellent temporal and spatial setting for such research. This is because the region is often considered to have been a destination for migrating populations during these periods, and there is considerable archaeological evidence with which to examine these processes, even though they remain poorly understood at present.

The Tano Origins Project was accordingly designed as a study of the relationship between migration and conflict in the Galisteo Basin between A.D. 1250 and 1325. The name "Tano Origins" was chosen because this period of time encompasses the beginning of villages that were inhabited by Tewa-speaking "Tano" people at the time of the Spanish *entradas*, and because "origins" refers in part to the processes through which these circumstances came to be. We have conducted research at multiple scales, emphasizing how the dynamics of conflict shaped and were reflected by the organization of community landscapes. Targeted strategies of archaeological excavation, survey, and collections research have each been adopted to maximize information acquisition and make efficient use of resources.

RESEARCH CONTEXT

The Galisteo Basin is a major physiographic province of the northern Río Grande region of New Mexico (Fig. 1.2). It comprises much of the watershed of the Galisteo Creek, an intermittent stream (in the modern era) that flows south and west out of the Sangre de Cristo foothills south of Santa Fe. The shallow central basin, roughly 16 km north-south by 19.3 km east-west, is bounded to the west by the Cerrillos Hills and Ortiz Mountains, separated by a gap through which the river passes to empty into the Rio Grande just north of Kewa Pueblo (Santo Domingo). In geological terms the northern perimeter of

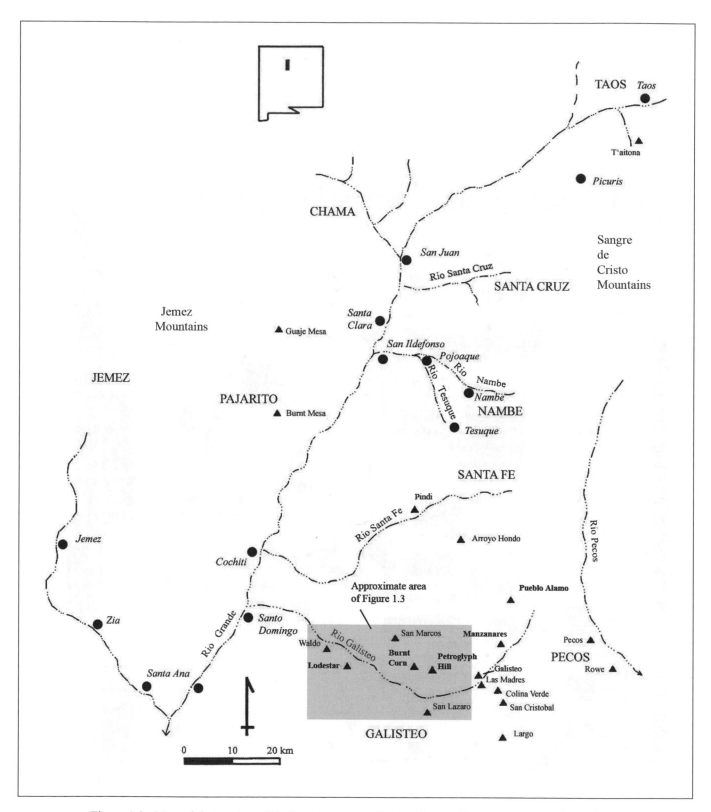

Figure 1.2. Map of the northern Rio Grande region of New Mexico, illustrating archaeological districts, modern Pueblos, and selected large Ancestral Pueblo sites. Cartography by James Snead.

the Galisteo Basin consists of a wide plain of outwash gravels that have eroded from the Sangre de Cristos in relatively recent times, with lower strata including Oligocene volcanics and Eocene sandstone exposed along the basin's dissected flanks and open floor (Disbrow and Stoll 1957). A similar plain extends beyond the basin to the south, towards the dry *playas* near Estancia. The ecology of the basin margins is dominated by piñon-juniper woodland, which is also prevalent in the subsidiary hills at the basin's center. Open grassland occurs at the lowest elevations.

The archaeological resources of the Galisteo Basin have attracted attention for more than a century. This is due to the basin's proximity to Santa Fe and awareness that the presence of substantial indigenous populations in both the precolumbian and Colonial eras provide a distinct window into the Southwestern past (Reed 1943). Existing information about the Galisteo Basin was synthesized by Cordell (1979), and I provide a brief synopsis here.

The first recorded archaeological reconnaissance in the Galisteo Basin was made by Adolph Bandelier (1892), who visited the region in 1882. Among other observations, he first identified the fragmentary remains near Lamy now known as the Lamy Junction community (LA 27, LA 362–368, LA 31774–31779), describing them as "a typical small-house settlement" (Lange and Riley 1966: 329). Following Bandelier, the next major archaeologist to work in the region was Edgar Lee Hewett, who took little interest in the Galisteo Basin. It was not until 1912 that substantive fieldwork began, under the direction of Nels Nelson of the American Museum of Natural History. During the course of five field seasons Nelson excavated large sections of the major Galisteo sites, emphasizing the large pueblo villages that had been occupied into the Colonial period. San Cristobal, in particular, received detailed attention. Some of the information Nelson collected was published in ground-breaking reports (Nelson 1914, 1916, 1919), and extensive collections were curated at the American Museum of Natural History, but no comprehensive account was completed (for a detailed discussion, see Snead 2001a).

The impression that Nelson had exhausted the archaeology of the Galisteo Basin seems to have been widespread, and for 30 years after his return to New York only modest research was conducted. Tree-ring samples were collected at some locations (see Chapter 2 herein; Smiley and others 1953; Stallings 1937), and many of the large sites in the basin were mapped and surface collected as part of Harry P. Mera's survey of Southwestern sites (Mera 1940). In 1947 Bertha Dutton launched a new program of Galisteo research that lasted 15 years. Like Nelson, Dutton produced influential but ultimately incomplete reports on her work (Dutton 1964, 1980; see also Schaafsma 1969, 1993). Only a few other field studies were conducted during the Dutton era, such as work by Erik Reed (1954).

In more recent times archaeological research in the Galisteo Basin has been conducted under the auspices of cultural resources management (CRM) (for a few examples, see Batten and Dello-Russo 1992; Doleman and others 1979; Kayser and Ewing 1971; Kurota 2006; Phillips and Seymour 1982). The most influential of these projects was Richard Lang's (1977a) survey of the San Cristobal drainage, conducted on behalf of the State of New Mexico. The 1,373.8 ha of land surveyed by Lang represented the largest contiguous area systematically examined in the region to that date. Although never published, Lang's summary of the project continues to be the primary source for reconstructing indigenous Galisteo history (for example, Cordell 1979a: 56).

In addition to continuing work for CRM, there have been several research projects in the Galisteo Basin in recent decades, many of which were focused on the archaeology of the Colonial era. These include fieldwork at San Lazaro (Lycett 1995), Paa-Ko (Lycett 2001, 2002), and San Marcos (see Ramenofsky 2001; Thomas 2001). Major work on earlier occupations of the Galisteo Basin includes excavations at Pueblo Blanco (Creamer and others 1993), study of indigenous agricultural landscapes associated with San Marcos (Eddy and others 1996; Lang 1995; Lightfoot 1990; Lightfoot and Eddy 1995), and documentation of petroglyphs (for example, Brody and Brody 2006; Schaafsma 1990). Laboratory research, particularly focused on issues of ceramic production, has been important in Galisteo Basin studies, particularly because lead from the Cerrillos Hills was used in the manufacture of Rio Grande glaze wares (Chapter 3 herein; compare Habicht-Mauche and others 2000; Welker 1995). Field-based studies of the lead sources have also produced important results (Bice 2003).

The research history of the Galisteo Basin has produced some interesting biases in our understanding of the region's past. On a general level, the relative rarity of archaeological survey in the region stands in contrast to surrounding areas, such as the Pajarito Plateau (for instance, Powers and Orcutt 1999). Thus only relatively low intensity survey, such as that conducted by Lang (1977b; see also Futch 1997), or smaller-scale projects (see Kurota 2006) provide evidence of the cultural landscape of the region. This dearth of survey data is changing but review of information on site location maintained by the New Mexico State Historic Preservation Office (SHPO) reveals thousands of hectares of land in the Galisteo Basin, including areas close to Santa Fe, which have never been archaeologically investigated.

The research that has been done in the Galisteo Basin is heavily slanted toward the late precolumbian and early historic eras. This emphasis is in part the legacy of Nels Nelson, who selected this area for research precisely because it had good resources representing this late era (see Snead 2001a). In addition, the visibility and magnitude of the late sites, and the existence of historical records pertaining to their seventeenth-century occupation, have contributed to the research focus. A poor understanding of the time periods preceding the Classic period in the Galisteo Basin, however, is a serious weakness. We have basic information for several major sites occupied during the thirteenth century but few details, and we know even less about sites that were inhabited in earlier periods.

Our archaeological understanding of the Galisteo Basin thus has significant gaps. One premise of the Tano Origins Project is that interpretations of Puebloan history of the region, both in terms of internal social dynamics and external relationships to cultural transformations across the Southwest, are crippled by our lack of information about the thirteenth-century communities. Ideas about the significance of the celebrated late precolumbian villages, as well as the role played by the Galisteo Basin in the demographic reorganization of the Southwest, cannot be pursued until we gain a better understanding of the organization of the Coalition population across the Galisteo landscape. Our theoretical questions pertaining to conflict and migration are particularly apt for approaching this complex era.

CULTURE HISTORY

The following synopsis of culture history draws upon two recent discussions of the post–A.D. 1150 periods (Spielmann 1996; Snead and others 2004). Very little new information is available for earlier periods. The discussion of chronology is derived from these sources and a selective review of relevant CRM reports. I use a

Table 1.1. Period and Phase Designations in the Galisteo Basin

Period	Phase	Date
Preceramic		10,000 B.C.– A.D. 600
Developmental Pueblo		A.D. 600–1200
Coalition (early)	Tesuque	A.D. 1200–1250
Coalition (late)	Pindi	A.D. 1250–1300
	Galisteo	A.D. 1300–1350
Classic (early)		A.D. 1350–1425
Classic (late)		A.D. 1425–1550
Colonial-Historic		A.D. 1550–1950

modified version of the chronological sequence (Table 1.1) developed for the northern Rio Grande region by Wendorf and Reed (1955) and Lang (1977a).

Preceramic Period (10,000 B.C. – A.D. 600)

According to Lang (1977a: 13–14), Paleoindian and early Archaic occupations are extremely scarce in the San Cristobal drainage, with apparently only two documented sites dating to the Cody complex. A similar pattern is described for the Vista Grande area in the western Galisteo Basin, with only ephemeral evidence for early hunting and gathering occupations. There is better evidence for occupations in subsequent Archaic phases, with a low but consistent frequency of Bajada, Armijo, and Cochise phase sites (Futch and others 1996; Lang 1977a: 14–16). These sites are variably termed "campsites" and "hunting camps." The only excavated Galisteo Basin site occupied during this long interval is La Bolsa (LA 356), located in the flood pool of the Galisteo Dam in the western basin (Honea 1971).

Developmental Pueblo Period (A.D. 600–1200)

Evidence for early Puebloan occupation (Basketmaker–Pueblo II/Developmental) has been recorded in the eastern Galisteo Basin, particularly in the San Cristobal drainage, where Lang (1977a: 19–20) recorded sites with components that appear to be short-term occupations, probably resource-collection camps. Subsequent work in the greater San Cristobal area, however, has documented more substantial Basketmaker sites (Charles Hannaford, personal communication, 2006). The early Puebloan occupation further west in the basin appears to have been much smaller, with none of the surveys in that region recording components dating to this period. Possible exceptions are the oft-noted "Bronze Trail" sites (Wiseman and Darling 1986), a series of small structures hypothetically associated with Chaco-era turquoise extraction from the Cerrillos Hills. If this interpretation is correct, these sites represent a unique circumstance.

Coalition Period
(A.D. 1200–1325)

The beginning of the Coalition period, often called the "Tesuque phase" (A.D. 1200-1250), is traditionally associated with the appearance of Santa Fe Black-on-white ceramics, but in the Galisteo context this has not been securely fixed in time. There are only a few sites in and around the Galisteo Basin that date to the Tesuque phase, and these include the extensive Pueblo Alamo (LA 8), with multiple room blocks and adobe-masonry construction (Allen 1973; Robinson and others 1973; Wiseman 1999; Chapter 2, this volume). The only other well-dated Tesuque phase site in the Galisteo Basin, LA 3333, includes pit structures with limited surface architecture (Dutton 1964). Lang (1977a: 222) used surface ceramics to identify other probable early thirteenth-century occupations but these evaluations must be considered preliminary. The Tesuque phase appears to have been an era of gradually increasing population, with small villages and hamlets established in the relatively well-watered eastern flanks of the basin.

The subsequent Pindi phase (A.D. 1250–1300) was a time of significant expansion, with both individual pueblos and small clustered communities established throughout the Basin. The Lamy Junction community originally described by Bandelier, for example, is only one part of a notably dense settlement cluster extending for at least 3 km along terraces above the Galisteo Creek. Other Pindi phase sites along the eastern margins of the basin include Colina Verde (LA 309) and Pueblo Largo (LA 189). Farther west, the Galisteo Community includes at least four small pueblos (LA 8843, La Alesna; LA 8844, El Pipo; LA 8845, Los Danitos; and LA 83703). The western Galisteo Basin also has a substantial Pindi phase occupation, including the Waldo site (LA 9147; Hammack 1971), LA 9146, and LA 9148. The residential sites studied by the Tano Origins Project, including Burnt Corn Pueblo (LA 359), Pueblo Escondido (LA 358), and the Lodestar sites were also occupied during the Pindi phase. We presume that many, if not all, of the major Classic period villages in the Galisteo Basin were established during this period. Ann Ramenofsky (2001) suggests that San Marcos may have been founded in the late A.D. 1200s. However, the early components at the site excavated by Reed (1954: 324) that had Santa Fe Black-on-white ceramics also included glaze ware, and were thus post-Coalition in date. There is a substantial black-on-white ceramic component at San Lazaro that has not been well documented (Jan Orcutt, personal communication, 2000).

Despite the evidence for an expanding population, there were significant settlement gaps in the Galisteo Basin during the Pindi phase. The almost complete absence of sites with Santa Fe Black-on-white pottery in systematically surveyed areas near the Galisteo Dam at the western periphery of the basin is notable (see Batten and Dello-Russo 1992; Doleman and Brown 2000; Lang 1976, 1977b; Phillips and Seymour 1982). A similar absence of Pindi phase sites characterizes the southeastern basin near Pueblo Blanco (Kurota 2006). There are also remarkably few surface sites of this phase in the vicinity of San Cristobal, despite the presence of Colina Verde to the north and the Largo-Wildhorse Community to the south (Lang 1977a: 393).

The low frequency of Pindi phase sites in some parts of the Galisteo Basin contrasts with neighboring areas with numerous smaller settlements characterized by black-on-white ceramics that presumably date to the Pindi phase. These include parts of the northern and western basin as well as the flanks of the Ortiz mountains (Futch 1997; Snead 2004). Such discontinuous distribution of sites indicates that the Galisteo Basin population during this time was using the landscape selectively, and that some topographic zones were less desirable, including the lower elevations to the far west.

The nature of the thirteenth-century occupation of the eastern Galisteo Basin has often been invoked as reflecting the movement of population into the area in response to demographic shifts elsewhere in the Southwest. LA 3333 thus has been considered a preliminary "camp" of migrants built prior to the construction of more substantial villages in the area (Dutton 1964). The architecture and layout of Pindi phase sites might provide information about the origins of their builders but the evidence is complex. Lang (1977a: 224) describes several site plans, including room block clusters, isolated room blocks, large L-shaped room blocks, clusters of large and small room blocks, and large room blocks with some outliers. The longevity of these settlements differed widely. Colina Verde, a substantial complex built atop a low summit, appears to have been inhabited well into the following century (Smiley and others 1953: 30), whereas other sites were only briefly occupied. The appearance of clustered settlements is a notable aspect of Pindi phase settlement, such as the Lamy Junction Community, the ancestral Galisteo Community, the Burnt Corn Community, and the Lodestar Community.

The subsequent Galisteo phase (A.D. 1300–1325) is controversial on several points. Traditionally the advent of this phase is marked by the appearance of Galisteo Black-on-white pottery, which is technologically similar to Santa Fe Black-on-white but with some arguably distinctive features. Eric Blinman and Dean Wilson suggest that these ceramics are simply a variant of Santa Fe Black-on-white made with local materials (Eric Blinman, personal communication, 2000; see Chapter 3 herein). This would imply that the phase itself is a result of archaeological misinterpretation rather than a manifestation of a change in Ancestral Pueblo society.

Whether or not Galisteo Black-on-white is "real," there was a distinctive shift in Galisteo Basin settlement during the early 1300s. The occupation of many of the more prominent Pindi phase pueblos, such as Burnt Corn and Manzanares, ceased during this interval, and relatively few new pueblos appear to have been established. The complex histories of well-dated settlements in the adjacent Santa Fe region, particularly Pindi Pueblo (LA 1) and Arroyo Hondo (LA 12, or Kuaa-Kay) (Ahlstrom 1989; Creamer 1993; Stubbs and Stallings 1953) suggest alternating periods of growth and abandonment, and similar processes were probably ongoing in the Galisteo Basin. Whether this can be attributed to some form of settlement cycling or to other mechanisms such as warfare, a possible explanation we consider in Chapter 8, will hinge upon better chronology based on more accurate tree-ring dates (see Chapter 2, this volume).

Classic Period (A.D. 1325–1550)

The Classic period was marked by the dramatic expansion of Galisteo Basin settlements, the appearance of Rio Grande glaze ceramics, and the advent of the new Rio Grande style iconography manifest in rock art and ceramic design motifs. The appearance of these characteristic features was not entirely synchronous but over the course of the A.D. 1300s local society was transformed. For more than two centuries the Galisteo Basin was at the center of the eastern Pueblo world. The list of major villages of this era includes Galisteo (LA 26), Blanco (LA 40), Pueblo Colorado (LA 62), Pueblo Largo (LA 189), Pueblo She (LA 239), San Cristobal (LA 80), San Lazaro (LA 90/91), and San Marcos (LA 89).

Despite the prominence of the Classic period pueblos in the Galisteo Basin, however, we know little more about them than we did in 1915. All were built to a relatively similar plan with linear room blocks arranged around plazas, with some multiple-story construction using adobe and stone masonry. The major villages contain hundreds or thousands of rooms, and the four largest villages contain more than 2000 rooms. A small number of tree-ring dates from these sites makes their occupational history difficult to interpret (see Chapter 2). It is thus challenging to determine whether the large Galisteo Basin sites were continuously occupied throughout the Classic period, as is often presumed, or were repeatedly vacated and reoccupied. Ann Ramenofsky (2001) has suggested that differential distribution of dated ceramics across the surface of San Marcos indicates that they were not continuously used throughout this period.

Whether or not there were significant population increases and decreases during the period, the Galisteo Basin landscape contains substantial evidence for intensive use. A few smaller residential settlements are known, such as the 31-room Wheeler Site (LA 6869; Alexander 1971). In some cases elaborate networks of agricultural features have been documented. Surveys of the San Marcos community have documented linear borders and other elements of Pueblo farming technology distributed across hundreds of hectares surrounding the pueblo (Lang 1995; Lightfoot 1990; Lightfoot and Eddy 1995). Work beyond this zone has recorded gravel mulch fields (Haecker and Haecker 1997; Legare 1994, 1995) and field houses at distances of up to 10 km from San Marcos (Hill 1998; McGraw 1998).

By modern standards the Galisteo Basin is a marginal environment for farming, and the fact that such a seemingly large number of people lived there for centuries requires further investigation. Various explanations for the success of the Classic period pueblos in the Galisteo Basin have been put forward, most suggesting that some sort of economic specialization by the local population played a role. Economic specialization might have included mining and control of mineral resources such as lead ore for ceramic decoration (Bice 2003; Habicht-Mauche and others 2000; Huntley 2004, 2008; Snead and others 2004) or turquoise (Warren and Mathien 1985), or large-scale ceramic production (Warren 1979; Welker 1995). There has also been considerable debate over the possibility that the spatial cluster of settlements represented by the Galisteo Basin pueblos reflects some form of supracommunity organization (see Plog 1983; Reed 1988; Spielmann 1994; Upham and Reed 1989; Wilcox 1981, 1984, 1991). Each of these scenarios has appeal but none have been substantively tested. This is another issue that would be clarified by a better understanding of the occupational histories of the pueblos. Ultimately, projections as to how people supported themselves are based on how many people lived in the Galisteo Basin at different times.

Colonial–Historic Period
(A.D. 1550–1950)

Evidence for the early Colonial period in the Galisteo Basin has been thoroughly summarized (in particular, Lycett 1995; see also Schroeder 1979) but our knowledge of this period is being transformed as recent projects are published (Lycett 2001, 2002; Ramenofsky 2001; Thomas 2001). In contrast, little has been published about eighteenth, nineteenth, and twentieth century archaeology, and this means that there is little empirical evidence available to complement text-based, historical studies for these periods.

PROJECT SETTING

The chapters in this volume use information collected during the Tano Origins Project between 2000 and 2007. Considering the multi-centric aspect of this research, the different sites, landscapes and collections studied in the course of the project are summarized here with reference to the chapters of this volume in which the associated details are presented. The spatial context of the research program is depicted in Figure 1.3.

The Burnt Corn Pueblo Landscape

Burnt Corn Pueblo is located in the western Galisteo Basin, approximately 2 km north of the Galisteo Creek and east of Highway NM 14, not far from the better-known site of San Marcos. There is no evidence that Burnt Corn Pueblo was known to any of the early archaeologists who worked in the region, and it was apparently first recorded by H. P. Mera in the early 1930s. Designated LA 359 at that time, it was accidentally renumbered LA 9144 and LA 8748 in later years, evidence that it remained remote and poorly understood through most of the twentieth century. This isolation exposed it to vandalism, and dozens of old looter's pits are visible. Modern ownership is divided between the Bureau of Land Management and a private landowner.

On the surface, Burnt Corn Pueblo consists of nine masonry-adobe structures distributed in a north-south line along the top of a narrow ridge overlooking the Cañada de la Cueva, a major intermittent drainage. Surface ceramics are almost entirely black-on-white types, with some trade wares of western origin, indicating a Coalition period occupation. An extensive community is associated with Burnt Corn Pueblo, including a small plaza site (Pueblo Escondido, LA 358) immediately across the Cañada and several associated structures, petroglyphs, shrines, and other features. Preliminary reconnaissance by an Elderhostel team in 1999 located some of these sites and affirmed the research potential of Burnt Corn Pueblo (Peck 1999).

Our work in the Burnt Corn landscape had three components. Survey of the Burnt Corn Community was conducted in 2000 and 2006, recording 47 sites and 95 isolated occurrences in 70 ha surrounding the pueblo. Some of the survey research has been published (Snead 2004, 2008a) but landscape-related studies continue, as described in Chapter 4 by Gregory Greene and Phillip Leckman. Excavations were conducted at Burnt Corn Pueblo in 2002 and 2005, and these are summarized by James Snead, Monica Smith, and Elizabeth Baker Brite in Chapter 6. In 2006 additional excavations were conducted at two small room blocks within the Burnt Corn community, Cholla House (LA 134186) and Slope House (LA 134193). Results of this work are presented by Mark Allen in Chapter 7. Post-excavation research included tree-ring dating, discussed in Chapter 2 by James Snead and Anthony Thibodeau, and ceramic analysis, described in Chapter 3 by Lori Barkwill Love and Leslie Cohen. Information needed for management of Burnt Corn Pueblo as a cultural resource was collected during the fieldwork.

Petroglyph Hill

Petroglyph Hill lies approximately 5 km east of Burnt Corn Pueblo in a similar topographic and ecological

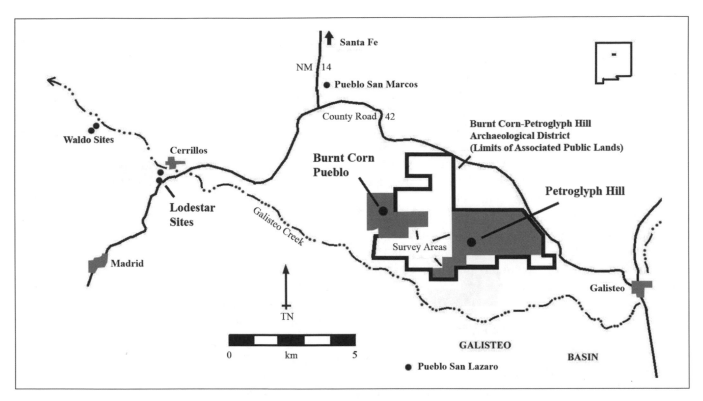

Figure 1.3. Northern Galisteo District, illustrating selected modern features, archaeological sites, and the research setting of the Tano Origins Project. Cartography by James Snead.

zone. Despite the provocative name and the occasional visit to the site by rock art specialists, neither the hill itself nor any other archaeological feature in its vicinity had been formally recorded prior to our work. The opportunity to document this site and conduct survey in the vicinity came about when the property was acquired by Santa Fe County in 2002.

Petroglyph Hill provided two important opportunities for the Tano Origins Project. Proximity to Burnt Corn Pueblo allowed us to study the landscape beyond the core of the Burnt Corn community. The density of rock art at the Petroglyph Hill site provided a unique resource for studying ritual activity. We have little information about ritual features in the Galisteo Basin or elsewhere in the region during the Coalition period. As at Burnt Corn Pueblo, we collected information needed to manage Petroglyph Hill as a cultural resource. Like other open space in Santa Fe County, Petroglyph Hill has the potential to serve multiple uses, including recreation. A thorough understanding of the nature and distribution of archaeological resources is critical for arriving at informed decisions about making the vicinity accessible to the public and managing fragile resources.

Archaeological survey in the vicinity of Petroglyph Hill was directed by Genevieve Head from 2004 through 2006. This survey identified 184 sites and 288 isolated occurrences distributed across 630 ha. In 2004 Marit Munson recorded the rock art at Petroglyph Hill in extensive detail (Munson 2005a). The archaeological data generated by these tandem efforts is discussed in Chapter 7.

The Lodestar Sites

Lodestar is a small ranch located approximately 8 km west of Burnt Corn Pueblo, immediately abutting State Road 14 south of the town of Cerrillos. Small, farmstead-scale sites had been previously recorded on this property (Jager 1995), and when the owner decided to transfer them to the Archaeological Conservancy in 2005, we were asked to conduct preliminary research. Reconnaissance identified five room blocks and related features clustered into four sites, all dated to the Coalition period by the exclusive presence of black-on-white ceramics.

Work at Lodestar offered a significant opportunity to broaden our excavated sample. The landscape of the western Galisteo Basin during the Pindi phase was dominated by small structures in loose clusters rather than aggregated settlements, and it presented a distinctly different picture than that in the vicinity of Burnt Corn Pueblo. The only similar site that has been excavated is the Waldo Site, a linear adobe-masonry structure containing four rooms with an associated jacal room and two adjacent pit houses (Hammack 1971: 97). Lodestar thus represented an opportunity to collect information that was both unique in its local context and comparable to that derived from our work upriver at Burnt Corn Pueblo. Excavations in 2005, directed by Mark Allen (2006; Snead 2005b), concentrated on two of the sites, Lodestar South (LA 105759) and Lodestar North (LA 158557). The two small structures at Lodestar South were both tested, as was the single structure at Lodestar North with an associated depression. The excavations at the Lodestar sites are discussed in Chapter 7.

ARCHIVAL AND COLLECTIONS RESEARCH

Study of collections and field notes from previously excavated sites in the Galisteo Basin has been a priority of the Tano Origins Project since the inception of research. A considerable quantity of unpublished and unanalyzed material is available, creating the opportunity to assemble a body of information that can be compared with the results of our fieldwork. Some Galisteo Basin collections are curated out-of-state, including the artifacts from the Nelson excavations that are stored at the American Museum of Natural History in New York. Other relevant material, however, is maintained by state institutions in Santa Fe, with collections housed at the Museum of Indian Arts and Culture/Laboratory of Anthropology (MIAC/LOA) and documents archived by the State Historic Preservation Division.

Our archival and collections research has focused on three sites excavated between the 1950s and the mid-1970s. These are Pueblo Alamo (Allen 1973), Manzanares (LA 1104/10609; Steen 1980); and Pueblo Largo (LA 183; Dutton 1951, 1953, 1955). All of these sites date, at least in part, to the Coalition period, and they have substantive collections that show promise for archaeological interpretation. Preliminary evaluation of the field notes for these sites has been completed (Snead 2004), as has the analysis of ceramics from the Manzanares collection (Barkwill Love 2006). These studies have led to new dating initiatives, described in Chapter 2, and the ongoing ceramic studies of Lori Barkwill Love and Leslie Cohen, presented in Chapter 3. Volunteer researchers at the Laboratory of Anthropology are working on an independent project to study the ceramics of Pueblo Largo. The completion of an inventory of Bertha Dutton's archives by Diane Bird will make it possible to evaluate the Largo excavations.

The following chapters outline the results of the Tano Origins Project as of 2010. The culmination of the National Science Foundation grant that funded our research has brought a hiatus in fieldwork, and we are using this break to complete analyses, share information, and design the next phase of research. One of our goals for this volume is to engage the archaeological community in the Southwest in assisting us with that prospect by reviewing our work. We hope that the legacy of Burnt Corn Pueblo, including the dramatic events of the early fourteenth century and the archaeological endeavor that has tried to understand them, will continue to unfold.

CHAPTER TWO

Dating the Galisteo: Pueblo Settlement in Context

James E. Snead and Anthony J. Thibodeau

Archaeology in the Galisteo Basin is severely hampered by poor chronometric dating. Our excavations at Burnt Corn Pueblo and related sites offered the opportunity to increase the number of tree-ring dates available for the region, particularly since the apparent widespread destruction by fire implied good preservation of carbonized wood. Since excavation elsewhere in the region is increasingly rare, the best opportunity to collect additional dates lies in preserved collections from older projects. Our collections research at the Museum of Indian Arts and Cultures/Laboratory of Anthropology (MIAC/LOA) identified promising samples for dendrochronological analysis. The preliminary results of our dating program are described in this chapter.

The American Southwest is renowned as the heartland of tree-ring dating, and archaeology in the region benefits from a temporal framework anchored by thousands of secure dates (Nash 1999). Yet this reputation masks considerable uncertainty, particularly on a regional and local level. Although our control over time allows us to ask questions that would be impossible elsewhere, the persistence of gaps in tree-ring data often interferes with satisfactory answers.

The Galisteo Basin unfortunately provides an example of the limits of the existing chronology. Although there are hundreds of tree-ring dates available for the region, they are less useful than the casual glance suggests. Most of the dendrochronological research that produced this evidence was conducted between the 1930s and 1960s. This research began with a sampling program conducted by W. S. Stallings (1937). There is little provenience information available for Stallings' dates, however, so they are suggestive but difficult to fully evaluate (Robinson and others 1973; Smiley and others 1953). Many of these dates were derived from wood that does not appear to have been building material, increasing the uncertainty of their context.

A second round of dating was stimulated by the extensive fieldwork of Bertha Dutton (for instance, 1955). We thus have good dates for Pueblo Largo (LA 183) and Las Madres (LA 25) but these chronological sequences are not supported by correlative data from other sites. Dates from San Cristobal, for instance, are almost entirely associated with a single room block originally investigated by Nelson and sampled in the 1930s (Robinson and others 1973: 45; Stallings 1937). Despite recent efforts to revive interest in dating Galisteo sites (Wiseman 2004), much of our absolute chronology in the region is based entirely on Stallings and Dutton.

One irony presented by the poor dating of Galisteo sites is that the region actually provides a good environment for dendrochronology. In a letter to Bertha Dutton about the collections from Pueblo Largo, Terah Smiley remarked that the Galisteo samples were "about as easy to work as anything I have ever encountered. I have never seen such chronology as that area has. It is almost perfect" (T. Smiley to B. Dutton, 5 March 1953. 95PLE.011, Archives, MIAC/LOA). The presence of numerous burned sites in the region enhances the potential of tree-ring dating. Excavated materials from sites in the region that are curated at MIAC/LOA in Santa Fe include many undated wood samples, and some of the dates that were processed in the past remain unpublished.

Our approach to tree-ring dating of Galisteo sites took advantage of these conditions. The following discussion includes some of the results of this work, divided into three sections that illustrate different types of opportunity: (1) new dates from previously undated specimens, using Pueblo Alamo (LA 8) as case study; (2) "old" dates from previously unpublished sources, with a focus on Manzanares (LA 1104/10607); and (3) new dates from new specimens, derived from our intensive dating program at Burnt Corn Pueblo (LA 359).

OLD WOOD, NEW DATES
PUEBLO ALAMO

Pueblo Alamo, dating to the Coalition period, is a large residential complex at the heart of an Ancestral Pueblo community along the Cañada de los Alamos south of Santa Fe (Fig 1.2). Although the site is technically outside the Galisteo Basin, the geographical and cultural associations are clear. The cultural landscape surrounding Pueblo Alamo is complex, including several smaller structures (LA 8028), at least one major hilltop shrine (LA 125568), and a large Classic period pueblo (Chamisa Locita, LA 4). This evidence indicates that the foothills of the Sangre de Cristos and the upper Cañada de los Alamos and Cañon Ancha drainages were hospitable environments for settlement in the Coalition and Early Classic periods.

Archaeological research at Pueblo Alamo was inaugurated by Nels Nelson in 1915. Nelson identified four large room blocks in a linear, north-south arrangement, which he numbered I through IV (from south to north; Fig. 2.1a). He completely excavated 24 rooms in these structures and sampled others. He also excavated a room in the much smaller Building V, which does not appear on his site map, but is described in his transcribed field notes as "Located directly S. of main pueblo on a steep, rounded knoll, close to the S. Bank of creek and marked by two pine trees." These notes are archived at the American Museum of Natural History (AMNH) (accession 1915–85), with photocopies at the New Mexico Historic Preservation Department (NMHPD) (NMCRIS 42654). Nelson's notes are relatively limited and include no feature plans, but the general descriptions of contexts and lists of artifacts provide useful information. At some point in the late 1920s Pueblo Alamo was mapped by H. P. Mera (Fig. 2.1b). This work was followed between 1932 and 1937 by Stallings' tree-ring sampling program (Stallings 1937).

Pueblo Alamo is unfortunately located in the right-of-way of Interstate 25, and in 1971 a large-scale excavation project was launched in advance of interstate expansion. Under the supervision of Stewart Peckham of the Museum of New Mexico, the fieldwork was directed by Joseph Allen and staffed by a rotating crew of museum personnel and day laborers provided by the State of New Mexico. Over the course of several weeks, 78 rooms in three of the four room blocks (labeled A–D, from north to south) were fully or partially excavated and a number of preliminary reports were ultimately prepared (Fig.

2.1c; Allen 1973; see NMCRIS 31018). Substantial collections are curated at MIAC/LOA, with field notes and maps archived by NMHPD. The site is discussed in a handful of reports and articles written during the past 40 years (Dickson 1979: 81; Habicht-Mauche 1993: 91; Wiseman 1999, 2004). All that remains of Pueblo Alamo today are the extreme northern and southern ends of the site, separated by hundreds of meters of the I–25 and US 285 interchange.

Chronology

Nine tree-ring dates derived from the specimens collected by Stallings at Pueblo Alamo were published in the 1950s (Smiley and others 1953: 17), and an additional 43 dates from Stalling's samples were published in the 1970s (Robinson and others 1973: 31–32). There is limited published provenience data for these 52 samples, although four came from two rooms in the northernmost room block (presumably IV/A) and five came from Nelson's building V (Smiley and others 1953: 17). All were apparently derived from "charcoal fragments" (Robinson and others 1973: 32), and there were few cutting dates in the assemblage. The pueblo is typically considered to have been occupied in the A.D. 1300s, with "vv" dates distributed across the first half of the century and a cluster of cutting dates in the 1260s (Robinson and others 1973: 31). These dates form an insubstantial basis for understanding the occupation of Pueblo Alamo. Our review of the available information suggested that no tree-ring samples from the 1971 excavations were processed. Wood with apparent dating potential was collected, however, and we were able to locate many of these samples in the Pueblo Alamo storage boxes. With funding from the small grant program of the New Mexico Archaeological Council and permission from the MIAC/LOA Collections Committee, we submitted nine specimens to the Laboratory of Tree-Ring Research (LTRR) at the University of Arizona in the spring of 2006. Ultimately, dates were derived from three of the submitted samples, identified as GALB–62, GALB–63, and GALB–64 (Table 2.1). All represented burned architectural wood, probably *vigas* or *latillas*. Fortuitously, each came from a different room block (Fig. 2.2). GALB–63 and 64 originated within sealed contexts overlain by architecture. Although none of the samples provided cutting dates, they collectively suggest construction during the first half of the A.D. 1200s, probably preceding 1230.

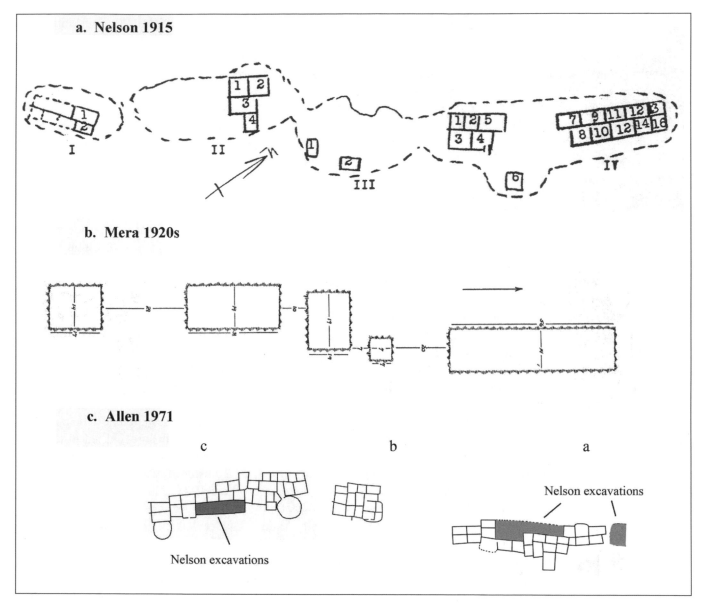

Figure 2.1. Pueblo Alamo (LA 8) as mapped by Nels Nelson (a), H. P. Mera (b),
and Joseph Allen (c). Adapted from maps on file at NMHPD.

Collectively, these new dates indicate that Pueblo Alamo had a complex history. The apparent contemporeneity of the three different room blocks is an important piece of new information. As discussed in Chapter 1, it has been argued that the room blocks at some of the large, Classic Period pueblos were occupied sequentially, and thus that what appears to be a single large site today actually represents a series of somewhat smaller occupations (see Ramenofsky 2001). Pueblo Alamo was built in an earlier era, but the fact that several large structures on the site were built at roughly the same time implies a substantial resident population. That this occupation preceded A.D. 1230 is also significant, since very few sites in the region date to those decades.

The 1971 notes indicate that many of the rooms had multiple floors, some separated by trash fill, and there was evidence for wall reconstruction and blocked doorways. Numerous floor features were present. The sealed contexts of GALB–63 and GALB–64 are thus consistent with an early occupation followed by renovation and renewal. If the cluster of cutting dates in the 1260s is factored in, two major phases of construction are indicated.

Table 2.1. Tree-ring Dates from Pueblo Alamo (LA 8)

Sample Numer GALB-	Provenience	Date A.D.
62	Room 10, Room block IV/A. Fill. "Burnt roof material small dia. vigas (8 cm); small willow sabinos [*latillas*] (1 cm to 2 cm dia)" (field notes).	1086–1223+vv
63	Room 124, Room block III/B. "Subfloor kiva or pit under F66" (field notes).	1130–1200+v inc
64	Room 61, Roomblock II/C. "From fill between floors 1 and 2" (specimen label).	1117–1193+vv

NOTE: All wood is piñon pine.

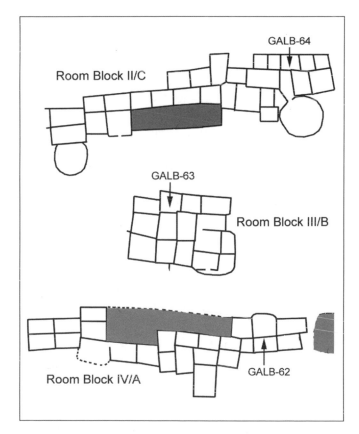

Figure 2.2. Detail of Pueblo Alamo, illustrating context of newly-dated tree-ring samples. Nelson's excavations depicted with gray shading.

The picture of Pueblo Alamo that emerges from this preliminary analysis is one of a long-term settlement that may have been occupied for generations. This is an important finding, particularly given the short occupation span of some later settlements (see below). The significance of the site as a place occupied for decades needs to be incorporated into future analyses of settlements of the Tesuque Phase in general and the Santa Fe and Galisteo districts in particular. In practical terms, our work demonstrates the research potential of curated collections of artifacts and notes, and indicates there is clearly more to be learned from Pueblo Alamo.

OLD DATES, NEW PUBLICATION MANZANARES PUEBLO

Manzanares is a complex of adobe structures located approximately 1.6 km east of the town of Lamy on the north bank of the Galisteo Creek (Fig. 2.3). Topographically the setting is a broad, open terrace along the north bank of the creek with the sides of the valley rising more steeply to the east. An extensive Coalition period community is evident in the vicinity. The pueblo itself has been estimated to contain more than 200 rooms with multiple stories built around a central plaza (Steen 1980: 129). Today the site is visually undistinguished, consisting of an amorphous mound covered by chamisa and juniper, but it is one of the largest Coalition period settlements in the entire region.

Nels Nelson excavated at Manzanares in 1915 while testing several sites in the vicinity of Lamy. Nelson (1915) referred to the site as "Mansanaria no. 2," which his notes describe as "an old communal pueblo with several regularly arranged buildings." The site was designated LA 1104 by Mera, although the absence of a site map and clear locational information caused considerable confusion thereafter. Nelson's use of the name "Mansanaria" provides priority for referring to LA 1104 as "Manzanares." The site has also been referred to as "Lamy," although that name should properly be applied to LA 27.

Tree-ring specimens were collected at Manzanares in 1933 (Stallings 1937). In the early 1970s the extensive tract of land that includes Manzanares was included in the El Dorado residential development, and the archaeologist Charlie Steen was engaged to excavate the site with an eye toward "interpreting" it for future neighbors. Steen referred to the site using the designation LA 10607 because he considered Mera's description of the

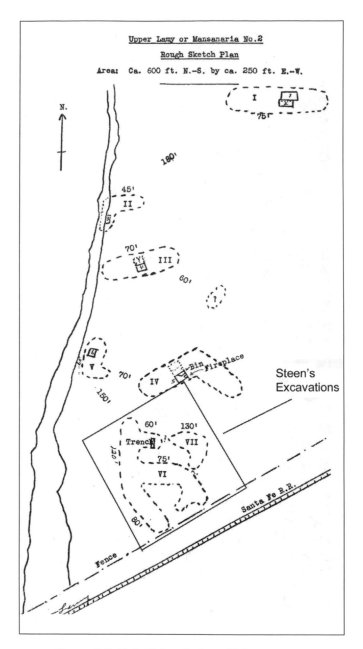

Figure 2.3. Nels Nelson's plan of Manzanares, modified to indicate general area of Steen's excavations in the 1970s. Adapted from map in Nelson's notes on file at NMHPD.

site to be "indefinite" (Steen 1980: 129). Working with a volunteer crew associated with the College of Santa Fe, Steen conducted episodic fieldwork over several years, typically with summer and fall sessions. The last recorded Steen excavations at Manzanares took place on April 19, 1976, although an article he published on his work gives 1977 as the completion date. In total,

27 rooms were tested, 21 of which were excavated completely (Steen 1980: 132). No detailed analyses or reports were published, although extensive collections are housed at MIAC/LOA (Chapter 3 herein). Manzanares is now privately owned.

Chronology

The tree-ring samples collected at Manzanares by Stallings are described as coming from two proveniences, an "Upper Room" and a "Lower Room" (Robinson and others 1973: 24). There are no indications as to how these locations relate to the pueblo in general. Only two "vv" dates were derived from the Upper Room, and although they suggest the possibility of an early thirteenth-century occupation, the data are thin. The 17 samples from the Lower Room are much more substantive, and they include cutting dates clustering between A.D. 1295–1301 (see also Smiley and others 1953: 37). Regrettably, we do not know the location of this "lower room," although correspondence in the LTTR file for this site implies that Stallings sampled Nelson's backdirt. One of the challenges posed by Manzanares is that an excavation unit that was not backfilled, arguably dug by Nelson, is present at the site, but does not appear in Steen's maps, making it difficult to correlate the two projects. We assume that the major structure excavated by Steen was also exposed in the trench excavated by Nelson but this cannot be verified at present.

Although Steen's brief report refers to new dates, they are only generically presented as associated with the late thirteenth and early fourteenth century (Steen 1980: 135). Useful details, however, are archived in the LTTR file and the site files curated by NMHPD. Associated correspondence indicates that the samples were processed in 1977, and the 15 dates that were derived are here published for what we believe is the first time (Table 2.2). From this assemblage, we infer a construction episode in the A.D. 1290s. Of particular interest is the fact that all but one of these samples came from three contiguous rooms (16, 22, and 23), and that the samples were derived from burned architectural wood that was part of the collapsed first story ceiling (Fig. 2.4).

Viewed together with the poorly provenienced Stallings dates, the Steen material suggests a notably tight construction sequence for the portion of the pueblo covered by the sample, with dates ranging from the A.D. 1290s through 1302. The limited variability in these samples indicates that no repairs or reconstruction took

Table 2.2. Unpublished Tree-ring Dates from Manzanares (LA 1104/10607)

Sample number MAN–	Provenience	Date AD
8	Room 8	1259p–1307vv
9	Room 13	1121p–1276+vv
10	Room 16	1242–1303r
16	Room 22	1071–1270++vv
13	Room 22	1204p–1296+r
14	Room 22	1231p–1296+r
15	Room 22	1235p–1296+r
18	Room 22	1244p–1302r
12	Room 22	1252p–1302c
19	Room 22	1219p–1304vv
6	Room 23	1233p–1269r
4	Room 23	1224p–1276vv
5	Room 23	1210p–1277+vv
1	Room 23	1236p–1296r
3	Room 23	1270p–1304vv

NOTE: The specimens are organized by provenience and then by date rather than by sample number. All wood is piñon pine.

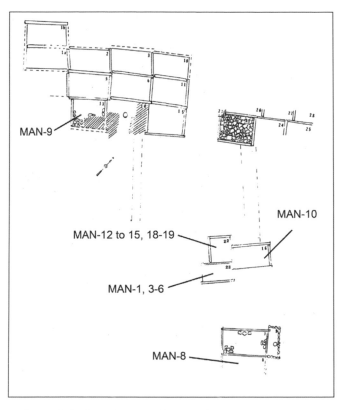

Figure 2.4. Steen's map of excavations at Manzanares, modified to illustrate location of rooms with dated wood. Adapted from map on file at NMHPD.

place after the first decade of the fourteenth century. Consistency between these different sets of dates implies that the occupation of Manzanares was relatively brief, or at least unlike the long-term settlement suggested for Pueblo Alamo, only a half-day's walk away. This evidence thus underlines a potentially significant shift in settlement mode between the early and late thirteenth centuries.

NEW SAMPLES, NEW DATES BURNT CORN PUEBLO

Prior to the beginning of fieldwork at Burnt Corn Pueblo in 2000, there were only three published tree-ring dates from the site, all from surface finds, and these indicated an occupation in the second half of the thirteenth century A.D. (Robinson and others 1972: 25). The overwhelming dominance of black-on-white ceramic types confirmed this attribution, but further specificity was impossible.

Chronology

Our 2002 excavations were designed to expand this chronology as much as possible and gain perspective on the architectural history of the site as a whole (Chapter 4 herein). Additional chronological information was derived from the 2006 excavations. One hundred and thirty-one samples of potentially datable architectural wood were collected from four units (1, 4, 5, 6A/B; see Fig. 2.1). These samples produced 94 tree-ring dates, including 52 cutting dates (Table 2.3). The dates were derived primarily from the plaza pueblo designated as Structure 2 (Units 5 and 6B) and from Structure 5 (Unit 1). These two structures are more than 100 m apart, providing good spatial sampling.

Several interesting patterns are evident, the first being that the range for significant construction at Burnt Corn Pueblo, A.D. 1288–1302, is notably narrow. There is a cluster of dates in 1292, including 7 dates from Unit 1 and 14 dates from Unit 6B. This suggests that construction was in progress throughout the pueblo in that year.

**Table 2.3. Tree-ring dates from Burnt Corn Pueblo (LA 359) from Samples
Collected during the 2002 and 2005 Excavations**

Sample number	Provenience	Date
GALB–33	Unit 1 Lot 3; burnt roofing material against E wall	1236–1290 r inc
GALB–17	Unit 1 Lot 5; burnt roofing material against E wall	1144p–1288"++r inc
GALB–07	Unit 1 Lot 5; burnt roofing material against E wall	1145p–1290"+r
GALB–16	Unit 1 Lot 5; burnt roofing material against E wall	1224p–1290"+r
GALB–08	Unit 1 Lot 5; burnt roofing material against E wall	1245±p 1291"+r
GALB–06	Unit 1 Lot 5; burnt roofing material against E wall	1160–1292w
GALB–10	Unit 1 Lot 5; burnt roofing material against E wall	1263p–1292r inc
GALB–11	Unit 1 Lot 5; burnt roofing material against E wall	1266p–1292r inc
GALB–12	Unit 1 Lot 5; burnt roofing material against E wall	1266p–1292r inc
GALB–13	Unit 1 Lot 5; burnt roofing material against E wall	1267p–1292rB inc
GALB–05	Unit 1 Lot 5; burnt roofing material against E wall	1263–1293r inc
GALB–14	Unit 1 Lot 7	1230p–1291"+r inc
GALB–31	Unit 1 Lot 9; burnt roofing material just above or on floor	931–1015w
GALB–32	Unit 1 Lot 9; burnt roofing material just above or on floor	1127p–1237w
GALB–30	Unit 1 Lot 9; burnt roofing material just above or on floor	1154–1255"+w
GALB–28	Unit 1 Lot 9; burnt roofing material just above or on floor	1203–1285w
GALB–33	Unit 1 Lot 9; burnt roofing material just above or on floor	1251p–1292r inc
GALB–34	Unit 1 Lot 9; burnt roofing material just above or on floor	1262p–1292v inc
GALB–35	Unit 1 Lot 11; burnt wood in pit cut into floor adjacent to E wall	1210p–1292r inc
GALB–61	Unit 1 Lot 11	1265p–1292r inc
GALB–43	Unit 4 Lot 8; Fill: burned roof fall?	1132–1247vv
GALB–25	Unit 4 Lot 8; Fill: burned roof fall?	1177–1267vv
GALB–24	Unit 4 Lot 8; Fill: burned roof fall?	1237p–1294vv
GALB–19	Unit 5 Lot 3; Fill: burned roof fall?	1234p–1299"+vv
GALB–18	Unit 5 Lot 3; Fill: burned roof fall?	1262p–1302r inc
GALB–38	Unit 5 Lot 3; Fill: burned roof fall?	1267p–1302v
GALB–39	Unit 5 Lot 3; Fill: burned roof fall?	1268p–1302r
GALB–40	Unit 5 Lot 3; Fill: burned roof fall?	1272p–1302r inc
GALB–59	Unit 5 Lot 4; Fill; burned roof fall	1165p–1281vv
GALB–49	Unit 5 Lot 4; Fill; burned roof fal	1278p–1301r
GALB–58	Unit 5 Lot 4; Fill; burned roof fall	1276p–1301r
GALB–44	Unit 5 Lot 4; Fill; burned roof fall	1244"±p–1302r inc
GALB–46	Unit 5 Lot 4; Fill; burned roof fall	1269p–1302r inc
GALB–47	Unit 5 Lot 4; Fill; burned roof fall	1265p–1302r inc
GALB–48	Unit 5 Lot 4; Fill; burned roof fall	1262p–1302r inc
GALB–50	Unit 5 Lot 4; Fill; burned roof fall	1250"±p–1302r inc
GALB–51	Unit 5 Lot 4; Fill; burned roof fall	1268p–1302r inc
GALB–52	Unit 5 Lot 4; Fill; burned roof fall	1265p–1302r inc
GALB–53	Unit 5 Lot 4; Fill; burned roof fall	1271p–1302r inc

**Table 2.3. Tree-ring dates from Burnt Corn Pueblo (LA 359) from Samples
Collected during the 2002 and 2005 Excavations (continued)**

Sample Number	Provenience	Date
GALB–55	Unit 5 Lot 4; Fill; burned roof fall	1257p–1302r inc
GALB–56	Unit 5 Lot 4; Fill; burned roof fall	1201-1302r
GALB–57	Unit 5 Lot 4; Fill; burned roof fall	1270p–1302r
GALB–60	Unit 5 Lot 4; Fill; burned roof fall	1244p–1302r
GALB–54	Unit 5 Lot 4; Fill; burned roof fall	1175p–1302v
GALB–82	Unit 6 Room A Lot 32; Fill: along S. wall	1246p–1286w
GALB–71	Unit 6 Room B Lot 43; Fill: burned roof fall	1244p–1292v inc
GALB–72	Unit 6 Room B Lot 43; Fill: burned roof fall	1246p–1292r inc
GALB–75	Unit 6 Room B Lot 43; Fill: burned roof fall	1261p–1292r inc
GALB–79	Unit 6 Room B Lot 43; Fill: burned roof fall	1259–1292r inc
GALB–80	Unit 6 Room B Lot 43; Fill: burned roof fall	1262p–1292r inc
GALB–65	Unit 6 Room B Lot 45; Roof fall just above or on floor	1254p–1292r inc
GALB–66	Unit 6 Room B Lot 45; Roof fall just above or on floor	1261p–1292r
GALB–68	Unit 6 Room B Lot 45; Roof fall just above or on floor	1262p–1292r inc
GALB–70	Unit 6 Room B Lot 45; Roof fall just above or on floor	1248p–1292r inc
GALB–73	Unit 6 Room B Lot 45; Roof fall just above or on floor	1259–1292r inc
GALB–76	Unit 6 Room B Lot 45; Roof fall just above or on floor	1259p–1292r inc
GALB–77	Unit 6 Room B Lot 45; Roof fall just above or on floor	1238p–1292r inc
GALB–78	Unit 6 Room B Lot 45; Roof fall just above or on floor	1244p–1290+r inc
GALB–81	Unit 6 Room B Lot 45; Roof fall just above or on floor	1241p–1292r inc
GALB–89	Unit 6 Room B Lot 45; Roof fall just above or on floor	1260p–1292v inc

NOTE: With one exception, all wood is piñon pine. GALB–31 is ponderosa pine; the anomalously early date of this specimen suggests some divergent source.

Another cluster is evident at 1302, with 16 of the 18 cutting dates from Unit 5 dating to that year. This indicates that a second substantial construction episode took place in the plaza pueblo. In total, 71 percent of the Burnt Corn cutting dates are for the years A.D. 1292 and 1302.

The sets of dates in the three rooms are also internally consistent. The wood cut for Unit 1 spans a 6-year range, but the 1- and 2-year ranges for wood cut for Units 5 and 6B are particularly discrete. No later repairs are evident in any of these examples, suggesting a relatively short use-life for the rooms. In fact, none of the dated roofs from Burnt Corn show any evidence of reconstruction.

It is possible that this sample of dated wood is inadvertently biased, and that other room blocks on the site are older or younger, but the clarity of the pattern is compelling. The A.D. 1272 cutting date from the surface find

RG–4566 (Robinson and others 1972: 25) suggests the possibility of an earlier occupation (Chapter 6 herein), as do a few of the dates in Table 2.3, but no later occupation is implied. The almost complete absence of glaze ceramics from the site argues against any substantial Early Classic occupation. It is generally assumed that Glaze A pottery types appeared in the Galisteo Basin no later than the A.D. 1340s (Schaafsma 1995: 162), although since it was being produced in the Albuquerque district by 1315 some traded glazes can be expected some years earlier. Either way, the occupation at Burnt Corn was over before this new development.

The only indication of a later date for the Burnt Corn occupation comes from an archaeomagnetic sample taken from a burned feature in Unit 4 (Structure 1), processed by Jeff Cox of the Office of Archaeological Studies. The sample was taken well above the floor, and no further excavations were conducted at that location, so the archaeomagnetic sample cannot be more securely interpreted. Additional archaeomagnetic samples collected by Gary Hein in 2005 are being processed.

DISCUSSION

This body of tree-ring dates—the new, the old, the forgotten—delineates interesting trends in Galisteo chronology that deserve to be further examined. Wiseman's recent analysis of cutting and non-cutting dates from the region, suggests that the existing chronological record documents expansions and contractions of settlement across the Coalition and Classic periods (2004). Our information supports this assertion and provides relevant details about such transformations.

Securing good dates for Pueblo Alamo further clarifies the position of this important site in the precolumbian history of the northern Rio Grande. There are surprisingly few well-dated sites of the early A.D. 1200s in the vicinity, with only LA 3333 from the southeastern Galisteo Basin demonstrably contemporary (Dutton 1964). This is a critical interval, because many of the traditional arguments about the Pueblo settlement of the Galisteo in the mid–1200s are based on the idea that the region was relatively empty. The scope of construction at Pueblo Alamo in the 1220s and earlier will not change this scenario, but the size of the pueblo and the consistency of these dates across it is at least good evidence for a large resident population at the beginning of the thirteenth century. Renewed research in the vicinity of LA 3333, recently designated the Wildhorse Community (Charles Hannaford, personal communication in 2007), may provide further detail on this pivotal era.

The "sealed" contexts of these new Pueblo Alamo dates, and thus evidence for subsequent reconstruction, are also important. Multiple building phases at the pueblo support other indications that it was a center of population for decades. The only other known pueblo in the vicinity with similar longevity is Colina Verde, which was apparently occupied from the mid–1200s through the early fourteenth century (Smiley and others 1953: 330). Other Coalition period occupations appear to have been more brief, suggesting that some complex settlement dynamic was at work. The newly dated samples also add to the body of evidence indicating that Pueblo Alamo was destroyed by fire. The dispersion of burned samples across the pueblo suggests that this catastrophe was widespread, and the fact that much of the additional evidence for burning is apparently associated with the later occupation implies that catastrophic burning occurred more than once. Further review of the Pueblo Alamo field notes will clarify this pattern.

The precise overlap of the Manzanares and Burnt Corn dates indicates considerable construction across the Galisteo Basin at the end of the A.D. 1200s. This trend is evident in other regional sites as well, particularly Pueblo Largo (Dutton 1955: 40). The expansion was as brief as it was significant. Neither Manzanares nor Burnt Corn shows signs of substantive activity after the first few years of the 1300s. Wiseman's (2004) review suggests that little construction took place in the Galisteo during this period, and the Pueblo Largo sequence is also characterized by "a notable absence of cutting dates in the 14th century" (Robinson and others 1973: 38). Evidence for construction during this interval is minimal even at regional sites with greater longevity, such as Pindi (LA 1; Ahlstrom 1989: 369).

Thus there is increasing evidence for a brief population "pulse" across the Galisteo Basin in the waning years of the Coalition period. Such shifts have been noted before and argued to reflect migration (Lang 1977a: 229) or local movement in response to shifting opportunities for farming (Habicht-Mauche 1993: 90) or some form of population cycling (Lang and Schieck 1991: 105). Dates derived from surface ceramics elsewhere in the region have also been used to identify short-term population shifts (Crown and others 1996). For example, evidence from the Pajarito Plateau identifies the late 1200s as a time of population decline or dispersal (Powers and Orcutt 1999: 559).

Whatever process produced this pattern of Galisteo Basin settlement—population expansion, internal reorganization, or immigration—it arguably came to a dramatic end. Manzanares, Burnt Corn, and Pueblo Largo all show evidence that this construction phase was terminated by burning. Largo was eventually reoccupied, but Manzanares and Burnt Corn remained "empty" through the remainder of the precolumbian era (Chapters 4 and 5 herein; Snead 2004, 2008b). As more evidence becomes available it is evident that our preferred models for change, such as abandonment, reorganization, and cycling, may mask a harsher reality for the people of the northern Río Grande. Better dates make nuanced interpretations possible, and as we dig new sites and delve in existing collections the attention that we can pay to strengthening the chronology is clearly worthwhile.

CHAPTER THREE

Late Coalition Ceramics from the Galisteo Basin

Lori Barkwill Love and Leslie Cohen

Ceramic analysis has been an important element of the Tano Origins Project, with particular emphasis on the black-on-white and utility wares of the Coalition period. These ceramics have received limited attention, and considerable confusion exists about their typology and associated attributes. The excavated and curated collections studied by the Tano Origins Project have provided opportunities to take a detailed look at this artifact class, shedding light on the characteristics of the ceramics themselves, and on possible patterns of exchange and population movement.

In general terms the late Coalition period ceramics from the Galisteo Basin have received less attention than the Classic period glaze wares from the region. Reports on the black-on-white and utility wares from Coalition sites are sparse and often incomplete (e.g. Allen 1973; Steen 1980). Research to better understand these ceramics is thus timely, both because of expanding archaeological fieldwork in the area and because of renewed interest in the topic of migration among Southwestern archaeologists. The Galisteo Basin was a possible destination for migrants from the Colorado Plateau in the A.D. 1200s, and ceramics have been found useful in the study of migration processes. Documenting the complex associations of black-on-white and utility wares during the Coalition period clarifies our understanding of how local assemblages are associated with population movement and social interaction.

This chapter presents data about late Coalition period ceramic assemblages in the Galisteo Basin. To understand these ceramics, we use descriptions of pottery types from sites outside the basin, many of which derive from large multi-component settlements occupied well beyond the Coalition period. We are therefore faced with several questions: how do the ceramics from the Galisteo Basin compare to standard pottery descriptions? What do the ceramic assemblages from late Coalition sites in the Galisteo Basin actually look like? What are the similarities and differences between the local types? We address these questions using ceramic data from six late Coalition sites studied by the Tano Origins Project.

WHITE WARE

Traditionally, Santa Fe Black-on-white and Galisteo Black-on-white are considered to be the two local decorated types in the Galisteo Basin during the late Coalition period (Wendorf and Reed 1955: 145). Variability in these and other black-on-white pottery types in the Northern Rio Grande has made classification difficult (Honea 1968: 111; Kidder and Amsden 1931: 14, 22; Kidder and Shepard 1936: 470; Lang 1982: 158). Regarding the ceramic assemblages from Forked Lightning (LA 672) and Pecos Pueblo (LA 625), Amsden remarked that "[s]o great is the variability of the Pecos Black-on-white that one gets the strong feeling that easily recognizable, quite valid types must lurk within it" (Kidder and Amsden 1931: 22). Although consistent attributes are difficult to isolate, over the years widely-accepted types have been defined. Descriptions of Santa Fe Black-on-white and Galisteo Black-on-white are derived from Coalition–Classic period sites across the Northern Rio Grande, and are most commonly cited from the Forked Lightning and Pecos assemblages (Kidder and Amsden 1931; Kidder and Shepard 1936), as well as those from Pindi Pueblo (LA 1) (Stubbs and Stallings 1953) and Arroyo Hondo (LA 12) (Habicht-Mauche 1993).

Santa Fe Black-on-white is one of the most widely distributed and longest-lived carbon-painted white wares in the Northern Rio Grande region (Habicht-Mauche 1993: 19). Associated tree-ring dates place initial production at A.D. 1175 to 1200, and the type continued to be produced until A.D. 1350 to 1400 in some places (Habicht-Mauche

1993: 19). In fact, the production of Santa Fe Black-on-white is considered to be the hallmark of the Coalition period (Wendorf and Reed 1955). The diagnostic attributes of Santa Fe Black-on-white include a uniform paste color, typically a bluish-gray; fine tuff or sand temper, or both; unslipped interior and exterior surfaces; unpolished exterior surface; and round rims (Habicht-Mauche 1993: 21; Kidder and Amsden 1931: 24; Wilson 2007: 30). The technological variability and design style similarity of Santa Fe Black-on-white throughout the Northern Rio Grande has been attributed to an open network of interaction that existed among the communities in the region during the early to middle Coalition period, from A.D. 1150 to 1250 (Habicht-Mauche 1993: 88–89; Ruscavage-Barz 1999: 234).

The history of Santa Fe Black-on-white as a ceramic type is complex. As initially named and described by Amsden and Kidder, the type was placed within the "rough exterior" category, and was initially called the "Blue-gray type" because of its distinctive bluish tint (Kidder and Amsden 1931: 23). Amsden found that the Blue-gray type was almost always in bowl form, generally had a thin slip applied only to the interior, most commonly had thin or round rims, and the painted designs frequently extended to the rim without a framing line (Kidder and Amsden 1931: 23–24). Amsden also identified a subtype, Whitewash slip ware, which was similar to the Blue-gray type in paste, decoration and lack of exterior polish, but associated with a thin whitewash slip on the exterior and occasional flared rims (Kidder and Amsden 1931: 24). Anna Shepard's microscopic and petrographic analyses of the Blue-gray type found that there were three distinct temper groups: fine sand (silt), tuff, and sherd (Kidder and Shepard 1936: 461). However, she noted that there was no correlation between the temper groups and different surface treatments. The tuff-tempered Blue-gray type was found more frequently at Pecos than Forked Lightning and the sherd-tempered Blue-gray type was only found in the earliest levels at Fork Lightning (Kidder and Shepard 1936: 471–472).

The Blue-gray type was renamed Santa Fe Black-on-white by H. P. Mera (1935: 12) to conform to the standard binomial type-naming convention. Mera suggested that Santa Fe Black-on-white developed out of the earlier mineral-painted Kwahe'e Black-on-white and the carbon-painted Gallina Black-on-white. LA 742, a small pueblo in the Tesuque Valley, was designated the type-site for Santa Fe Black-on-white (Mera 1935: 12). Mera also suggested that naming of subtypes or varieties

should be avoided until an extensive study of the pottery was completed.

Assemblages from other excavated sites expanded the archaeological understanding of Santa Fe Black-on-white. At Pindi Pueblo the type was described as having a light gray to dark blue-gray paste color, and semi-polished to well-polished interiors that may have a white slip that occasionally extends over the rim on the exterior or that covers the entire exterior of the bowl (Stubbs and Stallings 1953: 48). Santa Fe Black-on-white was the predominant decorated type associated with the late thirteenth-century occupation of Pindi Pueblo. After A.D. 1300 Santa Fe Black-on-white declined in frequency at Pindi Pueblo, although there was a slight increase towards the end of the occupation in the mid-fourteenth century (Stubbs and Stallings 1953: 15, 23).

Santa Fe Black-on-white at Arroyo Hondo is described as having a uniform paste and texture, with a fine silt/sand or tuff temper (Habicht-Mauche 1993: 20-22). Over time, the use of tuff temper increased. Bowls had either a polished slipped or unslipped interior, with unslipped exteriors, and there was frequent use of framing lines. As at Pindi Pueblo, the frequency of Santa Fe Black-on-white at Arroyo Hondo is variable throughout the site's occupation. The type occurred in high frequency at the beginning of the early fourteenth-century Component I, but then dramatically decreased. There was a resurgence in the frequency of Santa Fe Black-on-white at the beginning of Component II, ca. A.D. 1370, that persisted until the end of the occupation in the early fifteenth century (Habicht-Mauche 1993: 5-7, 19). Sourcing analyses demonstrate that the Santa Fe Black-on-white at Arroyo Hondo was a trade ware, most likely produced in the Española Basin to the north (Habicht-Mauche 1995: 173).

Several black-on-white types were produced in the Northern Rio Grande region during the early fourteenth century, with Galisteo Black-on-white most prevalent south of the Santa Fe River (Habicht-Mauche 1993: 92). The initial production of Galisteo Black-on-white is thought to have begun by A.D. 1300, but an earlier production date around A.D. 1270 has been suggested (Habicht-Mauche 1993: 28). The type was apparently produced into the fifteenth century. Diagnostic attributes include a light grey to white paste, often with a distinct dark core; sherd temper; slipped interior and occasionally slipped exterior with a tendency to crackle or craze; polished interior and exterior; and square rims with occasional rim decoration (Habicht-Mauche 1993:

28; Kidder and Amsden 1931: 29; Stubbs and Stallings 1953: 50; Wilson 2007: 37). The introduction of new black-on-white types has been attributed to the "emergence of competing ethnic groups during the late Coalition period" (Habicht-Mauche 1993: 98). In addition, some archaeologists think there is a striking similarity between Galisteo Black-on-white and Mesa Verde Black-on-white (Mera 1935: 19, 21; Stubbs and Stallings 1953: 48, 50), and interpret this as evidence that Mesa Verde migrants moved into the Galisteo Basin (Cordell 1995: 206; Riley 1952: 78).

As with Santa Fe Black-on-white, the descriptions of Galisteo Black-on-white come from sites outside the Galisteo Basin. Amsden categorized Galisteo Black-on-white under his polished exterior category and called it Crackle type (Kidder and Amsden 1931: 25-26). He found that it had a thick, finely crackled, smooth slip on the interior and exterior, but the exterior often had a thinner slip than the interior. Amsden noted that a dark core, a single thick framing line with a narrow top banding line, and square (flat) rims were common attributes with the Crackle type. In the earliest levels of Forked Lightning, the surface appearance of Crackle type closely resembled Blue-gray type (Santa Fe Black-on-white); however, by the middle of the occupation it became more distinct and was the dominant decorated type during the late Forked Lightning and early Pecos occupations.

Anna Shepard's technological analysis of the sherds at Forked Lightning and Pecos found that, with a few exceptions, the temper in Crackle type was ground sherd (Kidder and Shepard 1936: 464-466). Only a third to a half of the Crackle type was slipped on the interior as well as the exterior, and the crackle slip was not universally found on the sherds. Furthermore, an exterior slip was found more often in the later levels than the earlier levels in the stratigraphic tests, suggesting that an exterior slip was a temporal variation (Kidder and Shepard 1936: 480). Based on the composition of the ground sherds used as temper in Crackle type, Shepard suggests that Crackle type was produced at sites in the Galisteo Basin (Kidder and Shepard 1936: 485).

Mera (1935: 21) changed the name from Crackle type to Galisteo Black-on-white but did not alter the type description, although he noted that in the central and western portions of the distribution area it was more polished and less crackled (1935: 21). He also suggested that the type-site for Galisteo Black-on-white be changed from Forked Lightning to Burnt Corn Pueblo

(LA 359) because he believed that Burn Corn was closer to the center of its distribution.

Stubbs and Stallings (1953: 15, 23, 50) note that the Galisteo Black-on-white from the A.D. 1250-1300 component at Pindi Pueblo closely resembled Mesa Verde Black-on-white. In the later occupations, however, the two were more distinguishable. Stubbs and Stallings describe early Galisteo Black-on-white as having either sherd or crushed andesite temper; a well-polished interior and exterior white slip that is often crackled or crazed; square rims, often with rim ticks; and designs similar to Mesa Verde Black-on-white (Stubbs and Stallings 1953: 15, 50).

Galisteo Black-on-white in the Arroyo Hondo assemblage was universally sherd tempered with light gray to white paste, with dark cores present in about 30 percent of the sample (Habicht-Mauche 1993: 28). The majority of the Galisteo Black-on-white bowls had flat (square) rims, and they were slipped on the interior and exterior (Habicht-Mauche 1993: 28, 40–41). The petrographic and XRF analyses of the Galisteo Black-on-white from Arroyo Hondo suggest that this pottery came from at least three distinct sources, all probably from the Galisteo Basin (Habicht-Mauche 1993: 67, 81, 85).

UTILITY WARE

Standardized type descriptions for the utility or culinary ware are virtually nonexistent for the Northern Rio Grande region (Bice and Sundt 1972: 146; Habicht-Mauche 1993: 12–13). Habicht-Mauche suggests that these wares are "often neglected because they generally reflect much slower rates of stylistic change and have fewer easily observable and measurable attributes" (1993: 13).Thus, their usefulness in detecting chronology and cultural change is limited. Utility ware is typically classified by surface treatments or types of corrugation. However, this too can cause confusion because many different terms are used to describe a type of corrugation, such as smeared, smoothed, blind, or obliterated indented corrugated. There is also the problem that a single vessel may have more than one type of corrugation (Habicht-Mauche 1993: 13).

The lack of consistency in terminology for utility ware makes it difficult to compare assemblages from different sites in the Northern Rio Grande. However, some generalizations can be made about these wares for the Coalition period, when jars represented the primary vessel form (Cordell 1998: 67). In terms of surface treatment, there appears to have been a general transition from clearly indented corrugation to partially obliterated or smeared corrugation, although this was not universal (Cordell 1979b: 144; Stubbs and Stallings 1953: 56-57; Wendorf and Reed 1955: 145–146). There was also an increase in the use of micaceous clay/temper over time (Habicht-Mauche 1993: 15; Stubbs and Stallings 1953: 56; Wendorf and Reed 1955: 145). However, Mera (1935: 14, 18, 21) noted that the utility ware at sites associated with Galisteo Black-on-white was made less often with micaceous clay than the utility ware at sites associated with Santa Fe or Wiyo Black-on-white ceramics.

TRADE WARES

The trade wares commonly found at late Coalition sites in the Galisteo Basin are Wiyo Black-on-white, Chupadero Black-on-white, and White Mountain Red Ware, specifically St. Johns Black-on-red and St. Johns Polychrome. Wiyo Black-on-white was initially named Biscuitoid by Amsden (Kidder and Amsden 1931). It is currently described as having a highly polished slipped interior, an unslipped and unpolished exterior, and a softer, browner paste than Santa Fe Black-on-white (Wilson 2007: 32). The modern consensus is that Wiyo Black-on-white developed from Santa Fe Black-on-white (Habicht-Mauche 1993: 22, 25; Mera 1935), and was produced between A.D. 1300 and 1400 (Wilson 2007). The types are quite similar, and it is interesting that when Helene Warren reexamined a sample of sherds from Forked Lightning, she found that all 10 of the Biscuitoid sherds in the sample were actually Santa Fe Black-on-white (Warren 1971). The core area of production and distribution of Wiyo Black-on-white was the Española-Chama region, and the type only became common in the Santa Fe area after A.D. 1300 (Habicht-Mauche 1993: 22, 23, 85).

The association of Chupadero Black-on-white with other black-on-white wares is uncertain. Some of its common attributes include mineral paint, a thin white-to-gray slip, and heavy striations on jar interiors (Habicht-Mauche 1993: 17; Wilson 2007: 29). The production span for Chupadero Black-on-white is over 300 years, from A.D. 1175 to the 1540s (Habicht-Mauche 1993: 17). It was produced primarily to the south of the Galisteo Basin, in the Chupadero Mesa, upper Jornada del Muerto and Socorro areas (Habicht-Mauche 1993: 17). Nonetheless, the type has been reported in small quantities at sites across the Northern Rio Grande in components dating around the late thirteenth and early fourteenth centuries, such as at Pindi Pueblo and Forked Lightning (Lang 1993: 180).

White Mountain Red Ware was produced in the Cibola region and widely distributed in an area extending from Mesa Verde in the north to Casa Grandes in the south, and from the Pecos River in the east to the Chino Valley in Arizona in the west (Carlson 1970: 37). The various types in this ware include St. Johns Black-on-red and St. Johns Polychrome (Carlson 1970: 31). Production dates range from A.D. 1175 to 1300, with St. Johns Black-on-red more common earlier in the date range (Carlson 1970: 31, 41). Small quantities of St. Johns Black-on-red and St. Johns Polychrome have been noted at Coalition period sites in the Galisteo Basin, including Pueblo Alamo (Allen 1973; Smiley and others 1953: 17), Lamy Pueblo (Smiley and others 1953: 17), and LA 3333 (Dutton 1964: 450–451).

QUESTIONS AND CONTRADICTIONS

The complexity of classifying black-on-white and utility ceramics provokes questions regarding the reliability of the types themselves and their use for understanding the Coalition period. Contradictions also abound, one of which is that the assemblages used to analyze ceramics found at late Coalition sites in the Galisteo Basin are typically from sites *outside* the basin itself, and some of these occupations postdate the Coalition period. Our central approach to ceramic analysis in the Tano Origins Project was thus to compare our materials to these diverse type descriptions. This approach has proven useful both for understanding our own collections and for making comparisons with assemblages documented elsewhere. Here we use this information to address a basic question: what does Galisteo Black-on-white look like at late Coalition period sites in the Galisteo Basin?

Methodology

We analyzed excavated material from six sites in the Galisteo Basin, including Burnt Corn, Manzanares, Lodestar North, Lodestar South, Cholla House, and Slope House (Chapters 4 and 5). Given the absence of whole vessels, only sherds were examined. In some cases, the ceramic assemblages were sampled. Ceramics

Table 3.1. Ceramic Assemblages

Ware	Burnt Corn Pueblo n	%	Manzanares n	%	Lodestar North n	%	Loadstar South n	%	Cholla House n	%	Slope House n	%
White Ware	887	20.78	694	36.45	3	1.52	24	16.11	34	21.25	23	21.90
Utility Ware	3173	74.34	1203	63.18	186	93.94	125	83.89	126	78.75	82	78.10
White Mountain Red Ware	9	0.21	7	0.37	9	4.55						
Indeterminate	199	4.66										
Total	4268		1904		198		149		160		105	

were classified on the basis of surface treatments or by a combination of temper and surface treatments. For sherds classified by temper and surface treatments, the temper was determined by making a fresh break on the sherd and examining it under a binocular microscope.

Santa Fe Black-on-white was identified by surface treatment that featured unpolished and unslipped exteriors and unpolished to semi-polished, slipped or unslipped interiors, and sand or sand-tuff temper. Wiyo Black-on-white was distinguished on the basis of unpolished, unslipped exteriors, with highly polished slipped interiors, and temper consisting of sand or sand and tuff. Galisteo Black-on-white was identified on the basis of slipped exteriors and slipped or crackled slipped interiors, and sherd temper. Utility wares were classified primarily using the type of corrugation. However, the temper of utility wares from Lodestar North and South, Cholla House, and Slope House were also analyzed.

Burnt Corn Pueblo

A total of 4,268 sherds were recovered from the 2002 and 2005 excavations at Burnt Corn Pueblo (Table 3.1). Roughly 20 percent of the total ceramic assemblage comes from the five small units excavated in 2002, with the remaining 80 percent derived from the two larger units excavated in 2005 (see Chapter 6, this volume; Smith 2005). The initial classification was based on visual inspection of surface treatments. Decorated ceramics in this assemblage consisted of Galisteo Black-on-white, Santa Fe Black-on-white, Wiyo Black-on-white, St. Johns Polychrome, St. Johns Black-on-red, and Indeterminate White Mountain Red Ware. The utility ware consisted of Smeared Indented Corrugated, Smoothed Corrugated, Indented Corrugated, Plain Corrugated, Plain Grayware, Clapboard Corrugated, Indeterminate

Smudged, and Neck Banded Corrugated. Sherds classified as indeterminate made up 51.46 percent of the white ware and 27.14 percent of the utility ware.

There were inconsistencies in the type naming conventions used during analysis of the 2002 and 2005 assemblages, so a detailed discussion of the entire assemblage awaits reanalysis. However, one potentially significant aspect of the Burnt Corn assemblage is the absence of Chupadero Black-on-white. In contrast, small quantities of Chupadero Black-on-white are reported at other Galisteo sites, including Manzanares (Steen 1980:137 and see below), Pueblo Alamo (Allen 1973; Smiley, et al. 1953: 17), Lamy Pueblo (Smiley and others 1953: 17) and the earliest levels of Pueblo Largo (Dutton 1953: 350). If future reanalysis of the Burnt Corn ceramic assemblage confirms the absence of Chupadero Black-on-white, this will provide useful information about trading patterns in the Galisteo Basin.

Two separate samples of the black-on-white ceramics from the Burnt Corn assemblage were classified according to temper and surface treatments. Bowl sherds represented 96 percent of the black-on-white assemblage, and only this vessel form was analyzed.

The first sample, designated the rim study, included 67 rim sherds, about 8 percent of the total number of black-on-white ceramics (Table 3.2). Rim sherds were selected for analysis when the design, surface treatment, and rim form were clearly visible. The provenience, temper, rim shape, rim decoration, design orientation, interior and exterior treatments, paste color and type were recorded for each sherd. The second sample, designated the stylistic study, included a total of 106 body and rim sherds, or 12 percent of the black-on-white ceramics. This sample was drawn from sherds that exhibited visible paint designs and surface treatments, and which were classified as Santa Fe Black-on-white or Galisteo Black-on-white.

Table 3.2. Frequency of Black-on-white Types by Sample

Type	Sample 1 (Rim Study) n	Sample 1 (Rim Study) %	Sample 2 (Stylistic Study) n	Sample 2 (Stylistic Study) %
Santa Fe Black-on-white	21	31.34	44	41.51
Galisteo Black-on-white	44	65.67	62	58.49
Wiyo Black-on-white	2	2.99	0	0
Total	67		106	

NOTE: Sherds classified as Wiyo were not included in the Sample II analysis.

Initially a minimum sherd size of 3 cm was used to select the sherds. Too few sherds met all the criteria, however, so the minimum size was dropped. Nonetheless, the average size of the selected sherds was 3.6 cm^2. The analysis included the same attributes as those investigated in first sample, with the addition of design elements.

Both samples show Galisteo Black-on-white as the predominant black-on-white type at Burnt Corn. Although Galisteo Black-on-white was in the majority, Santa Fe Black-on-white constituted 41.5 percent of the sherds in the stylistic study and 31.34 percent of the sherds in the rim study. There was a low frequency of Wiyo Black-on-white, which is not surprising given that this pottery type is generally found north of the Santa Fe River (Habicht-Mauche 1993: 22, 85). Wiyo Black-on-white is noticeably more common in the Santa Fe area after A.D. 1300, when Burnt Corn Pueblo was no longer occupied

Manzanares

Manzanares is a large late Coalition site located in the northeastern portion of the Galisteo Basin along the north bank of the Galisteo Creek (see Chapter 2, this volume). Forty boxes of sherds from this site were produced by excavations sponsored by the College of Santa Fe in the 1970s (Steen 1980). This collection is curated at the Museum of Indian Arts and Cultures/Laboratory of Anthropology, and it provides an excellent comparative assemblage. Despite the fact that detailed provenience information is not available for the majority of these artifacts, further study has proven useful (Barkwill Love 2006).

Two separate analyses were conducted on the Manzanares ceramic assemblage. For the first analysis, 13 of the 40 boxes were selected based on the catalog description of the boxes as only containing sherds, or inspection of the boxes confirming that sherds made up the majority of the box contents. Four of the 13 boxes were selected at random, and all the sherds from randomly selected, unlabeled bags within them were selected for analysis. For the remaining nine boxes, only bags labeled with locational information were selected for analysis. Nine bags were analyzed but only two of them had locational information that corresponds to the excavation map. It appears that there was a change in the site and unit terminology used during the excavation (Snead 2005a). Consequently, even though the remaining seven bags had locational information, the location listed did not correspond to the excavation map.

A total of 1,904 ceramics were selected for analysis using this sampling procedure, and these were classified by a visual inspection of surface treatments (Table 3.1). The decorated ceramics included Galisteo Black-on-white, Santa Fe Black-on-white, Wiyo Black-on-white, Chupadero Black-on-white, Kwahe'e Black-on-white, St. John's Polychrome, and St. John's Black-on-red (Table 3.3). Small or eroded sherds were classified as indeterminate black-on-white. For the decorated ceramics, bowls were the most common vessel form (95.44%). The utility ware consisted of Smeared Indented Corrugated, Smooth Corrugated, Indented Corrugated, Plain Corrugated, Clapboard Corrugated, and Plain Gray Ware (Table 3.4).

The second analysis of Manzanares ceramics was based on a selection of Black-on-white bowl rim sherds that were classified by temper and surface treatments. This analysis was done in conjunction with the rim study (Sample I) at Burnt Corn Pueblo, and the same criteria were used to select the sherds for analysis. A total of 157 black-on-white rim sherds were included in this analysis (Table 3.5).

Galisteo Black-on-white was the predominant decorated type in the Manzanares assemblage, constituting 51.8 percent of the sherds in the initial analysis and 53.5 percent of the sherds in the rim study. As at Burnt Corn, Santa Fe Black-on-white was the second most commonly found type, constituting 23.4 percent of the sherds in the initial analysis and 46.5 percent of the sherds in the rim study. Wiyo Black-on-white and Chupadero Black-on-white were found in low frequencies in the initial analysis; and Wiyo Black-on-white was not found in the rim

Table 3.3. Decorated Ceramic Types

Type	Manzanares n	Manzanares %	Lodestar North n	Lodestar North %	Loadstar South n	Loadstar South %	Cholla House n	Cholla House %	Slope House n	Slope House %
Galisteo Black-on-White	363	51.78			6	25.00	12	35.29	3	13.04
Santa Fe Black-on-White	164	23.40	1	8.33	16	66.67	20	58.22	18	78.26
Wiyo Black-on-White	12	1.71			1	4.17	1	2.94	1	4.35
Kwahe'e Black-on-White	3	0.43								
St. Johns Polychrome	3	0.43								
St. Johns Black-on-red	4	0.57								
Indeterminate Wh. Mnt. Red Ware			9	75.00						
Indeterminate Black-on-white	149	21.26	2	16.67	1	4.17	1	2.94	1	4.35
Total	701		12		24		34		23	

study. Chupadero Black-on-white sherds are typically jar pieces, and none were included in the study of bowl rims.

The most common utility ware at Manzanares was Smeared Indented Corrugated. One interesting note was that mica was present in 56.69 percent of the utility ware sherds. It is unknown whether the mica occurred naturally in the clay or was added as temper. Steen (1980: 138) observed that flakes of mica were commonly found in the fill of the rooms at Manzanares, although he could not determine the use of this mica. However, Wendorf and Reed (1955: 146) noted that the use of mica in the temper of utility ware was characteristic of the Galisteo Phase from A.D. 1300 to 1325. At Pindi Pueblo, Stubbs and Stallings (1953: 56) found that utility ware with micaceous temper increased in the later levels. Additional research into the paste and temper of the utility ware at Manzanares is needed to determine how the mica was being used.

Lodestar North

Lodestar North is located about 13 km west of Burnt Corn Pueblo (see Chapter 7, this volume). A total of 198 sherds were recovered during the 2005 excavation, and the entire assemblage was analyzed (Table 3.1). The ceramics were classified by temper and surface treatment. The decorated ceramics were very small and few in number (Table 3.3).

It should be noted that the nine tiny, indeterminate red ware sherds had similar paste and, although none could be refitted, possibly belonged to two vessels. All the decorated ware was found within the top 30 cm of fill, while ceramics from the lower units, in proximity to

the floor, were exclusively utility ware. Therefore, the decorated sherds may not necessarily be associated with the structure at the site, but may have been transported from the surface. The utility ware was comprised of only two types: Smeared Indented Corrugated and Plain Gray Ware (Table 3.4).

Lodestar South

Lodestar South is a cluster of small structures within the dispersed Lodestar community 13 km West of Burnt Corn Pueblo (see Chapter 7, this volume). Only 149 sherds were found during the 2005 excavation (Table 3.1). As with Lodestar North, the ceramics were classified by temper and surface treatment. The decorated ceramics consisted of Santa Fe Black-on-white, Galisteo Black-on-white, and Wiyo Black-on-white (Table 3.3). No red ware was found at Lodestar South. The utility ware included Smeared Indented Corrugated, Indented Corrugated, Plain Corrugated, and Plain Gray Ware (Table 3.4).

The decorated sherds at Lodestar South, weighing slightly more than 80 g, were larger than the decorated ceramics at Lodestar North, weighing less than 10 g. The predominant decorated type found at Lodestar South was Santa Fe Black-on-white. Unlike Lodestar North, the decorated ceramics were found throughout the structure, with 45.83 percent of the decorated ceramics found 30 cm or lower below datum. There was also more variety in the kinds of utility ware at Lodestar South than Lodestar North. Although for both, Smeared Indented Corrugated was the most frequently found utility ware (excluding indeterminate).

Table 3.4. Utility Ware Surface Treatments

Surface Treatment	Manzanares n	Manzanares %	Lodestar North n	Lodestar North %	Loadstar South n	Loadstar South %	Cholla House n	Cholla House %	Slope House n	Slope House %
Smeared Indented Corrugated	732	60.85	107	57.53	21	16.80	28	22.22	31	37.80
Indented Corrugated	155	12.88			14	11.20	17	13.49	5	6.10
Smoothed Corrugated	117	9.73								
Plain Gray Ware	45	3.74	1	0.54	9	7.20	4	3.17	6	7.32
Plain Corrugated	7	0.58			12	9.60			1	1.22
Clapboard Corrugated	4	0.33					7	5.56	2	2.44
Indeterminate Corrugated	143	11.89	78	41.94	69	55.20	70	55.56	37	45.12
Total	1203		186		125		126		82	

Cholla House

Cholla House is a small structure or farmstead in the Late Coalition Burnt Corn community (see Chapter 7). A total of 160 sherds was excavated during the 2006 excavation (Table 3.1). The classification of the ceramics was based on temper and surface treatment. The decorated ceramics were composed exclusively of Santa Fe Black-on-white, Galisteo Black-on-white, and Wiyo Black-on-white (Table 3.3). The utility ware included Smeared Indented Corrugated, Indented Corrugated, Clapboard Corrugated and Plain Gray Ware (Table 3.4).

The predominant decorated type at Cholla House was Santa Fe Black-on-white. Bowls were the most common vessel form for the decorated ceramics, constituting 91.18 percent of the assemblage. One Santa Fe Black-on-white sherd found on the surface had a basket-impressed exterior. Among the utility wares, Smeared Indented Corrugated was the predominant surface treatment.

Slope House

Slope House, like Cholla House, is a small structure or farmstead within the Burnt Corn community (see Chapter 7). A total of 105 sherds were found during the 2006 excavation (Table 3.1). The ceramics were classified by temper and surface treatment. The decorated ceramics included Santa Fe Black-on-white, Galisteo Black-on-white and Wiyo Black-on-white (Table 3.3). The utility ware was found throughout the site and consisted of Smeared Indented Corrugated, Indented Corrugated, Clapboard Corrugated and Plain Gray Ware (Table 3.4).

Santa Fe Black-on-white was the predominant decorated type at Slope House. However, it should be noted that 78.26 percent of the decorated ceramics came from the uppermost 20 cm of the fill. This differs from Cholla House, where 23.53 percent of the decorated ceramics came from the equivalent stratigraphic units. Given that the site was at the bottom of a slope, it is likely that some of these ceramics were washed into the site. Of the three decorated sherds found in the stratigraphic units below 20 cm, one was a large Galisteo Black-on-white worked sherd, possibly a scoop. Smeared Indented Corrugated was the most common utility ware surface treatment at this location.

DISCUSSION

The late Coalition ceramic assemblage was predominately composed of utility ware, with Smeared Indented Corrugated constituting the most common surface treatment. The decorated ceramics consisted almost entirely of white ware with a low frequency of White Mountain Red Ware. For Burnt Corn and Manzanares, Galisteo Black-on-white was the most commonly found white ware; however, at Lodestar South and Cholla House, Santa Fe Black-on-white was the predominate type. This difference may reflect a slightly earlier occupation for Lodestar South and Cholla House. Lodestar North and Slope House cannot be included in the discussion because the decorated ceramics were primarily found on or near the surface, and may not be associated with the occupation of the structures at the sites. Caution must be exercised in comparing these ceramic assemblages because of significant differences in sample size.

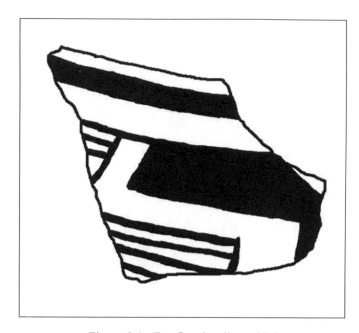

Figure 3.1. Top framing line with lower incorporated design orientation.

Table 3.5. Frequency of Black-on-white Types for Rim Study

Type	n	%
Galisteo Black-on-white	84	53.50
Santa Fe Black-on-white	73	46.50
Total	157	

Table 3.6. Examination of Utility Sherd Temper

Site	n	Temper Examined %	Temper Not Examined %
Cholla	126	56.35	43.65
Slope House	82	71.95	28.05
Lodestar North	186	65.05	34.95
Lodestar South	125	50.40	49.60
Total	519		

To further investigate the black-on-white ceramic assemblage, white ware data were examined from the rim study of Burnt Corn and Manzanares. These data were chosen because the same methods and attributes were used in the analysis. At Burnt Corn and Manzanares, the majority of the black-on-white sherds had round rims, moderately polished interiors, unslipped and unpolished exteriors, a top framing line with lower incorporated design orientation (Fig. 3.1), and sherd temper. Statistical tests of the attributes between the two sites were inconclusive. This ambiguity is attributable in part to the variability among the ceramic attributes in the sample (Fig. 3.2). However, when the temper category is reduced to the sherd, sand, and tuff temper groups that reflect the main inclusions, the difference in temper groups between the two sites is not significant (x^2 = 2.897, p = .23).

With the exception of temper, a comparison of the black-on-white assemblages at Cholla House and Lodestar South was limited because of sample size, small number of rim sherds, and differences in recording attributes. The predominant temper group was fine tuff and sand for Lodestar South (43.48%) and very fine sand and silt for Cholla House (55.56%) (Fig. 3.3). However, when the temper groups are reduced to sherd, sand, and tuff categories, the difference in temper groups between the two sites is not significant (x^2 = 3.971, p = .14).

We also examined utility wares by analyzing the temper groups that were recorded for ceramics from Cholla House, Slope House, Lodestar North, and Lodestar South. With the exception of Lodestar South, temper was recorded for the majority of sherds (Table 3.6). Temper was not examined on very small sherds. The temper was determined by making a small break on the sherd and examining the fresh break under a microscope. Multi-lithic sand was found to be the predominant temper group for the utility ware at Cholla House (39.44%) and Lodestar North (62.81%) (Table 3.7). At Lodestar South the predominant temper group was anthill sand (30.16%) and at Slope House it was granite without abundant mica (35.59%).

At all the sites, very fine sand (silt) was found to be the predominant temper group for Plain Grayware, except at Lodestar South where it was fine tuff and sand. At Cholla House and Lodestar South, the temper group for the Plain Gray Ware matched the predominant temper group for the white ware. It is interesting to note that while anthill sand was frequently found in the different utility types at Lodestar North and South, it was only found in one Clapboard Corrugated sherd at Slope House and two Indented Corrugated and two indeterminate corrugated sherds at Cholla House. Anthill sand,

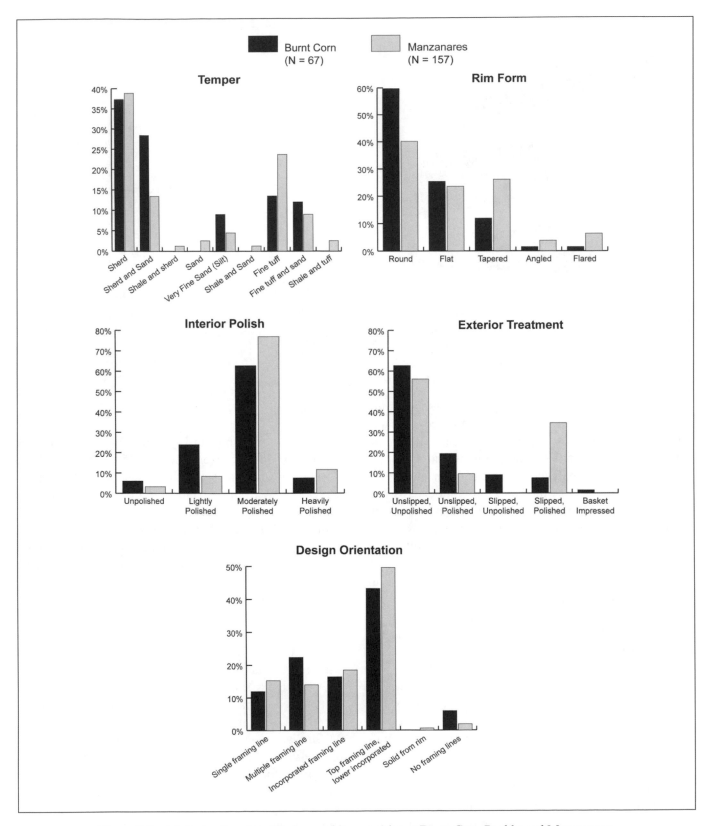

Figure 3.2. Attributes found on black-on-white ceramics at Burnt Corn Pueblo and Manzanares.

Table 3.7. Percentage of Temper Groups by Site

Temper Group	Cholla House n = 71	Slope House n = 59	Lodestar North n = 121	Lodestar South n = 63
Andesite/diorite with sherd	1.41	0	0	0
Andesite/diorite with sand	0	3.39	1.65	4.76
Anthill sand	5.63	1.70	33.06	30.16
Crushed andesite/diorite	0	13.56	0	0
Fine tuff and sand	2.82	1.70	0.83	6.35
Granite with abundant mica	7.04	3.39	0	4.76
Granite without abundant mica	30.99	35.59	0.83	7.94
Large tuff fragments (vitric tuff)	7.04	10.17	0	0
Multi-lithic sand	39.44	20.34	62.81	26.98
Sand	1.44	0	0.83	12.70
Sand and mica	1..44	0	0	1.59
Sherd and sand	0	0	0	1.59
Tuff and anthill sand	0		0	0
Very fine sand (silt)	2.82	10.17	0	1.59

Table 3.8 Attributes of Galisteo Black-on-white at Burnt Corn Pueblo and Manzanares

Site	n	Rim Shape	Interior Polish	Exterior Slip	Exterior Polish
Burnt Corn	44	54.44% Round	54.55% Moderate	79.55% Unslipped	72.73% Unpolished
Manzanares	84	34.53% Flat	61.45% Moderate	55.95% Slipped	64.29% Polished

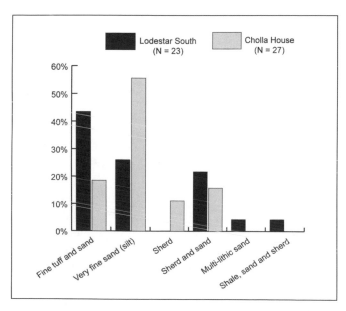

Figure 3.3. Temper Groups for black-on-white ceramics at Lodestar South and Cholla House.

sometimes referred to as phenocrysts, was typically found as temper, usually in combination with tuff, in the utility ware on the Pajarito Plateau (Wilson 2008a: 128). However, in the sample we analyzed, only one Plain Corrugated sherd from Lodestar South had anthill sand and tuff temper. Another temper group of interest is andesite or diorite, which was frequently found as temper in pottery from the northern San Juan or Mesa Verde region (Wilson 2008a: 129). The use of andesite or diorite, either crushed or in combination with sand or sherd, was most frequently found at Slope House where it was present in Indented Corrugated, Clapboard Corrugated, and Smeared Indented Corrugated sherds.

Overall the assemblages of utility ware and decorated ceramics analyzed here are comparable to other Coalition period ceramic assemblages in the Northern Rio Grande (Habicht-Mauche 1993; Powell 2002; Wilson 2008a). The variability found in the temper groups for both the utility ware and white ware from late Coalition period ceramic assemblages from the Galisteo Basin may mean that the inhabitants participated in an extensive trade network. Such an exchange system has been documented for the Santa Fe-Pecos district and the Pajarito Plateau during the Coalition period (Habicht-Mauche 1993: 92; Ruscavage-Barz 2002: 264).

CHARACTERIZING GALISTEO BLACK-ON-WHITE

Our findings are significant for questions regarding the origins and associations of Galisteo Black-on-white (Cordell 1995; Dutton 1964; Riley 1952; Wilson 2008b). At Burnt Corn, Galisteo Black-on-white most frequently has a moderately polished interior, unslipped and unpolished exterior, and round rims (Table 3.8). At Manzanares, Galisteo Black-on-white most frequently has a moderately polished interior, slipped and polished exterior, and flat (square) rims. Therefore, while the Galisteo Black-on-white at Manzanares closely resembles the general description of Galisteo Black-on-white, at Burnt Corn it does not. It is also interesting that Mera (1935: 21) thought that Galisteo Black-on-white from the western Galisteo Basin was more polished than that from the eastern basin. We found, however, that 63.6 percent of the Galisteo Black-on-white sherds at Burnt Corn Pueblo have a moderately to heavily polished interior. In contrast, 95.2 percent of the Galisteo Black-on-white sherds at Manzanares in the eastern Galisteo Basin have a moderately to heavily polished interior.

One of the attributes we were particularly interested in examining was crackled slip. The stylistic study of Burnt Corn ceramics was used to examine the presence or absence of crackle slip on bowl interiors and exteriors. At Burnt Corn, only 16.13 percent of the interiors and 15.25 percent of the exteriors of the Galisteo Black-on-white sherds had a crackle slip. Only four sherds (6.45%) had crackle on the interior and exterior. Therefore, a crackle slip was uncommon at Burnt Corn, and this is congruent with Mera's (1935: 21) finding that crackle slip is rare in the western portion of the Galisteo Basin.

To further examine the similarities and differences between Galisteo Black-on-white and Santa Fe Black-on-white, we use the stylistic study of Burnt Corn ceramics, excluding the indeterminate category of the attributes from the analysis. For some attributes, more than 20 percent of the expected values were less than five; therefore, the chi-square comparison was omitted.

Table 3.9. Interior Slip on Black-on-white Ceramics at Burnt Corn Pueblo

Type	Count	Unslipped %	Slipped %	Crackled %
Santa Fe	44	56.82	40.91	2.27
Galisteo	62	35.48	48.39	16.13

Table 3.10. Exterior Slip on Black-on-white Ceramics at Burnt Corn Pueblo

Type	Count	Unslipped %	Slipped %	Crackled %
Santa Fe	44	93.18	6.82	0
Galisteo	59	69.49	15.25	15.25

Table 3.11. Interior Polish on Black-on-white Ceramics at Burnt Corn Pueblo

Type	Count	None %	Light %	Moderate %	High %
Santa Fe	44	4.54	25.00	63.64	6.82
Galisteo	61	0	18.03	68.85	13.11

Interior and Exterior Slip and Polish/Treatment

In general, a slip was found on the interior and exterior more often on Galisteo Black-on-white than on Santa Fe Black-on-white (Tables 3.9 and 3.10). The difference in the use of interior slip between Santa Fe Black-on-white and Galisteo Black-on-white was significant ($x^2 = 8.699$, $p = .0129$). The difference in the use of exterior slip on Santa Fe Black-on-white and Galisteo Black-on-white was also significant ($x^2 = 13.424$, $p = .0012$). Like the use of slip, Galisteo Black-on-white is distinguished by more frequent polishing, particularly on the exterior, than Santa Fe Black-on-white (Tables 3.11 and 3.12).

Additional surface treatments for both Santa Fe Black-on-white and Galisteo Black-on-white were noted. For instance, one sherd of each type from the Burnt Corn assemblage was basket impressed, and basket-impressed sherds were also recorded in the surface scatter associated with Slope House. It has been suggested that basket-impressed vessels were an early variety of Santa Fe Black-on-white (Habicht-Mauche 1993: 22). However,

Table 3.12. Exterior Treatments on Black-on-white Ceramics at Burnt Corn Pueblo

Type	Count	Unpolished %	Lightly Polished %	Moderately Polished %	Highly Polished %	Basket Impressed %	Striated %	Corrugated %
Santa Fe	44	70.46	11.36	13.63	0	2.27	2.27	0
Galisteo	61	31.15	29.51	34.43	1.64	1.64	0	1.64

Table 3.13. Primary Elements on Black-on-white Ceramics at Burnt Corn Pueblo

Type	Line %	Triangle %	Rectangle %	Terrace/Step %	Key/Flag %	Scroll %
Santa Fe	56.82	22.73	15.91	4.55	2.27	2.27
Galisteo	70.97	29.03	8.06	9.68	0	0

NOTE: The percentages represent the sherds with a primary element present ; more than one primary element could be found on a single sherd.

Sundt (Bice and Sundt 1972: 117) reported a basket-impressed sherd of what he called Chaco-McElmo Black-on-white, later referred to as San Ignacio Black-on-white (Bice, Davis and Sundt 1998: 2), at Prieta Vista, an early thirteenth century site located in the eastern San Juan Basin region. Therefore, it is possible that basket-impressed vessels represented an early variation of black-on-white ceramics in general. Other types of exterior treatments included a striated exterior on a Santa Fe Black-on-white sherd and corrugations left exposed on one Galisteo Black-on-white sherd.

Designs

There are conflicting reports on the decoration of Galisteo Black-on-white (Kidder and Amsden 1931: 26; Stubbs and Stallings 1953: 15, 50). Therefore, we compared the decoration of Santa Fe Black-on-white and Galisteo Black-on-white in our sample by examining primary elements (design shapes that stand alone as a basic unit of analysis), secondary elements (design shapes that attach to primary elements), and the use of hatching (Hegmon 1995: 204).

Seven different types of primary elements were recorded in the sample (Table 3.13). There was no significant difference between Galisteo Black-on-white and Santa Fe Black-on-white in the usage of any of the primary elements (Table 3.14). Straight lines were the most frequently used primary element on both Santa Fe

and Galisteo Black-on-white. No curvilinear lines were found on either type. When straight lines are present, 72 percent of the Santa Fe Black-on-white sherds and 82 percent of the Galisteo Black-on-white sherds have more than one line present. We found that there was not a significant difference between Galisteo Black-on-white and Santa Fe Black-on-white in terms of single verse multiple line use ($x^2 = 883$, $p = .3474$). In terms of use of secondary elements, there was a significant difference between Galisteo Black-on-white and Santa Fe Black-on-white ($x^2 = 7.932$, $p = .0049$). Secondary elements were present on 27.42 percent of the Galisteo Black-on-white sherds and only 6.82 percent of Santa Fe Black-on-white sherds. Ticking (Fig. 3.4) was the most frequently found secondary element on Galisteo Black-on-white (35.29%), but it was not present on Santa Fe Black-on-white.

Amsden (Kidder and Amsden 1931: 24, 26) noted that hatching was uncommon on Crackle type at Fork Lightning and Pecos Pueblo, but that hatched triangles were frequent on Blue-gray type. Using a simple presence or absence comparison, we found hatching on 52.27 percent of the Santa Fe sherds and on 25.81 percent of the Galisteo sherds, a significant difference ($x^2 = 7.750$, $p = .0054$). When we examined the design composition of triangles, we found that triangles were most frequently solid filled on both Santa Fe and Galisteo Black-on-white. On Santa Fe Black-on-white, a solid fill was found in 70 percent of the triangles. Therefore,

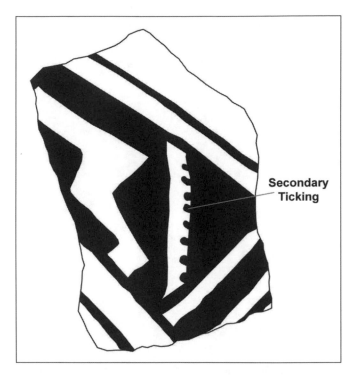

Figure 3.4. Ticking as secondary design element found on Galisteo Black-on-white ceramics at Burnt Corn Pueblo.

Table 3.14. Chi-Square Comparison on the Use of Primary Elements on Santa Fe Black-on-white and Galisteo Black-on-white at Burnt Corn Pueblo

Line	Triangle	Rectangle	Terrace/Step
$x^2 = 2.256$	$x^2 = .532$	$x^2 = 1.551$	$x^2 = 1.028$
$p = .1331$	$p = .4658$	$p = .2129$	$p = .3015$

while hatching was found more frequently on Santa Fe Black-on-white at Burnt Corn, it was not necessarily associated with triangles.

Rims

There were a total of 43 rim sherds in the sample, including 27 Galisteo Black-on-white and 16 Santa Fe Black-on-white sherds. A round rim was the most frequent rim form on both types (Table 3.15). Three Galisteo Black-on-white rim sherds, or 11.11 percent of the sample, were decorated with dots or squares; however, this rim decoration is found on three different rim forms (round, tapered, and flared). Rim decoration was not found on Santa Fe Black-on-white. The most common orientation for how a design is laid out on the rim is a top framing line with lower incorporated design for Galisteo Black-on-white (45%) and a single framing line (31.25%) for Santa Fe Black-on-white (Table 3.16).

CONCLUSION

The ceramic assemblages from sites studied by the Tano Origins Project were dominated by utility wares, followed by white wares and a very small quantity of White Mountain Red Ware. The frequencies of these ceramics are similar to other late Coalition sites in the Northern Rio Grande, including Arroyo Hondo (Habicht-Mauche 1993) and Pindi Pueblo (Stubbs and Stallings 1953). However, upon closer examination, there are many questions surrounding the ceramics, especially the black-on-white types.

Burnt Corn and Manzanares were virtually contemporary (see Chapter 2), and overall their black-on-white assemblages are similar. There are significant differences, however, in Galisteo Black-on-white. Galisteo Black-on-white at Manzanares matched the general description of the type in the literature. At Burnt Corn Pueblo, however, this type exhibits a moderately polished interior, an unslipped and unpolished exterior, and round rims, thus differentiating it from the published type descriptions. This is significant both because of the implied diversity of the type and because Burnt Corn is the proposed type-site for Galisteo Black-on-white (Mera 1935: 21). Furthermore, Mera's (1935: 21) observation that Galisteo Black-on-white was generally more polished and less crackled in the central and western portion of the Galisteo Basin does not necessarily hold with our sample. We found that Galisteo Black-on-white was less polished and less crackled at Burnt Corn, on the western side of the basin, than at Manzanares, on the eastern side of the basin. Examining the variability between contemporary sites in the Galisteo Basin may be a productive avenue for future research.

The question of whether Galisteo Black-on-white may be a variety of Santa Fe Black-on-white is not straightforward. Although the general description of Galisteo Black-on-white at Burnt Corn is similar to Santa Fe Black-on-white, differences also exist between the two types. We found that there was no significant difference in the use of lines as primary design elements and in the use of the interior as a decorative field. Furthermore, round rims were found to be the most frequent rim form for both types. However, we found that there was a significant

**Table 3.15. Rim Forms on Santa Fe Black-on-white and
Galisteo Black-on-white at Burnt Corn Pueblo**

Type	n	Round %	Flat %	Tapered %	Angled %	Flared %
Santa Fe Black-on-white	16	62.50	31.50	0	6.25	0
Galisteo Black-on-white	26	46.15	38.46	7.69	3.85	3.85

**Table 3.16. Design Orientations on Santa Fe Black-on-white and
Galisteo Black-on-white at Burnt Corn Pueblo**

Type	n	Single Framing Line %	Multiple Framing Lines %	Incorporated Framing Line %	Top Framing Line/Lower Incorporated %	No Framing Lines %
Santa Fe Black-on-white	16	31.25	25.00	6.25	25.00	12.50
Galisteo Black-on-white	27	33.33	7.41	3.70	48.15	7.41

difference between the two types in the use of slip for both the interior and exterior, the use of secondary design elements, and the use of hatching. Additional differences included use of rim decorations and design orientation, but these could not be statistically evaluated. Although Galisteo Black-on-white at Burnt Corn does not match the descriptions for the type, it is clearly different from Santa Fe Black-on-white.

We have to question whether what we were calling Galisteo Black-on-white is actually this ceramic type. As discussed, the classification of the ceramic types for these analyses were based primarily on temper, which is traditionally not the means for classifying these ceramics. We agree with Shepard (Kidder and Shepard 1936: 470, 476) that the variability in the surface treatments on the black-on-white ceramics is so great that temper is probably the best means for classification. However, in doing so, we acknowledge that this overlooks the sherd-temper variety of Santa Fe Black-on-white, as noted by others (Eckert 2006: 170; Habicht-Mauche 1993: 89; Kidder and Shepard 1936: 461; Warren 1974: 5). A sherd-tempered Santa Fe Black-on-white is usually only found in very small percentages (Habicht-Mauche 1993: 62; Kidder and Shepard 1936: 461; Ruscavage-Barz 1999: 201, 203) and generally in the earliest occupation levels, such as at Forked Lightning (Kidder and Shepard 1936: 461).

If we consider only surface treatments, the predominantly black-on-white assemblages at Burnt Corn and Manzanares have moderately polished interiors,

unslipped and unpolished exteriors, and round rims. This description fits more closely with Santa Fe Black-on-white than Galisteo Black-on-white, implying that although Galisteo Black-on-white was the predominate type in late Coalition site components outside the Galisteo Basin (Habicht-Mauche 1993; Stubbs and Stallings 1953), it may not have been the predominant type in the Galisteo Basin itself.

There is thus a clear need for a comprehensive study of Coalition period ceramics in the Galisteo Basin. Intensive sourcing would be particularly useful, since some of the patterns we identify may be linked to regional exchange. Sourcing studies will enhance our understanding of the ceramic types, and provide needed information on the social dynamics of late Coalition period sites in the Galisteo Basin and beyond.

While the classification of black-on-white types may be in question, there is no doubt that the classification of utility ware is also in need of serious investigation. The absence of any standardized typology for utility ware makes it virtually impossible to make inter-site comparisons. The examination of utility ware from Lodestar North, Lodestar South, Cholla House, and Slope House found considerable variability within the temper groups at each site. The temper groups found at these sites, including anthill sand and andesite-diorite, are commonly found in the Pajarito Plateau and the Mesa Verde region, respectively (Wilson 2008a: 128, 129). This is intriguing. Ethnographic studies have shown that utility ware is of low value and is generally exchanged among kin or people with close social ties (Duff 1999: 2.25). Therefore, we ask if the people who lived in the Galisteo Basin were engaged in exchange with other regions, or whether they were just using locally available tempering materials.

We think that future sourcing analyses of utility ware will provide valuable information on the late Coalition period social networks. Utility wares should not be treated as the "poor stepchild of Southwestern ceramics" (Habicht-Mauche 1993: 12); they need to be in the forefront of ceramic studies for the late Coalition period in the Northern Rio Grande. Our analyses of utility ware assemblages from the Tano Origins Project sites provide a brief indication of the opportunities that exist in this direction.

The late Coalition period falls in the middle of two major events in the Southwest, that is, the depopulation of the Mesa Verde region and the social reorganization and introduction of glaze ware in the Northern Rio Grande. However, the ceramics of this period are not well understood. Our preliminary study finds that standard type descriptions are not necessarily representative of Coalition period ceramics. Future research needs to include a more detailed technological and stylistic analysis of black-on-white and utility wares, as well as sourcing studies to determine where the pottery at these sites was being made. By examining the relationship of technological style, design style, and production source in future research, we will gain a better understanding of the late Coalition period ceramics in the Galisteo Basin and how these relate to the larger issues in Southwest archaeology.

CHAPTER FOUR

Construction and Destruction: A Life History of Burnt Corn Pueblo

James E. Snead, Monica L. Smith, and Elizabeth Baker Brite

In our early visits to Burnt Corn Pueblo, two obvious factors in the surface record of the site impressed us: the widespread evidence for destruction by fire and the dominance of black-on-white pottery on the surface. These two patterns signified that Burnt Corn Pueblo had been constructed during the Coalition period, had been destroyed in some single event, and its inhabitants had never returned. Such a dramatic history could only be verified through excavation, and we developed a program of subsurface testing. Results from the two excavation seasons that followed supported our initial observations and provided explicit context for further interpretation of the history of Burnt Corn Pueblo.

Excavations conducted at Burnt Corn Pueblo (LA 359) in 2002 and 2005 were designed to establish a "life history" of the site. Our research interests in conflict and population movement required as detailed a chronology as possible, something that was largely lacking from previous research in the vicinity (Chapter 2; Wiseman 2004). Chronology was important both in absolute terms in dating the settlement and longevity of Burnt Corn itself, and in a relative context by establishing associations between different parts of the settlement. Critical questions included whether the various structures in the complex were built simultaneously as a planned unit or in distinct episodes; whether there was evidence for reconstruction or reoccupation; and whether the burning of the pueblo was in fact a single event.

Part of our research included gathering information for the future management of Burnt Corn Pueblo. Widespread looting at the site in the 1960s and 1970s had disrupted subsurface contexts but the details of this damage were not clear. It was possible that few intact deposits remained at Burnt Corn, and that some sort of mitigation to ensure long-term preservation of what remained would be necessary. Managerial decisions could not be determined from surface evidence alone.

Our strategy had two components. First, we needed a broad spatial sample to collect as much chronological information as possible from different parts of the site. Our initial 2002 excavation season was thus devoted to sampling different room blocks. Second, our need for better context required more extensive exposure, and we implemented this in 2005 by excavating one and a half rooms in the plaza pueblo (Structure 2). Our approach was conservative, designed to collect information with minimal impact to the site.

In this chapter, we discuss site architecture at Burnt Corn Pueblo, making some comparison to the architecture of other sites documented in more extensive excavation programs elsewhere in the region (Carlson and Kohler 1990; Creamer 1993). Architectural information for Coalition period Galisteo sites is sparse. There has been limited attention to the architectural histories of "clustered" pueblos such as Burnt Corn (but see Fowles 2004). Thus our work not only provides a better understanding of Burnt Corn Pueblo and its legacy of conflict but also contributes a useful body of information regarding settlement history in the critical thirteenth century A.D. for the northern Rio Grande as a whole.

EXCAVATIONS

There are nine distinct mounds at Burnt Corn Pueblo, representing collapsed structures distributed along the high ground of the ridge top (Fig. 4.1). They range from 5 m to 20 m apart, with the layout conforming to the topographic contour of the ridge. Eight of the mounded structures (Nos. 1, 3–9) represent single-story, rectilinear room blocks encompassing 10 to 20 rooms.

Structure 2 differs from the other mounds in size and design, representing a "plaza pueblo" or group of connected room blocks enclosing a central space. Structures of this type have been documented throughout the

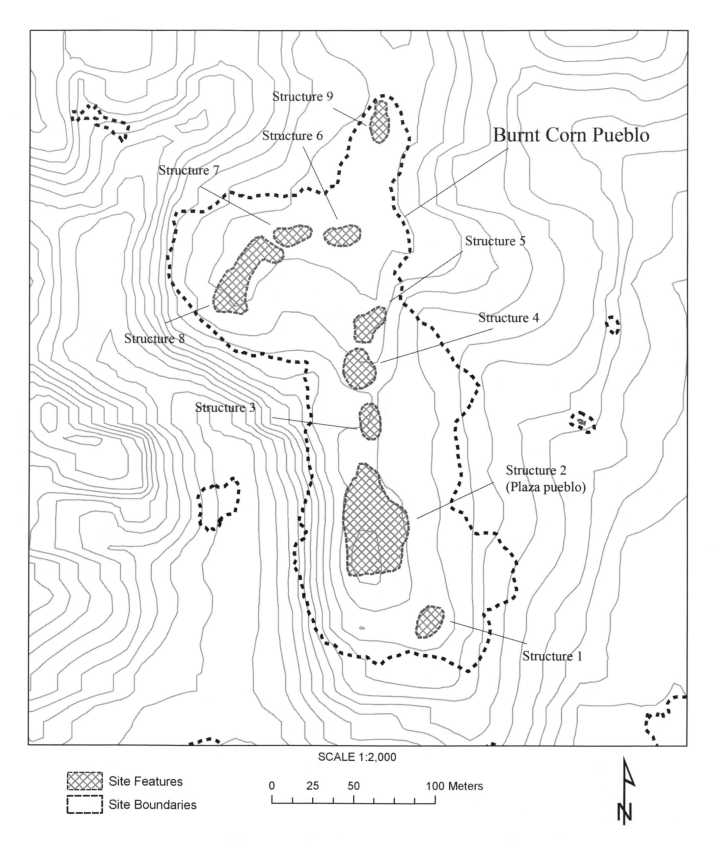

Figure 4.1. Structures and topography at Burnt Corn Pueblo (LA 359). Cartography by Gregory Greene.

northern Rio Grande region and widely discussed (for summary, see Van Zandt 2006). No entrance to the plaza at Burnt Corn Pueblo was evident, and the height of the southern end of the structure indicates the presence of multiple stories. The reduction of the room blocks to a mound makes it difficult to determine the total number of rooms, but we estimate there were 50 to 75 rooms in the plaza pueblo, with perhaps 150 to 200 rooms in the site as a whole.

Other features are also present at Burnt Corn Pueblo. These include dozens of grinding slicks, probable midden areas, and an apparent central shrine in an open area between two of the structures. Some additional small mounds appear on H. P. Mera's map of the site made in the 1920s or early 1930s, but these are no longer clearly recognizable. Based on analogy with other sites, we think the room blocks were predominantly domiciles and work areas for extended families or slightly larger social groups, with the associated features reflecting related domestic activities.

Gregory Greene made a GPS map of the site in 2005 and 2006 that included architecture, artifact scatters, and associated small features. Elements of the modern landscape, such as vegetation, the trail, and looters' pits, were also included. In 2005, a more detailed contour map of Structure 2, the plaza pueblo, was produced by Stephen Post and Jessica Badner of the Office of Archaeological Studies, Museum of New Mexico (OAS), using a total station (Fig. 4.2).

The 2002 excavations consisted of five 1 m by 2 m units placed in Structures 1 (Unit 4), 2 (Unit 5), 5 (Unit 1), 7 (Unit 2), and 8 (Unit 3). The 2005 excavations focused exclusively on Structure 2, with Unit 6 exposing all or parts of two rooms (A and B) in the north room block of the structure, and Unit 7 uncovering architectural debris west of the plaza. Units 3 and 7 were not completed so that the other five units produced most of the data used in this publication.

Our record-keeping strategy in both seasons was based on a lot system, in which a single continuous series of lot numbers was assigned to cultural features (such as walls, hearths, and postholes) and to arbitrary divisions in otherwise undifferentiated fill. We described each lot on a standardized form, and prepared Harris matrices for the units where more than one or two lots were excavated. We screened all excavated soil matrix, including topsoil, through one-quarter inch mesh. The following sections summarize general archaeological contexts and architectural information from the excavation units.

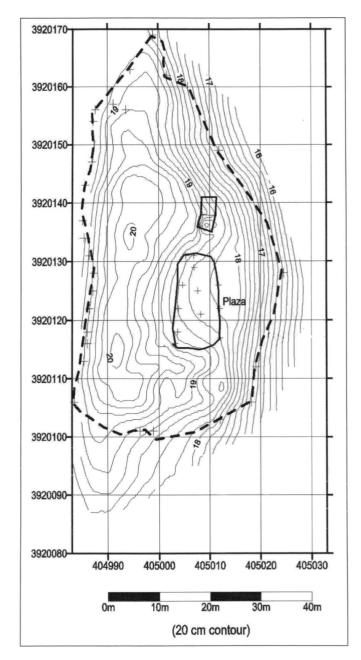

Figure 4.2. Topographic map of Burnt Corn Pueblo, depicting plaza and Unit 6. Cartography by Steven Post and Jessica Badner.

Unit 1 (Structure 5)

Unit 1 was a 1 m by 2 m excavation unit oriented along a masonry wall running roughly north-south. This wall had been exposed by a looter's trench. We defined 11 lots before reaching sterile soil. Slightly below the surface an adobe cross-wall abutted the stone masonry wall near the south end of the unit; the two walls defined the

Figure 4.3. Unit 1, Structure 5. Photograph by James Snead.

southeast interior corner of a room. Rodent burrowing disorganized some of the fill in this unit, and looting had disrupted the northern and western half. The masonry of the east wall consisted of small, shaped stones in regular courses. Wall plaster preserved in subsurface contexts showed discoloration of the outer 0.5 cm to 1 cm, indicating that it had been burned.

Fill along the eastern and southern walls appeared intact and consisted largely of hard-packed adobe melt and burned adobe chunks up to 10 cm in diameter, identified as debris from the collapse of the roof and walls. Much of this architectural fill showed evidence of burning. Numerous small pieces of carbonized wood were present throughout this deposit, including twigs and secondary beams (or *latillas*) up to 12 cm in diameter that we interpret as roofing material. We processed 51 wood samples from Unit 1 and submitted them to the Laboratory of Tree Ring-Research (LTRR) at the University of Arizona. A cluster of seven dates from this provenience indicates a construction episode in A.D. 1292 (Chapter 2).

Burned corn cobs and kernels in the fill occasionally occurred in discrete lenses or pockets a few centimeters wide and deep, with a larger lens of burned corn in uncertain context at the northwest margin of the unit. Some of the wood appeared to have burned in place against the masonry wall, perhaps after the roof's collapse (Fig. 4.3). Artifacts in the fill were predominantly ceramics, but we also recovered modest lithic debitage, tools including a quartzite chopper, and several fragments of turquoise. Faunal remains were sparse and of uncertain context because of the rodent burrows present within the fill.

We exposed a fragmentary floor with some charring at 71 cm below the surface. Some adobe roof-wall fall and burned corn lay directly atop this feature, representing the only cultural material in clear association with the floor. Nothing that could be identified as occupational debris was encountered in the excavation. A rough pit cut down into sterile soil was present in the southeast corner of the floor, from which a burned *latilla* protruded. Further study made it clear that the floor through which the pit had been cut was superimposed on top of a lower, prepared floor, with 4 cm of fill separating the two. Due to rodent damage the extent of this floor across the rest of the unit could not be determined. The lower portion of the adobe south wall was reddened as if burned. Although the unit incorporated a small area on the south side of this wall, no floor was identified in this narrow section of the unit, and limited access prevented us from excavating further.

Unit 2 (Structure 7)

Unit 2 originally consisted of a 1 m by 2 m excavation unit in Structure 7, placed in an approximate east-west orientation along the interior of a masonry wall visible on the surface (Fig. 4.4). As indicated by the slope of the mound, this represented the external wall of structure. One room was exposed, and in an unsuccessful effort to identify a cross-wall, we extended the unit eastward, to an ultimate size of 1 m by 2.3 m. We removed 13 lots from this structure before reaching sterile soil.

Rodent activity was common in Unit 2, and the southern portion of the unit had been disturbed by looting. Intact deposits were evident along the north wall, however, and adjacent to the east profile. Much of the fill was ashy in color but compact in consistency, with numerous chunks of adobe up to 15 cm in diameter mixed with masonry rubble. Carbon fragments, including burnt corn kernels and cobs, were present throughout the fill (Fig. 4.5). Wood was comparatively scarce. We encountered some burned *latilla* fragments, but the single sample submitted to the LTRR did not provide a date. We also recorded low frequencies of ceramics, lithic debitage, and faunal remains throughout the fill.

A prepared clay floor, designated Floor 1, was present at 72 cm below surface, and there was a thin, burned layer on top of it. On the western side of the unit, in direct contact with the floor, was a discontinuous, 1 mm thick carrot-yellow-brown deposit that appeared to be a vegetal substance, possibly a corn by-product. A bundle of nine burnt corn cobs in contact with or immediately above the floor was visible in the east profile of the trench. Once Floor 1 had been defined we made a small cut through it at roughly the center of the unit and exposed a lower floor, designated Floor 2. No fill separated the two floors, and Floor 2 was smoothed up onto the lower courses of the north wall. Floor 2 sat directly on the subsoil, with large tree roots exposed in this sterile matrix.

Figure 4.4. Unit 2, Structure 7.
Photograph by James Snead.

Unit 4 (Structure 1)

Unit 4 consisted of a 2 m by 2 m excavation unit in Structure 1, placed amidst a scatter of numerous unshaped blocks of building stone. We removed nine lots before ceasing excavations. A stone masonry wall bisected the unit from north to south, and the area to the west of this wall was disturbed by a looter's pit. Numerous rodent holes were evident on the surface. As excavation proceeded, it became clear that the masonry wall curved toward the southwestern corner of the unit. This wall had been plastered on the west face but, apparently, not on the east face. The excavators hypothesized that the east face of the wall was thus on the exterior of the building, but this could not be verified. The wall also

Figure 4.5. Burned and fused corn mass from Unit 2,
Structure 7. Photograph by Monica Smith.

articulated with a burned adobe feature, apparently the stub of another wall, at its southwestern extension.

The deposits that appeared the most intact were on the west side of the wall, which we infer to be the interior of the building. These deposits consisted of compacted adobe roof-wall fall with numerous lenses of burned corn kernels and cobs. Wood was not common, and only six tree-ring samples were submitted for dating (Chapter 2). At least one adobe fragment was highly vitrified, with a glassy and bubbly appearance. Ceramics, faunal remains, and lithic debitage occurred at low densities in the fill.

We stopped excavating Unit 4 at 58 cm below the surface, before reaching any floor features, when two small fragments of human bone were discovered on the western side of the wall. The archaeological context for these human remains was fill associated with debris from roof and wall collapse. We think this deposit is disturbed, and that the human remains might be present due to rodent activity. It is also possible that the human bones had been incorporated into the adobe matrix along with sherds and other midden debris at the time of construction. In any event, the human remains could not be associated with the destruction event itself with any confidence. In accordance with procedures established through tribal consultation, we stopped work and backfilled the unit, reburying the human remains in the location they were discovered.

Unit 5 (Structure 2)

Unit 5 was a 1 m by 1 m unit at the east end of the south room block of Structure 2, below the southeastern corner of the plaza. The mound at this location was more than a meter high, indicating the possibility of multiple stories. The unit was placed at the northern margin of a looter's pit where surface evidence suggested the possible exposure of an east-west stone masonry wall, where we anticipated intact deposits. We removed four lots from this unit prior to the end of the 2002 season.

Subsurface deposits in Unit 5 proved to be complex, and rodent burrows were ubiquitous. Contrary to our

Figure 4.6. Coursed masonry wall collapsed atop fill in
Unit 5, Structure 2. Photograph by James Snead.

expectations, we did not find an intact east-west wall, although we think that a wall was present further north. Instead, there was considerable stone rubble slightly below the surface, evidently a collapsed north-south wall of coursed masonry that had originally stood to the east of the unit. This wall had probably been preserved above the mound until a relatively recent time (Fig. 4.6). Ceramic chinking was still preserved between the courses of the wall. A heavily burned, plastered adobe wall with a north-south orientation was exposed on the western side of the unit. This adobe wall had been truncated by the looter's pit.

Much of the intact fill consisted of building stone, chunks of adobe, and related melt. Carbonized material was scarce in the higher levels and, unlike the other units excavated in 2002, corn was entirely absent. We recovered ceramics and a single piece of unworked turquoise, along with fragmentary groundstone artifacts and faunal material that appeared to be related to recent rodent activity. A substantial quantity of burned roof material came from the lower lots. We submitted 25 samples of architectural wood from this unit to the LTRR for dating (Chapter 2), including a piece of a primary roof beam, 32 cm long and 15 cm in diameter. Fibrous material, interpreted to be a matting of grass stems and twigs, was also associated with this lot. Within the matting and wrapped in burnt cordage were two palm-sized pieces of a red slate-like material. Striations on the surface of these two artifacts indicated some sort of light grinding.

Our interpretation of the fill of Unit 5 is that it represented the collapse of the roof and floor of the upper story of the plaza pueblo, buried beneath later fall from the exposed walls. The matting, burnt cordage, and ground slates had apparently been cached in the roof of the first-story room at the time the pueblo was destroyed. There were few indications as to the nature of the fill below this level. Due to the lateness of the season and the narrowness of the exposure, we terminated excavation of Unit 5 at 138 cm below the surface. However, we think that floor of the lower room was only slightly deeper.

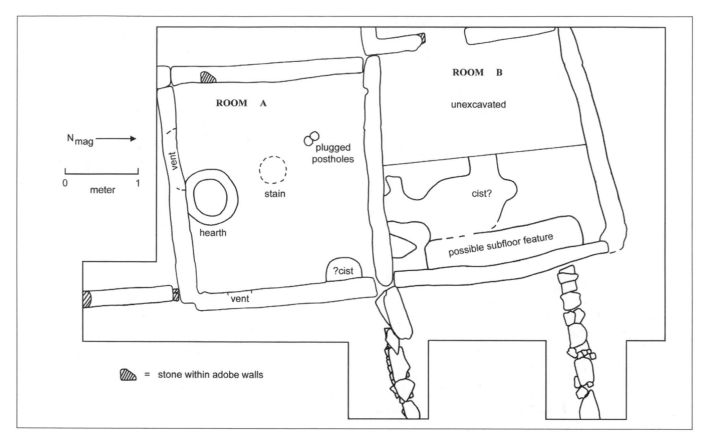

Figure 4.7. Plan of Unit 6, Structure 2, illustrating walls and floor features of rooms A (south) and B (north). Cartography by Monica Smith.

Unit 6 (Structure 2)

Unit 6 began as a 1 m by 1 m test pit. Within 10 cm of modern ground surface, we discerned a soil color and texture change that marked the presence of an adobe feature. We then expanded the unit by excavating successive 1 m x 1 m blocks to outline the adobe walls of Rooms A and B (Smith 2005).

Room 6A

The four adobe walls of Room 6A were preserved up to 83 cm high above a well prepared clay floor (Fig. 4.7). The walls were 20 cm to 22 cm thick, and covered with a 3–10 mm thick layer of clay plaster. Room 6A measured 2.6 m along its north-south axis and 2.3 m along its east-west axis. There were no discernable doorways in the room, and no evidence for an upper story. The walls were abutted rather than bonded, suggesting that they had been built sequentially. The clay floor ran beneath the west wall but appeared to have abutted the other walls, indicating that the room may have originally been larger and was subsequently subdivided.

The fill of Room 6A consisted of adobe lumps and stones ranging from 10 cm to 25 cm interspersed with loose, windblown soil. Although up to ten percent of the adobe lumps were fire-hardened, they were neither baked nor vitrified. The loose soil in the fill was bioturbated with rodent activity, with numerous rodent holes 4 cm to 6 cm in diameter, and the occasional faunal remains of rodents (possibly pocket gophers). In the eastern portion of the room, close to present ground surface, was a large flat stone slab measuring 42 cm by 34 cm by 7 cm. This flat stone may have been a portion of a roof hatch or other covering that fell into the room as the walls disintegrated. Additional evidence for the process of collapse came from a large utility jar base that had apparently tumbled into the northern side of the room. Otherwise, there were few artifacts or organic materials, and we typically recovered less than one kilogram of artifacts per cubic meter of fill. The quantity of carbonized material was much less than what had been recovered in the units excavated in 2002. Roofing material was relatively scarce. We collected 19 tree-ring samples for dating, but only one returned a date (Chapter 2). A 2 mm to 3 mm layer of windblown silt lay immediately above the floor, and this was covered by wall and roof fall consisting of adobe lumps and stones. One stone 20 cm in size was nestled into a slight impact crater in the floor that was apparently created during the collapse of the building. A small cluster of utility sherds was atop this windblown layer, but no artifacts were noted in direct contact with the floor itself.

The floor of Room 6A was remarkably well preserved. The smooth clay surface had been patched in several places, covering two possible postholes in the northwestern quadrant, a small ovoid area along the east wall that is possibly a subfloor cist, and a hearth in the south-central area of the room. This hearth had been constructed with a stone slab lining, and was completely filled with a white-gray ash and capped with a 3 cm to 5 cm layer of clay apparently designed so the hearth would blend into the floor after use (Fig. 4.8). An archaeomagnetic sample was taken from this feature for analysis at the Office of Archaeological Studies in Santa Fe. Two vents at the floor level, one in the east wall and one in the south wall, were not directly in line with the hearth, and had been carefully plugged with stone and adobe.

We made a small cut measuring 0.5 m by 1.5 m through the floor in the northwestern corner of Room 6A to investigate what lay below. The floor consisted of 5 cm to 8 cm of gray-brown clay, resting on top of a 3 mm to 5 mm layer of reddish clay. These two layers of the floor were superimposed on a thin layer of vegetal material. Underneath that was 40 cm to 45 cm of relatively loose gray matrix with an artifact density greater than what we had encountered in the fill above the floor. At this depth we reached sterile soil, with a single posthole cut into it containing a residue of organic material.

Room 6B

Room 6B is immediately adjacent to and north of Room 6A. It measured 2.8 m along its north-south axis and 2.6 m along its east-west axis. The architecture of Room 6B closely resembled that of Room 6A, with unbonded adobe walls of similar width. The adobe walls were, however, considerably less robust, unplastered and bent as if poorly constructed. One doorway measuring

Figure 4.8. Sealed hearth in Room A, Unit 6, Structure 2. Note thick deposit of clean ash below adobe cap. Photograph by Monica Smith.

50 cm wide was present on the west side of the room. Once the walls of Room 6B were articulated, we continued our excavation to the floor in the eastern half of the room.

As in Room 6A, the fill of Room 6B consisted of adobe lumps and stones ranging from 10 cm to 25 cm interspersed with loose, windblown soil. There was evidence for rodent activity in the top 20 cm to 30 cm of fill. The fill, however, contained a much larger percentage of wood roofing material, consisting of several unburnt and partially burnt wood fragments ranging from 4 cm to 12 cm in diameter and up to 70 cm in length. There were also dozens of carbonized branch fragments and some other vegetal remains, all of which appeared to be associated with the roof (Fig. 4.9). We collected 28 tree-ring samples of architectural wood from this unit for dating (Chapter 2).

Architectural debris occurred throughout the fill of Room 6B to floor level. As in Room 6A, approximately ten percent of the volume of adobe was fire-hardened, although not highly fired or vitrified. In the central area on the east side of the room, the 30 cm of fill above the floor contained a considerable number of household and special-purpose items, including ground stone, quartzite cobbles, a crystal, and a pipe of the "cloudblower" variety. These artifacts were mixed with burned roof material.

The floor of Room 6B consisted of a compact clay matrix that was not bonded to the walls. No floor features

Figure 4.9. Room B, Unit 6, Structure 2, illustrating burned ceiling timbers in fill. Photograph by Monica Smith.

were present, and there were no artifacts in direct association with the floor. The floor was heavily eroded, particularly on the southern side. There were two probable subfloor cists or burials pits that intruded through the floor but we did not excavate those features because it is likely that they may have contained human burials.

Architecture Adjacent to Unit 6

To assess the larger context of Rooms 6A and 6B, we placed three 1 m by 1 m test pits in areas where we detected additional walls extending away from the rooms. In these test pits we removed only topsoil to a level of 10 cm to 15 cm below modern ground surface. This revealed the presence of two masonry walls abutting Room 6B to the east, and an adobe wall abutting Room 6A to the south (Fig. 4.7). These test pits demonstrated that the plaza pueblo was constructed using both stone masonry and adobe walls, and that the room block on the north side of the central plaza was at least three rooms wide. Room 6A is in the middle row of rooms, between an unexcavated room fronting the plaza and Room 6B against the exterior wall on the north side of the structure. The absence of doorways in Room 6A indicates that this was not a suite of interconnected rooms.

Unit 7 (Structure 2)

In 2005 we excavated a 1 m by 1 m test pit at the top of the western room block of the plaza pueblo.

Removal of 10 cm to 15 cm of upper matrix revealed what appeared to be the eroded remains of adobe architecture. Articulation of this jumbled mass of material would have required exposing a significantly larger area. We decided to close Unit 7 and allocate our time and personnel to the excavation of Unit 6.

ARTIFACTS

The artifact assemblage from the Burnt Corn excavations was surprisingly modest. Ceramics recovered from the pueblo are discussed in Chapter 2. Painted sherds were overwhelmingly black-on-white types, with a tiny percentage of White Mountain Red Ware also present. Two substantial fragments of larger vessels were identified: several sherds from the same black-on-white bowl that had been used as chinking in the collapsed stone masonry wall exposed in Unit 5, and the base of a corrugated vessel from the fill in Room 6A. Both of these contexts suggested recycling, and nothing approaching a reconstructible vessel was identified. In fact, we were subjectively convinced that the sherds recovered from Burn Corn Pueblo are smaller than those from contemporary sites. One hypothesis is that many of these sherds were from secondary contexts and had been incorporated into the adobe walls during construction. Further comparison would be instructive. With the possible exception of a cluster of utility ware sherds slightly above the floor in Room 6A, no ceramics were found in primary association with the floors.

The flaked stone assemblage recovered from Burnt Corn Pueblo was modest. Low frequencies of debitage were recovered from the different fill contexts, and formal tools were scarce. Raw materials were primarily local cherts, with some basalt and obsidian. As with the ceramics, no lithic material was found in primary floor contexts.

We recovered a large number of ground-stone artifacts at Burnt Corn Pueblo. These were predominantly manos but there were also a few fragmentary metates and several pieces of indeterminate ground stone. These ground-stone artifacts were apparently made using locally available raw materials. They were recovered exclusively from fill contexts associated with wall and roof fall. Most of the ground-stone artifacts came from Unit 6, which is not surprising because it was the largest area we excavated at the site. Our interpretation is that ground-stone artifacts were originally situated in work areas on the roof tops, and that they fell into the rooms when the roofs collapsed, either during the fire or during later salvaging of primary beams.

A small number of finished artifacts and idiosyncratic finds were encountered during excavation. These included small, twine-wrapped slate tablets from Unit 5; a rock crystal and "cloudblower" pipe in Room 6B; and a possible hatch cover from Room 6A. A few small pieces of turquoise were identified in Units 1 and 5. We were alert to the possibility that ritual deposits may be present at Burnt Corn Pueblo but we found no evidence of formal organization of these artifacts or of stratigraphic "cuts" suggesting that they had been deposited after the fire that destroyed the site. If ritual placement of these artifacts had occurred prior to the fire, they were disrupted during the collapse. The only artifacts that seemed to have been intentionally placed were the slate tablets in Unit 4. These tablets were associated with burned secondary timbers, and we think they had been cached in the roof prior to the collapse of the building. The pipe and quartz crystal recovered in Room 6B appear to be ritual artifacts but their context does not provide clear evidence as to whether they were left in the room accidentally or intentionally at the time the site was destroyed.

The presence of turquoise is an interesting indication of activities at Burnt Corn Pueblo. The small size and unfinished appearance of the turquoise pieces from Units 1 and 5 imply that they were raw materials awaiting manufacture, perhaps bead blanks. Small pieces of turquoise were occasionally observed on the site surface as well. When considered along with finds from excavations at nearby Cholla House (Chapter 7), and the proximity of the Cerrillos turquoise source to Burnt Corn Pueblo, this raises the possibility that residents of the site were involved in procurement and processing of this mineral. There is no doubt that Cerrillos turquoise was a valued commodity throughout Puebloan history (see Mathien 2001; Wiseman and Darling 1986). Documentation of local turquoise exploitation in the Coalition Period would strengthen our sense for such practices throughout the Ancestral Pueblo era.

CORN

By volume, the corn from Burnt Corn Pueblo accounts for the largest share of the finds. The corn we recovered will be analyzed by Mollie Toll (OAS) in a future publication. The following remarks discuss the archaeological context of corn at Burnt Corn Pueblo,

and our initial impressions about the nature of this corn. Carbonized kernels and partially preserved cobs were found in varying quantities in all excavated units. The three units in the plaza pueblo (4, 6, 7) produced only traces of corn, but substantial quantities of the grain were present everywhere else. In most cases corn was overwhelmingly present in the fill, intermingled with collapsed wall and roofing material. This pattern is consistent with the inferred presence of corn on the roof tops, which correlates with the ethnographically documented post-harvest practice of drying corn to prepare it for winter storage. The corn was relatively "green" at the time of the fire, as indicated by the presence of cobs fused together by the heat. This context implies that the burning of the pueblo took place in the fall of the year, when the corn was dry enough to burn but not yet ready to be brought inside (Richard I. Ford, personal communication, 2002).

The only place where corn was found in a different context was Unit 2, where a small stack of carbonized cobs exposed in the profile sat on or directly above the floor. We think a thin deposit on the floor of this room was a corn by-product. This pattern is what one might expect for a "cleared" storage room. The fact that there was burned corn in a good interior context, as well as burned corn from exterior roof top contexts, has important implications for our understanding of how Burnt Corn Pueblo was destroyed.

CONTEXTS FOR SITE HISTORY

The data collected during excavation of Burnt Corn Pueblo provide a useful basis for constructing a site history. Integrating the architectural information discussed in this chapter with the chronological data discussed in Chapter 2 reveals several patterns.

It is clear that the site was occupied for a relatively short interval. The span of time indicated by the cutting dates in our tree-ring sample, A.D. 1288–1302, is remarkably short. Architectural data also denote a brief occupation. For instance, Units 1 and 2 had multiple superimposed floors but there does not appear to have been any significant interval of time between their use, and the lower floors were built on sterile soil. The internal consistency of the tree-ring dates from the units implies that repair work on the roofs was minimal throughout the duration of the pueblo's occupation.

The plaza pueblo is an exception to the general pattern of occupational brevity. The decade separating the tree-ring cutting dates of A.D. 1292 and 1302 from excavation Units 5 and 6 indicates that some augmentation or reconstruction of the structure took place during that span of time. Indications that Rooms 6A and 6B were once a single large room that was subsequently subdivided provide additional evidence for longer-term use. The trashy fill below the floor of Room 6A, and the posthole in the lowest deposit of that room, provide evidence that a substantial occupation preceded the construction of this part of the structure, dated to A.D. 1302 by wood from Room 6B.

A conservative interpretation of this chronological evidence is that the A.D. 1292 dates from Unit 5 mark the construction of the southern room block of the plaza pueblo, followed a decade later, in A.D. 1302, by the northern room block. The trash underlying Unit 6 may be associated with the A.D. 1292 occupation or even earlier activity, since a single A.D. 1272 cutting date exists from a tree-ring sample collected on the surface by Bertha Dutton in 1962 (Robinson and others 1972: 25). A few of the non-cutting dates in our own sample also hint at an earlier occupation (Chapter 2). In either case, the later division of Rooms 6A and 6B implies that occupation lasted for a period of time after A.D. 1302. Given the absence of tree-ring evidence for roof repair in any of the excavated units, this occupation does not appear to have been long.

As the focal point of architectural investment and habitation, the plaza pueblo may have sustained a longer and more intensive series of construction activities than other structures at Burnt Corn Pueblo. It is also much more massive than the other structures, and located at a point on the ridge where it could be seen for long distances (Snead 2008a). The A.D. 1292 and 1302 cutting dates at Burnt Corn Pueblo bracket a total construction period of perhaps 20 years.

There is little evidence that Burnt Corn Pueblo was constructed to a standard plan. The use of both adobe and stone masonry within the same architectural contexts was ubiquitous. Units 1, 4, and 5 contained both types of masonry, and the adobe walls of Rooms 6A and 6B were abutted with stone masonry walls. The use of adobe and stone masonry over a short period of time is a fundamental aspect of Burnt Corn architecture. This eclecticism in construction style is also seen in the use of different masonry styles. Figure 4.10 illustrates the stone masonry walls exposed in Structures 1, 5, and 7, each of which has distinctive characteristics. The most formal masonry wall is the collapsed feature below the

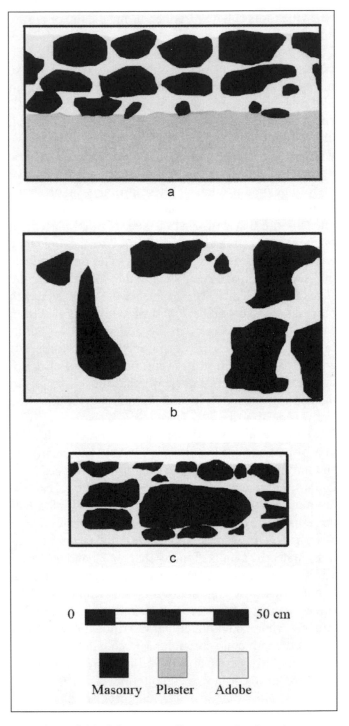

Figure 4.10. Masonry wall construction in units excavated in 2002: [a] Unit 1 (Structure 5), east wall, west (interior) face; [b] Unit 2 (Structure 7), north wall, south (interior) face; [c] Unit 4 (Structure 1) east wall, east (exterior) face. Drawing by Leslie Cohen.

surface in Unit 5 (Fig. 4.6). The elegant courses of this feature make a stark contrast to the expedient work evident in Structure 7. Building stone is readily available on the slopes of the ridge where Burnt Corn Pueblo is located, and we presume that the stone used to construct the walls of the pueblo came from similar sources.

The short occupation of Burnt Corn Pueblo and the easy availability of building stone in the vicinity indicate to us that differences in construction style represent neither temporal change nor material shortages, as has been suggested at other sites in the region where there are mixed architectural styles (Cordell 1998: 89; Creamer 1993: 14). The fact that some of the inhabitants of Burnt Corn took time to shape building stone and construct walls in distinctive ways is intriguing, particularly because most of the walls had been plastered and the different masonry styles would have been largely invisible while the pueblo was inhabited. This implies that Burnt Corn Pueblo was constructed rapidly by different builders, or at least builders working from different templates.

Our information about room function is limited by sample size. Room 6A, with a hearth, two vents and probable roof hatch, is the only room that can be clearly defined as a habitation space. However, the room with a floor pit in Unit 1 may also been used for domestic purposes. Room 6B and the room exposed in Unit 2 both abutted exterior walls, and were thus "deep" within their structures. This type of location was often used for storage in ancient pueblos. These rooms were located in single-story structures probably accessed by roof hatches rather than internal doors, however, so the architectural evidence for this inference is weak. A storage function is likely for the room exposed in Unit 2, with its stack of corn cobs exposed in the west profile.

Our difficulty in further defining room function highlights one of the central characteristics of the rooms excavated in Burnt Corn Pueblo: the almost total absence of floor assemblages. This pattern is particularly stark in Unit 6, where the complete excavation of one and half rooms exposed no artifacts in direct contact with the floor. This is not to say that Burnt Corn Pueblo was entirely devoid of evidence for human activities. Objects mixed with the roof collapse, including the ground slates in Unit 5, were clearly personal possessions. The dozens of grinding implements found in room fill are indicative of the work surfaces that existed on the roofs. Some large fragments of ceramic vessels recovered in collapse contexts probably represent the containers that

had been present on the roofs when they fell. Finally, the presence of what we think was corn drying on the roofs of the pueblo at the time it was destroyed implies that the inhabitants lived relatively normal lives until shortly before the conflagration that ended the occupation of the site.

CONTEXTS FOR SITE DESTRUCTION

Evidence from architecture and context sheds light on the ultimate destruction of Burnt Corn Pueblo. First, evidence from Unit 6 makes it clear that this area of the pueblo was in use immediately before the site was destroyed. This is particularly evident in the stratigraphy of Room 6A and Room 6B, where only a thin deposit of 3 mm to 4 mm separates the floor from the collapse debris above it (Fig. 4.11). As Matthews and his colleagues (1997) have noted, dust of this kind can accumulate under floor coverings or mats. If the thin deposit on top of the floor in Room 6A and Room 6B is associated with pre-conflagration activity, there would have been little or no time between the cessation of occupation and destruction of Burnt Corn Pueblo.

We suggest there was a rapid series of events associated with the conflagration, for which the term *perimortem* seems appropriate. It is likely that the formal sealing of the ash-filled hearth in Room 6B took place near the end of site occupation. We cannot be certain that the sealing of the vents in the same room took place at the same time, but it is a provocative idea. If we are correct that Unit 2 exposed a recently emptied storage room, then that room was cleared during the perimortem phase as well.

Our evidence indicates that the burning of Burnt Corn Pueblo was systematic and complete. All units showed evidence of the fire, some in quite dramatic fashion. Even in Room 6A, where the burning was least visible, flecks of carbon and small burnt fragments were dispersed through the fill, and there was an ephemeral smear in the center of the floor may have marked ash falling through the open roof hatch during the conflagration. The large pieces of burnt beams in the adjacent Room 6B demonstrate that this area of the room block was devastated. Excavated rooms also lacked secondary material that would have indicated partial abandonment of the pueblo. In all cases, collapsed debris from the upper walls and ceilings fell directly onto floors. The floor of Room 6A was "dimpled" where masonry rubble

Figure 4.11. Profile of Room B, Unit 6, illustrating relationship of wall and roof fall to other features. Drawing by Monica L. Smith.

fell onto it with some velocity. We think the pit in Unit 1 was open and empty when the pueblo burned, and that the *latilla* found in this pit at an oblique angle fell into it when the roof collapsed.

The fact that corn burned on the roof top is interesting. Fire on the outside of the building would not have easily penetrated the interior. If fires had been set exclusively inside the rooms, the layer of adobe roofing material would have provided considerable insulation to suppress the fire. We could also expect that a burning roof would collapse prior to complete immolation, dampening any remaining flames below (Tom Windes, personal communication, 2008). Conversely, the neatly stacked burned cobs exposed in Unit 2 could hardly have been lit by debris falling into the room from above. A single point of ignition for the conflagration thus seems improbable. Instead, the pattern of burning that is best accommodated by the evidence is the setting of fires both inside and outside of rooms at multiple locations.

In sum, we have the following series of perimortem events to make sense of: removal of corn from storage rooms, the clearance and sealing of at least some of the habitation rooms, and the systematic burning of flammable material both inside and outside of rooms throughout the Burnt Corn complex. Causal links between the three may not exist. We would argue that the emptying of the storage room and the "closure" of the habitation rooms reflect an orderly evacuation of the pueblo with ritual overtones. An alternative interpretation would be that the

storage room was cleared for some entirely different reason, such as to inspect the dried corn or to make room for the new harvest, an act that had no relation to subsequent events (Mark Allen, personal communication, 2009). For us the crux of the matter remains the general absence of floor assemblages in excavated areas. If the removal of artifacts from floors is as universal as it appears from present evidence, then this task would required some time to accomplish. Foreknowledge of the fire is thus implied, regardless of who wielded the torches.

Events at Burnt Corn Pueblo after the embers cooled can be inferred with caution. The absence of post-destruction trash in any excavated contexts suggests that there was no residential use of the site during the subsequent era. The almost total absence of later ceramics at the site indicates that this "abandonment" was real and, essentially, forever. We can infer, however, some modest activity in the months or years immediately following the fire. Most of the excavated architectural wood represents *latillas* or secondary roof beams, meaning that few *vigas* or primary beams were present. The excellent preservation at Burnt Corn Pueblo suggests that this is not simply a matter of decay. Reuse of roof material has been widely documented in the region (Windes 2002), and it is likely that vigas at Burnt Corn Pueblo were salvaged. Salvage may also explain the relative absence of windblown deposits in the rooms. Any post-destruction removal of beams would have been relatively destructive, bringing down unburned sections of roofs and the upper walls before natural deposition could accumulate on the floors.

DISCUSSION

Evidence for the construction and destruction of Burnt Corn Pueblo tells a story about the life of the community it sheltered. This narrative is necessarily broad in outline but bears on the research goals of the Tano Origins Project in interesting ways.

Population Origin, Settlement Longevity, and Community Organization

Architectural and contextual evidence from Burnt Corn Pueblo provides little direct evidence about the origins of the population who settled there. There are no obvious local antecedents for the Burnt Corn inhabitants, unless there is some temporal spread in the sites we have studied and the occupation of Burnt Corn was preceded by some of the dispersed, small-house settlements in the western Galisteo Basin, such as Waldo (Hammack 1971) and Lodestar (Chapter 7). There were clearly people living in the eastern Galisteo Basin in the decades prior to the establishment of Burnt Corn, and Pueblo Alamo may also be a candidate for a local source of population (Chapter 2). On a macroscale the date range of the Burnt Corn Pueblo occupation dovetails with the last construction episodes in the Mesa Verde region (Lipe 1995), once again bringing up the possibility that the Galisteo Basin may have been a destination for people from the Colorado Plateau.

Architectural evidence linking Burnt Corn Pueblo with thirteenth-century settlements in the Four Corners region, however, is inconclusive. The massing of architectural space in a position of high visibility, as seen in the Burnt Corn plaza pueblo, is reminiscent of "great house" design from the Colorado Plateau (Snead 2008a; see Fowler and Stein 2001; Lekson 2000: 159). However, in plan and construction Burnt Corn is not particularly reminiscent of settlements in the Four Corners region. Instead, the layout of the site with multiple room blocks in association with with a plaza pueblo closely resembles community clusters from the central and northern Pajarito Plateau, such as the Guaje Mesa site (LA 12700; Steen 1977: 33). These comparisons point in different directions, indicating that even though ceramics are the traditional proxy for social relationships among populations in the Southwest, architecture contributes to our evaluation of this issue.

The brevity of occupation at Burnt Corn Pueblo is one of the settlement's distinctive features. Some of the Coalition period pueblos in the Galisteo Basin appear to have had longer occupations. Pueblo Alamo, for example, shows evidence of repeated reconstruction, perhaps extending over decades (Allen 1973: 11), and dates from Colina Verde suggest an occupation of more than 50 years (Robinson and others 1973: 18). In some circumstances there appear to have been intervals when little construction was carried out or settlements were temporarily vacated, as at Pindi (Ahlstrom 1989) and Pueblo Largo (Wiseman 2004). It is possible that there were earlier occupations at Burnt Corn Pueblo, and that some of the undated room blocks were occupied at different times than those we excavated, but the short construction span still stands out as anomalous.

Although the destruction of Burnt Corn Pueblo cannot be precisely dated, we can make general inferences about the duration of the settlement. Patricia Crown (1991: 205) used detailed empirical evidence from Pot Creek Pueblo (T'aitöna, LA 260) to determine that a mean of 19 years had elapsed between construction and repair of rooms at that settlement. Applying her calculations to the Burnt Corn case would mean that the lack of repair in the Unit 1 roof, built in A.D. 1292, might have left it relatively uninhabitable after a twenty-year interval. In the absence of contrary evidence, we think it likely that the destruction of Burnt Corn occurred between A.D. 1303, following the final dated architecture at the pueblo, and 1311 when some of the roofs constructed earlier would have been disintegrating. Given our inference that the remodeling of rooms 6A and 6B took place after the A.D. 1302 cutting dates in the roof of 6B, some years may have passed in the interim. A rounded-off estimate of A.D. 1310 for the burning of the pueblo fits the available information.

The apparent absence of coordinated effort in the building of the various structures at Burnt Corn Pueblo also warrants further discussion. The different building styles used across the settlement implies minimal coordination or control of construction. The overall impression is of distinct groups building near to each other but using their own traditional techniques.

Jeffery Clark's discussion of architectural style and migrating populations (2001) is relevant to understanding how Burnt Corn Pueblo may have developed. He suggests that building techniques are culturally encoded practices, learned by observation and teaching during the course of everyday life. These activities may not be overtly symbolic but people are aware that architecture is meaningful. Thus it is in domestic contexts, away from more symbolically charged public spaces, where conservative practices are most likely to prevail (Clark 2001: 13). In other words, traditional methods of construction would be more predictably found in walls deep within a structure and hidden behind plaster than in some place where they would be "seen" by others. This observation is particularly germane in communities composed of different social groups, as might be the case in a time of high population flow or migration in the Galisteo Basin.

The eclectic masonry styles at Burnt Corn Pueblo may represent the presence of groups of people with distinct histories. These differences would not have been profound because there are numerous aspects of shared material culture present, particularly as manifested in a common ceramic tradition, but it is probable that many of the inhabitants had limited social experience with each other. This situation would be more akin to a settlement of people who once lived in different "neighborhoods" rather than a settlement of people who previously lived in different societies. In this scenario, Burnt Corn Pueblo was a coalescent community, as defined by Hill and others (2004).

The plaza pueblo is different from the other eight structures in scale and, possibly, planning. Buildings of this type are characteristic of the Coalition period in the northern Rio Grande and have been widely discussed (Cordell 1989: 322, 1998; Kohler and Root 2004; Kohler and others 2004; Ruscavage-Barz 1999: 159; Van Zandt 1999, 2006). These sites are variably interpreted as defensive structures (Wilcox and Haas 1994: 222), spaces designed to accommodate new communal ritual practices (Adams 1991: 125), or architectural proxies for specific social groups (Van Zandt 1999: 375). As such, plaza pueblos are considered to reflect the central tenets of social organization in the Coalition period.

Each of three scenarios for plaza pueblo construction implies a certain degree of centralized decision making, against which the apparent expedient construction strategy for the Burnt Corn plaza pueblo must be considered. Linda Cordell (1998: 89) has noted that the "planned" appearance of the Rowe plaza pueblo is not sustained by evaluation of the construction sequence, and it would appear that coordination in the building of Burnt Corn was similarly limited. The fact that the structure was built throughout at least a ten-year interval and perhaps longer also cautions against viewing it as an execution of a detailed plan.

It is thus possible that the central feature of the plaza pueblo, the enclosed plaza itself, did not exist until the very end of the occupation. It is also possible that the original structure was a room block like the others in the community, and that it was later remodeled into a new plaza pueblo architectural form. If, as Adams (1991:125) has argued, the significance of plaza pueblos relates to their providing stages for public ritual performances, the timing of the renovation of Burnt Corn Pueblo is provocative. At Burnt Corn Pueblo we may be seeing a social dynamic of coalescent communities, where residents from disparate origins responded to internal tension or external aggression by establishing an architectural context that promoted community identity.

The "End" of Burnt Corn Pueblo

The excavated evidence makes it clear to us that Burnt Corn Pueblo was destroyed in a conscious and systematic act. Evidence for this process is one of the things that brought us to the site in the first place, and we have made considerable progress in our interpretations of the event.

The indications are that the fire was widespread and probably set both inside and outside rooms. This makes it unlikely that the fire was accidental, a situation supported by evidence from other regional excavations. At Arroyo Hondo there were indications of accidental fires: 7 out of 66 rooms occupied in Component 1 were burned, and these appear to be represent occasional accidents over several decades of occupation. However, nearly half of Component 2 rooms at Arroyo Hondo were destroyed by fire, leading the excavators to infer that some other all-encompassing process was implicated in burning (Creamer 1993: 13–14, 42).

We consider a range fire to be an unlikely explanation for the conflagrations at Burnt Corn Pueblo because the piñon-juniper woodland surrounding the site rarely burns with high intensity, and the woodcutting and the trampling of vegetation associated with long-term occupation of a pueblo would have reduced the fuel load in the immediate vicinity of the settlement. Evidence for apparent preparation prior to the blaze also argues against a sudden decision to depart.

The fundamental question of "who did it," and whether the destruction caused by the fire was an act of vengeance by another group, of decommission by the residents themselves, or the result of some other scenario, hinges on evidence from the regional context of

Burnt Corn Pueblo. This evidence is discussed in Chapter 8. At this stage we note that the fire that terminated Burnt Corn's role as a domicile did not end its role as a landmark of significance in the western Galisteo Basin landscape. The buildings at Burnt Corn Pueblo may have provided a material resource for a brief time, and the architectural wood from the pueblo appears to have been salvaged for use elsewhere.

Over the longer term, Burnt Corn Pueblo served as another kind of resource, one with cultural meaning and moral implication. The smoldering remains of a formerly active place high on a ridgetop would have been a material talisman in the tales of the Tano people, redolent of actions and consequences in the way that keeps Pueblo landscapes alive with meaning (Malotki 2002; Snead 2004, 2008b). We cannot know the essence of such tales, nor whether they reflected actual events or were narratives imposed on the remains by others. Nonetheless, it is likely that the demise of Burnt Corn Pueblo was a meaningful event in Pueblo history, and that its place on the landscape continued to be recognized by subsequent generations.

Archaeological Investigations of Small Sites: Lodestar, Cholla House, and Slope House

Mark W. Allen

An important opportunity to expand the work of the Tano Origins Project came in 2005, when we were invited by the Archaeological Conservancy to conduct test excavations at the Lodestar sites near the town of Cerrillos. Investigation of these sites, 11 km west of Burnt Corn Pueblo, allowed us to obtain a more detailed look at the "neighbors" of the Burnt Corn community, and to examine small residential sites, a neglected aspect of the archaeological record of the Galisteo Basin. The test excavations were conducted by the Cal Poly Pomona team, and this work produced comparative information that significantly changed our perspective on Late Coalition period settlement in the region.

The archaeological landscape of the Galisteo Basin is dotted with the remains of many smaller pueblos. Long ignored, these sites represent aspects of settlement that provide a larger frame of analysis for the Tano Origins Project. Test excavations at a number of small Coalition period sites near Burnt Corn Pueblo revealed idiosyncratic architectural details, but similar assemblages and occupational spans. Evidence is persuasive that most of these small pueblos were burned at the end of their occupation, indicating that the destruction of Burnt Corn Pueblo by fire was not an isolated occurrence in the region.

This chapter describes archaeological investigations conducted at the Lodestar Ranch and in the Burnt Corn community, two Ancestral Pueblo settlements a few hours' walk apart. Student crews from Cal Poly Pomona conducted surface mapping and limited test excavations at several small, Late Coalition period archaeological sites in these two areas. The work was designed to obtain a more complete understanding of the nature and distribution of small communities and households in the hinterland of the short-lived Late Coalition period Burnt Corn Pueblo.

SMALL STRUCTURES IN THE GALISTEO BASIN AND ON THE PAJARITO PLATEAU

Comparative data for small site excavations are limited for the Galisteo Basin, but more information is available from the nearby Pajarito Plateau (Cordell 1979a: 61–64). Before summarizing our work at Lodestar and the Burnt Corn community, we review the investigation of smaller structures in the region.

The Waldo Site (LA 9147) is located in the western Galisteo Basin on a gravel bench above the river (Fig. 1.3). The site consists of a room block oriented northwest to southeast, with four contiguous stone masonry rooms in a row, and another incomplete room with remnants of adobe walls attached to the structure. There are also two pit house structures northeast of the rooms. All the rooms and structures at this site were excavated by Hammack (1971). Two of the four rooms constructed using sandstone masonry had interior walls plastered with gray clay. Some rooms had well made adobe plastered floors; others did not. Two of the rooms were likely used for habitation, and two were storage areas. Roofing materials lay directly on top of the floors. The attached room with adobe walls was possibly a ramada on the south side of the pueblo. There were few artifacts in the rooms, and artifacts in direct contact with the floors were rare. There was a small midden area about 30 cm deep located between the pueblo and the pit houses. The rooms appear to have been abandoned after a short occupation. The pueblo does not contain evidence of burning, and few valuables were left behind by the inhabitants. Roof beams were scavenged shortly after occupation ended.

A number of small Coalition pueblos on the Pajarito Plateau, about 25 km the north of the Waldo Site, were investigated by personnel at the Los Alamos National

Laboratory. Two sites located near each other on Mesita Del Buey provide useful comparative cases. Site LA 4624 is a 25 room linear pueblo that apparently dates to the Early-Middle Coalition period. Ten rooms were excavated at this site (Vierra and others 2002). Site LA 4618 appears to be a later Coalition period pueblo with 13 rooms, including one circular subterranean kiva and one above-ground square-shaped kiva. All of these rooms were excavated (Schmidt 2006). Both sites show consistent stratigraphy with four layers in the rooms. From bottom to top these stratigraphic layers include a prepared floor, roof fill, wall fill, and post-occupational fill. Schmidt (2006: 41) noted that this sequence is common at Coalition period sites at Los Alamos. These sites are nearly all oriented the same way, slightly east of north, with middens built up outside the rooms in front of the pueblo. The front rooms consistently are interpreted as habitation rooms, and adjoining back rooms are smaller and identified as storage rooms.

LA 4624, earlier and larger than LA 4618, has walls constructed of a mix of shaped and unshaped tuff blocks and hard-packed adobe. Some of the walls and floors were plastered. The four floors that were exposed at this site had intermittent areas of ash and smoke staining. There were many artifacts found on the floors, although no particularly valuable items were noted. Melted adobe, burnt daub, burnt wood fragments, and charcoal occurred in the roof and wall fall, and it was clear in some rooms that that the roof had burned and collapsed on top of the floor.

The later and smaller site, LA 4618, had two distinct kiva structures, and notably different wall construction. The walls were constructed using four to six courses of shaped tuff blocks, held together with adobe mortar. Each room had evidence of fine clay plastering on the walls and floors, sometimes smoothly blended together. Schmidt (2006: 43) wrote: "based on the high number of still-usable artifacts and the degree of burning on many of the artifacts associated with the floor, it is possible that the pueblo was rapidly abandoned."

Other small Pajarito sites include LA 12121, an east-west aligned eight-room structure with a corner kiva dated by dendrochronology to A.D. 1177 (Traylor 1990: 496). Saltbush Pueblo (LA 4997) was slightly larger, with 11 rooms aligned north-south and a detached kiva. It showed evidence of two components, one dated by dendrochronology to the early 1200s (Snow 1974). A few other examples of small sites are detailed in Kohler and Root (2004), Steen (1977), and Worman (1959).

These studies highlight the research questions that can be answered with excavation of small Coalition period pueblos. It is evident that architecture of this period is quite eclectic, exhibiting diverse layouts and building styles. Differences between the Waldo site and the small sites excavated on the Pajarito Plateau are clear, but we do not know whether this variability represents fundamental cultural and functional differences or a problem in archaeological sampling. There are many architectural sites on the Pajarito Plateau that resemble the Waldo site which have not been excavated (Van Zandt 1999, 2006). It is clear that more evidence about small sites is needed to understand their variability during the Coalition period.

Research Design and Methodology

Small structure excavations were investigated by the Tano Origins Project in two locales. The first of these was the Lodestar Ranch, where four pueblos were examined. Work in the Burnt Corn community concentrated on two small structures. Research at both locales included surface and subsurface investigation.

The primary goal of surface investigations was to document the presence and extent of artifacts and features visible on the surface. Each site was examined thoroughly by field crew members, and visible artifacts were marked with pin flags. Features were identified and delineated, and site boundaries were estimated using topography and the distribution of artifacts, features, and middens. Data were recorded using Trimble data loggers, and GPS (global positioning system) positions were later subjected to differential correction for submeter accuracy. These corrected data were then entered into a GIS (geographic information system) project using ARCMAP software. We used a digital camera to record surface evidence and views of each site. Crews left most observed artifacts in situ, collecting only a few diagnostic items. When artifacts were point-plotted, basic information on their type, material, and other diagnostic traits was recorded. We mapped identifiable pueblos by laying out long metric tapes along the major axis of each block and then measuring the locations of each constituent rock perpendicular to this axis. Datums on the site maps note the end points of the main axis mapping line.

We undertook subsurface investigations at sites to assess their depth, preservation, and chronology, and to determine the buried structure of the room blocks as discerned from the surface distribution of construction stones. The pueblos had visible rock alignments that were likely wall courses or foundations, so excavation units were placed adjacent to them in hopes of exposing intact structural features. We excavated in arbitrary 10 cm levels. All excavated material was screened in the field with one-quarter inch mesh, unless otherwise noted. Upon completion, all excavations were backfilled and the surface was restored to the original contour. Displaced rocks that were likely architectural remains were returned to their original positions. All collected materials are permanently curated at the Laboratory of Anthropology/Museum of Indian Arts and Culture in Santa Fe.

ARCHAEOLOGICAL INVESTIGATIONS AT THE LODESTAR COMMUNITY

We conducted archaeological investigations at four small pueblos on the Lodestar Ranch in July and August of 2005 (Allen 2006). Previous archaeological work in the vicinity was limited. At least one of the sites was designated LA 590 by Harry Mera in the 1930s, but aside from scattered references no further recording was conducted until the 1990s (Jager 1995). Several archaeological resources at this location are in the process of being acquired by the Archaeological Conservancy for preservation. Thus, in addition to the primary goal of expanding our sample of Coalition period communities in the region, our investigations were also intended to provide the Conservancy with basic information to assist in the long-term management of the sites.

The work at Lodestar Ranch involved three operations. The first was an intensive surface survey, recording, and limited subsurface testing of a previously unrecorded small pueblo that has been designated the Lodestar North Site (LA 158557). The second operation was to update the site record of another small pueblo, the Lodestar South Site (LA 105759; Jager 1995), where we also conducted limited subsurface test investigations. The final operation was the mapping and surface investigation of two other small pueblos in the Lodestar vicinity: a previously unrecorded site north of Lodestar North designated as the North Site and LA 107127, located between Lodestar North and Lodestar South. These can all be characterized as small pueblos with associated middens. These sites are located on small mesas directly west of a major drainage that flows northward in a meandering path into the Galisteo Creek (Fig. 5.1).

Decorated ceramics on these sites are exclusively black-on-white with a few trade wares (Chapter 3). These ceramics indicate an occupation in the Late Coalition Pindi phase or, possibly, the subsequent Galisteo phase (A.D. 1250-1325).

The Lodestar North Site (LA 158557)

Lodestar North is located on a small mesa directly west of a major drainage that runs parallel to Highway 14. The site measures approximately 230 m along the east-west axis and 181 m along the north-south axis. There is a distinct cluster of surface artifacts in the northeast corner of the site, and a much smaller density of lithics, ground stone, and ceramic sherds in other areas of the site. The seven features discerned from surface evidence included: Feature 1, a pueblo with surface rocks; Features 2, 3, and 4, circular depressions; Feature 5, a low circular mound; Feature 6, a small rock cluster near the southeastern extremity of the site; and Feature 7, a rock concentration (which may be modern) along the eastern edge of the site.

The site shows no obvious disturbances other than occasional motorcycle tracks, and there is a light scatter of modern cultural material across the surface. Ground cover is sparse, and about a dozen juniper trees are clustered near the eastern boundary of the site. Natural erosion is minimal due to flat topography, except along the edges of the mesa where erosion is probably pronounced during occasional heavy rains. Notable artifacts identified during the surface survey and mapping include a number of ground-stone fragments, hundreds of sherds, hundreds of large basalt flakes (mostly primary or secondary stage), and a chert projectile point.

Feature 1

The pueblo designated Feature 1 is approximately 7 m by 18 m in size, with the long axis oriented north-south. Several rock alignments on the surface denote the locations of rooms and walls. Unit 1 was placed in one of these alignments in the north end of the feature. The test unit was 1 m by 2 m in size, with one of the long sides placed exactly on the western edge of a discernible rock alignment. This alignment proved to be the only intact wall encountered within the unit. The unit datum was set approximately 5 cm above ground surface and about 20 cm from the northwest corner of the unit, and

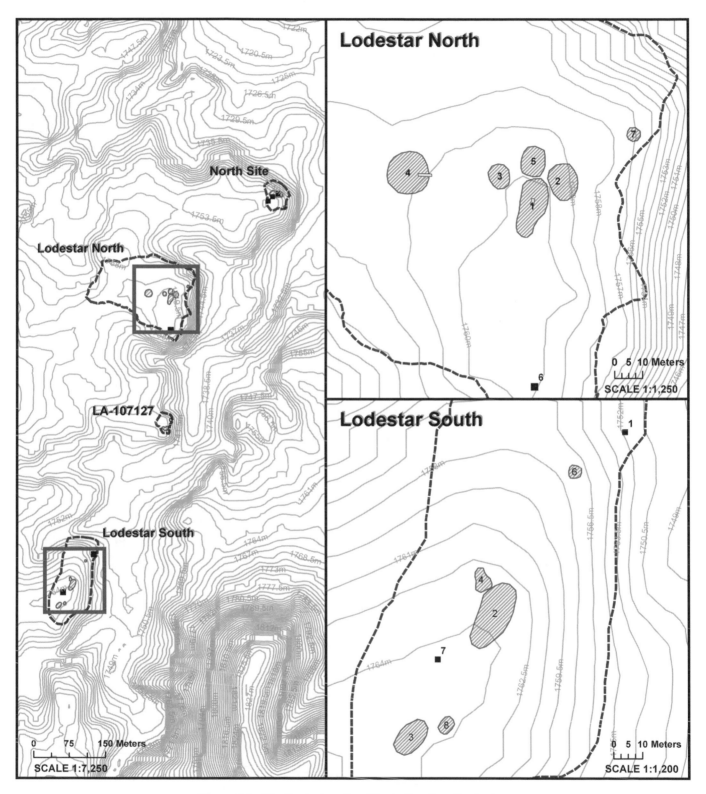

Figure 5.1. The Lodestar sites, illustrating the site cluster
with details of Lodestar North and Lodestar South.

all depth measurements were taken from this arbitrary elevation. The first four arbitrary levels were located in a stratigraphic level designated Zone A. This zone was approximately 50 cm to 60 cm thick, and it consisted of fine-textured and extremely compact adobe fill with a pale brown color and light yellowish brown mottling. Each arbitrary level within this zone contained a few sherds and lithics. Several ground-stone artifacts were also present within this level. Zone A appears to be fill from collapsed adobe, perhaps the upper courses of the walls of the pueblo. It was extremely difficult to excavate; in most areas of the unit a hand pick was required. Charcoal was scattered throughout the zone, with much higher concentrations toward the bottom. Two distinct courses of architectural stones ranging from 15 cm to 30 cm in diameter were exposed in the east profile wall of Unit 1. These architectural stones were laid in straight and level rows, one at the modern surface level and the second 6 cm to 12 cm below the first. They protruded from the east sidewall into the unit to a distance of 15 cm (Fig. 5.2). These stones were not removed or disturbed during the excavation of Unit 1 in order to preserve architectural integrity.

At the bottom of Zone A, just above a distinct prepared floor designated Zone B, we encountered a higher density of artifacts. These artifacts occurred in the 40 cm to 50 cm and 50 cm to 60 cm levels. We recovered a large number of burnt or charred utilitarian sherds, likely from one or a few different vessels. Some sherds had drilled holes, either for repair or for suspending the vessel from a roof beam. These two levels also yielded two pieces of turquoise, an obsidian projectile point, a core, several ground-stone artifacts, a hammerstone, and two polished bone tools. There were numerous animal bones in the two levels, some of which were burned. Most of these artifacts and ecofacts were point-provenienced. For the last level, we screened excavated deposits using one-eighth inch mesh in order to recover smaller pieces of turquoise.

We defined the floor designated Zone B in the southeastern corner of the unit at the bottom of the 50 cm to 60 cm level. It was further exposed by excavation of a 60 cm to 65 cm level. Zone B had a much lower density of artifacts than the bottom of Zone A. The floor appeared to be prepared using distinct yellowish-red clay, much softer than the clay in than Zone A. It contained some charcoal and ash, and it extended across the entire unit to the edge of the course of wall stones exposed on the east edge of the unit. The floor was approximately 10 cm thick in the northern half of the unit, and about 6 cm

Figure 5.2. Masonry wall in east profile of Unit 1, Feature 1, Lodestar North.

thick in the southern half of the unit. It was level, with some undulatation in the southeastern corner. A 30 cm by 30 cm square in the northwestern corner of the unit was excavated from 65 cm to 70 cm, reaching the bottom of Zone B. Located at a depth of approximately 75 cm below datum, Zone C was composed of natural soil or subsoil. It was light yellowish brown and much softer than Zone A. To make sure that there were no buried strata, an auger core was placed in the northwest corner of the unit and taken down to 1.02 m below datum. No artifacts or soil changes were observed.

In summary, Unit 1 exposed the eastern portion of a room with a prepared clay floor. Only the east wall was exposed but additional walls were probably present to the north, south, and west. A substantial quantity and variety of domestic artifacts and ecofacts, concentrated in the northern half of the room, provided evidence of domestic and residential activity. The walls consisted of at least two courses of stones laid straight in level rows, perhaps topped by adobe. The room appears to have burned and collapsed, possibly during a single event. There is no evidence of rebuilding or reoccupation of the room. Feature 1 apparently represents a short occupation, although the excavation of additional rooms would be needed to confirm this interpretation.

Features 2–4 (Circular Depressions)

Three of the surface features at the Lodestar North Site were circular depressions with maximum depths of 20 cm to 30 cm below the surrounding surfaces. Each feature filled with denser and greener vegetation than

Figure 5.3. Unit 2, Feature 4, Lodestar North, under excavation, illustrating
shallow pit cut into caliche with rim of basalt cobbles (upper right).

the rest of the site because the pits functioned as mois-
ture traps. Feature 2 was about 13 m in diameter, Feature
3 was about 8 m in diameter, and Feature 4, the largest pit, had a diameter of 15 m. All three features were
located close to the pueblo.

After discussion with representatives of the Archaeological Conservancy, we deemed it appropriate and
desirable to obtain a cross-section of one of these circular features to determine whether it was formed by cultural or natural processes, and if by cultural processes,
whether it dated to the prehistoric component represented by the pueblo and surface artifacts. A 1-m by 4-m
trench placed in Feature 4 provided a vertical exposure
of its profile. It extended from the lip of the pit, down
the slope of the pit, and on to the fairly flat center of
the feature. After excavation of the first level, the trench
was extended another meter at the top of the pit to better
expose a cluster of cobbles and pebbles encountered in
the easternmost edge of the trench (Fig. 5.3).

Because of the dense concentration of basalt cobbles
and pebbles along the rim of the pit, arbitrary excavation levels did not proceed by constant depths. Instead,
levels were created at points where we noted significant

changes in distribution of rocks. Different parts of
the trench were excavated to different depths and we
halted excavation when sterile soil was reached. The
maximum depth of Unit 2 was about 42 cm below the
surface of the lowest point inside Feature 4. We identified two stratigraphic layers in the unit. Zone A was
yellowish-brown in color, fine textured, and soft. It was
easily distinguished from Zone B below it, and could be
separated from it with a whisk broom. The upper zone
had a high density of cobbles, gravel, and pebbles in the
eastern half of the trench. In the western half of the unit,
Zone A yielded only small rocks, none as large as a fist.
The concentration of rocks in the feature was clearly
deposited from the excavation of the pit. It became clear
that Feature 4 was indeed a cultural rather than natural
feature. As the pit was excavated, the rock encountered
during this process was deposited at the edge of the pit,
and not hauled away. Several possible artifacts and a few
sherds were recovered during the excavation of Zone A,
but no charcoal was observed. Zone B was natural soil
or subsoil. It was compact, with a homogenous pale yel-
low color and fine texture. Zone B contained only small
pieces of basalt and was clearly sterile. The sidewalls of

Unit 2 showed that Feature 4 was a pit excavated with a gentle slope for about 2 m, then with a distinct vertical drop to a level floor in the pit's center.

Unit 2 seems to demonstrate that Feature 4 was excavated by hand before the modern era. Mechanical excavation or excavation with metal shovels and picks almost certainly would have left visible scars or cuts in Zone B, and none were observed. Nor were historical materials present. Likely, the entire lip of the pit was lined with the basalt cobbles and gravel that was originally part of the soil removed from the feature. This basalt occurs naturally in the soil covering the mesa top and is generally endemic in this region.

The function of Feature 4 is not entirely clear but the low density of cultural material and the absence of charcoal indicate that it may have been a borrow pit for fill or an agricultural feature rather than a kiva or similar structure. At nearby Pueblo San Marcos, pits have been documented as part of the agricultural landscape (Lang 1995: 155), and Kurt Anschuetz (1998: 328) described shallow, artificial depressions associated with farming practices in the Rio del Oso. Our work may thus represent the first excavations of a similar agricultural feature in the Galisteo Basin.

The Lodestar South Site
(LA 105759)

The Lodestar South Site is located approximately 445 m south of the Lodestar North Site. It was previously recorded as LA 105759 (Jager 1995: 25–27), although Snead's (2005b) comparison of site maps suggests that it is probably Mera's LA 590. The site is situated on a small mesa adjacent to a major drainage, a topographic setting similar to that of Lodestar North. Lodestar South Site measures 187 m north-south and 81 m east-west. Jager (1995) originally identified five surface features at the site, including two pueblos (Features 2 and 3), and a fairly dense distribution of surface artifacts directly east of the structures. Our initial reconnaissance in July of 2005 relocated these features, two of which, both rock alignments, may be modern in age. Three previously unrecorded features (Features 6 to 8) were identified in 2005 (Allen 2006: 12). The pueblos are recognizable as low mounds with distinct concentrations of masonry stones on the surface, some of which are still in discernible alignments or rows.

The most common surface artifacts are primary-stage and secondary-stage basalt flakes, but chert and obsidian debitage and several hundred sherds were also observed. Most of the pottery sherds are utility wares, but painted wares and biscuit wares are present as well. A few small pieces of turquoise were present on the surface of Feature 2, the largest pueblo, and an obsidian projectile point was recovered from the surface near Feature 3. Survey of the site identified two separate clusters of artifacts and darker soil; these were delineated and mapped as Locus A and Locus B, each directly east of the two pueblos. Few artifacts were observed in other areas of the site. The site is in good condition, with no obvious looter holes or substantial modern impact. The surface of the site is covered with sparse vegetation and about a dozen substantial juniper trees.

Feature 2

Feature 2 at the Lodestar South Site is a pueblo that measures 22 m along the north-south axis and 12 m along the east-west axis. Unit 1 was a 1-m by 2-m unit placed perpendicular to the main axis of the block in order to provide information on chronology, architecture, and preservation. The unit was placed alongside several rock alignments visible on the surface, with the hope of exposing at least one original wall course. Indeed, Unit 1 contacted two distinct masonry walls that ran roughly north-south along the main axis of the Feature 2 (Fig. 5.4). The first few levels of Unit 1 were exceedingly difficult to excavate because of the large number of rocks that apparently fell from the walls into the unit and the compact matrix, which consisted largely of melted adobe. We subsequently halted excavation of the unit east of the main wall so that efforts could be redirected toward reaching sterile soil on the west side of the unit during the available time for fieldwork.

At a depth of approximately 15 cm to 20 cm below the surface, we encountered a distinct layer of burning about 10 cm to 20 cm thick that ran through the west side of the unit. This burnt layer was thickest along the south wall. Interestingly, this zone did not extend eastward to the masonry wall in the middle of the unit. It is possible that the wall toppled over to the west prior to burning and thus prevented burning adjacent to the lower intact portions of the wall. Several large stones, possibly masonry blocks, were in the center of the unit below the burned zone. Somewhat contrary to this interpretation, however, several large and flat stones with ash and charring on their bottom were directly on top of the burnt layer, appearing to have landed on top of a fire.

Figure 5.4. Unit 1, Feature 2, Lodestar South, illustrating internal masonry walls and wall fall.

Several large pieces of charcoal, burnt wood, and burnt adobe chunks were in the burnt layer and in subsequent excavation levels.

Artifacts from Unit 1 included a number of small pieces of turquoise, recovered at a depth of 60 cm below the surface, and an obsidian projectile point located at about 20 cm below the surface. Ceramic sherds and ground stone occurred to a maximum depth of 80 cm. Sterile soil appeared about 80 cm below the surface. Also notable in this unit was the density of obsidian flakes, which was considerably higher than in Unit 1 of the Lodestar North Site.

Unit 1 probably exposed the western edge of the pueblo. Two distinct north-south walls were clearly visible just below the surface. It is unclear, however, if there were additional masonry walls west of the unit. Curiously, the two observed walls were only about 35 cm apart, certainly too close together to define a room. This positioning may reflect a rebuilding or modification

event, or conceivably two contemporary rooms placed close together without sharing a wall. The west portion of Unit 1, excavated to sterile soil, revealed clear habitation debris and evidence that at the end of occupation an intense fire burned along its western edge, at least in this location. Part of the westernmost wall inside the unit apparently collapsed westward before this fire started. Subsequently, several masonry stones fell on top of the fire after it began; they may have been from a different wall or perhaps were sitting on top of a roof structure.

Feature 3

Feature 3 at Lodestar South is a pueblo measuring 5 m to 6 m by 12 m in size at the south end of the site. Unit 2 began as a 1-m by 1-m test unit placed in a suspected room corner with three masonry walls at the southern end of the structure. After the first level, we extended Unit 2 another meter to the east to better define

Figure 5.5 Unit 3, Feature 3, Lodestar South, illustrating masonry wall possibly serving as a ramada foundation.

a substantial north-south wall running through the long axis of the pueblo. We excavated the east half of the unit and encountered sterile soil at 25 cm to 35 cm below the surface. The wall in the middle of the unit was carefully constructed and consisted of two courses of rock. The higher course was built of three rows of rocks: two outer lines consisting of fairly thin slabs placed on their edges and a middle course made up of rocks placed on their flat sides. The lower course was not exposed in plan by our excavations. In Unit 2 we also exposed a single line of rocks running east for about 2 m, but this did not appear to be a structural wall.

We further exposed the main wall by excavating Unit 3, positioned adjacent to Unit 2 but oriented north-south and thus parallel to the wall. Unit 3 began as a 1-m by 1.5-m unit, but in order to expose architectural elements it was extended a meter to the north to reach a final size of 1 m by 2.5 m. Thus, Unit 2 and Unit 3 formed an "L-shaped" trench with a north-south length of 3.5 m and an east-west dimension of 2 m. The maximum depths of this trench varied because all areas were not excavated to sterile soil. The deepest part of the excavation was the northernmost meter of Unit 3, where we encountered sterile soil at roughly 46 cm below the surface.

In Unit 2 and Unit 3 we recovered a low density of artifacts, mostly sherds, and charcoal was common. The key evidence we discuss here concerns the architectural elements that were exposed (Fig. 5.5). The well-made wall consisting of two existing courses extended a little over 2 m. At this point, it connected to a much more

substantial stone structure, which almost certainly was a sturdy structural masonry wall. Its constituent rocks were larger in size and were not placed flat. Our preliminary interpretation is that Units 2 and 3 exposed a point where a low but carefully made stone wall connected to the southwest corner of the pueblo. This stone wall may have had adobe elements stacked on top of it. We think the wall may have outlined a patio, ramada, or similar space. The shallow line of rock running east from this wall at the southern edge of Unit 2 outlined a space of perhaps 2 m by 2 m.

In Unit 3 we apparently exposed the southwestern exterior corner of the pueblo, and this might explain the relatively low density of recovered artifacts. Interestingly, the east side of the carefully made north-south wall, that is, the inside of the posited patio or ramada, had distinct burnt clay affixed to or in direct contact with the outer line of stone. This yellowish-red clay extended about 50 cm along the edge of the wall. The clay was about 5 cm thick in the middle, and tapered to less than 1 cm at the north and south edges. We obtained a profile of this clay with the excavation of a small cut perpendicular to the stone wall. This showed that the clay extended about 7 cm deep along the edge of the wall. The significance of this burnt clay is unclear, but it was in direct contact with the outermost line of stones that make up this wall.

Site LA 107127

An unnamed site recorded by Jager (1995) as LA 107127 is located 153 m south of the Lodestar North Site. This site measures 35 m by 46 m in size. LA 107127 is on a small mesa directly above a wash to the east. Two surface features documented by Jager were reidentified during our fieldwork. These include a circular rock alignment with some low mounding and a rectangular shaped stone feature that is likely the remains of a one-room structure. Jager noted there were 12 sherds and 42 flakes, mostly basalt, at the site. Our inspection turned up only a few sherds, suggesting that artifact collectors may have destroyed evidence on this site during the past decade.

The North Site

We briefly inspected a second site in the vicinity of the Lodestar North Site that we designated the North Site. Because the property status of this site was uncertain, our

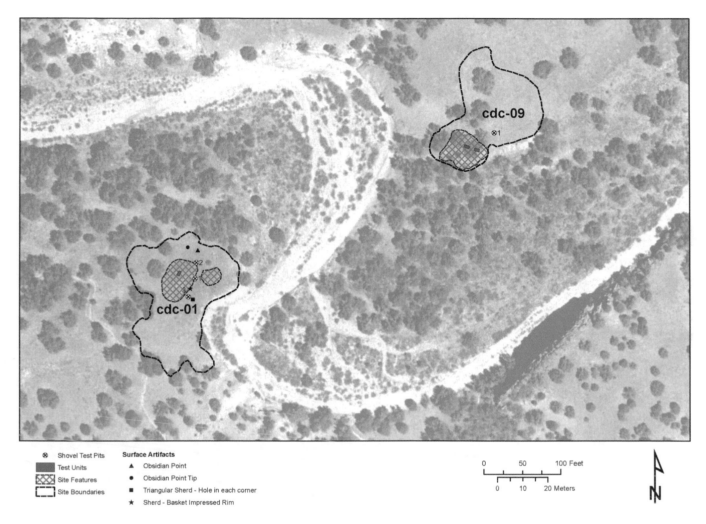

Figure 5.6. Cholla House (CD–1) and Slope House (CD–9),
excavated farmsteads within the Burnt Corn community.

reconnaissance of the North Site was brief and we did not complete an LA site form. The site measures 52 m by 63 m in size and is 205 m north of the Lodestar North Site. It is similar to the other mesa top sites already discussed but it has a low density of surface artifacts. The site encompasses a large pueblo that we designated as Feature 1. This pueblo measures 12 m by 28.6 m in size, and is the largest pueblo we observed during the 2005 field season at Lodestar. Feature 1 is oriented with the long axis east-west rather than north-south like all of the other pueblos. Collectors have cached several artifacts in the center of the pueblo, evidently within the past few years. We observed a few ground-stone artifacts close to the structure. We documented three features in addition to the pueblo. Feature 2 is a low circular mound, about 4 m in diameter and 0.5 m high. Feature 3 appears to be

a one-room rectangular structure measuring 3.2 m by 4.7 m in size, with associated basalt debitage. Feature 4 is a rock concentration about 2 m by 2.5 m in size, and it appears to be a pit filled with rocks.

ARCHAEOLOGICAL INVESTIGATIONS OF SMALL PUEBLOS IN THE BURNT CORN COMMUNITY

In July of 2006 we conducted archaeological investigations at two small pueblos within the Burnt Corn Community (Allen 2007). Surface inspection, mapping, and limited test excavations were completed at Cholla House (LA 134186, CDC–1) and Slope House (LA 134193, CDC–9). These small Pindi phase archaeological sites are located along the Cañada de la Cueva, about 200 m east of the substantially larger Burnt Corn Pueblo (LA 359). This work was a key component of the Tano Origins Project, designed to obtain a more complete understanding of the nature and distribution of smaller structures in the hinterland of the Burnt Corn community that existed at the end of the thirteenth century A.D. Survey in the community core has identified 17 probable field houses and farmsteads within 1 km of Burnt Corn Pueblo (Snead 2008a). Cholla House and Slope House are representative of these features.

The two sites investigated in 2006 can be characterized as small pueblos with associated middens. The archaeological investigations at each site included a thorough surface survey and a detailed point-plotted distribution map of tools and diagnostic artifacts, produced using submeter accuracy GPS data (Fig. 5.6). We mapped the pueblo features at each site using a tape measure and compass.

Cholla House
(LA 134186, CDC–1)

Cholla House is located on a terrace just above a bend in the Cañada de la Cueva, about 200 m southeast and below Burnt Corn Pueblo. Ceramics on the site point to a Late Coalition period component and a short occupation (Snead 2001b:14). Cholla House is a linear pueblo, oriented just east of north, probably comprised of four to six rooms. The mound is approximately 9 m by 16 m in size, though the pueblo itself may be only be 10 m to 12 m long. There is a midden immediately east of the structure with a relatively high frequency of surface artifacts, although the wider scatter occupies an area of 30 m by 35 m. Identified surface artifacts included debitage, sherds, a uniface, a side-notched obsidian projectile point, an obsidian biface tip that was probably a projectile point, and several ground-stone tools. One of the sherds was basket impressed, and another sherd had three drilled holes. Minor excavations consisting of three small shovel test pits, designated STP–1 through STP–3, were conducted in the midden area. Each of the shovel test pits was 35 cm by 35 cm in size, and excavated by shovel and trowel. All fill was screened with one-quarter inch mesh. STP–1, in the middle position, revealed a midden that was at least 35 cm in depth. The other two shovel test pits exposed sterile soil at 25 cm to 30 cm below the surface. Few artifacts were recovered from the shovel test pits.

Figure 5.7. Feature 1, Cholla House, illustrating wall construction and associated floor.

Feature 1

The pueblo was designated Feature 1, and we placed a single 1-m by 2-m test unit in what appeared to be a room corner at the southern end of the structure. The east-west alignment of rocks visible on the surface was confirmed as a wall segment, but no north-south wall was identified. Sterile soil was reached about 95 cm below the surface. A fine clay plastered floor above the sterile soil was sooty and blackened, and a side-notched chert projectile point lay on its surface. A large amount of roof debris, much of it burned, had fallen on the floor, including a shaped 40-cm square stone that might have been a hatch cover for the roof entry. A pair of well-formed two-handed manos with signs of scorching on their ventral surfaces may also have fallen from the roof. Several other ground-stone artifacts were in the fill, as well as a light density of sherds from utilitarian vessels. More than a dozen burned and unburned secondary wood beams appeared at various depths, suggesting that some parts of the roof fell in before others. Several valuable or useful tools were mixed in this fill, including a concentration of turquoise pieces (perhaps the contents of a sack or other container that had been stashed in the roof before it collapsed), five bone tools, and an obsidian projectile point. On top of the roof collapse was fill consisting of melted adobe and masonry stones that had fallen into the room.

As exposed in our excavation, Cholla House exhibits a construction method unique to similar sites previously excavated in the region (Fig. 5.7). A clay plaster surface extended from the floor up the south wall of the room for approximately 50 cm, topped by a flat, 30-cm thick layer of unshaped masonry. Above this was a course of adobe about 30 cm high, topped by another layer of stone masonry that was visible on the modern surface. Originally, the walls were several courses higher; their collapsed remains made up the mound and surface debris of Feature 1. The valuables in Cholla House, and the widespread evidence of fire and simultaneous roof collapse, likely indicate that the pueblo was not intentionally set on fire by its residents. The strongest argument for this interpretation is the cached turquoise.

Slope House (LA 134193)

Slope House (LA 134193, CDC–9) is also situated along the Cañada de la Cueva, less than a hundred meters from Cholla House. This pueblo is being rapidly eroded by a small arroyo along the south and east sides. Masonry debris from the structure is scattered across an area about 7 m by 10 m in size, oriented nearly east-west along the adjacent arroyo. Disturbance, erosion, and two large juniper trees at the site make it difficult to assess the number of rooms in the pueblo, but we estimate there were about six rooms present. The eastern edge of the pueblo has a distinct wall corner. An extensive midden up to 60 cm deep, as determined by a shovel test pit, is located directly northeast and upslope of the pueblo. Ceramics include Santa Fe Black-on-white and Galisteo Black-on-white. There are also lithics present, including basalt, chert, obsidian, andesite, petrified wood, and mica. These artifacts suggest a fairly heavy cultural use of the site during the late thirteenth or early fourteenth centuries. Two side-notched projectile points were also observed on this surface.

Figure 5.8. Unit 1, Slope House, under excavation.

Neither of the two 1 m by 2 m units placed inside the pueblo at the Slope House site revealed prepared floors or clear signs of burning. Unit 1, placed in an apparent corner of the easternmost room of the structure (Fig. 5.8), contained small amounts of charcoal, but this did not seem to indicate that the structure had burned. Melted adobe was particularly apparent in the west half of the unit. The crew recovered a low to moderate amount of ceramics, lithics, bone (some burned), one piece of turquoise, a bone bead, and a steatite pendant with a drilled hole in the fill.

Unit 2, placed within undefined but apparently interior space, exposed a mealing bin (Fig. 5.9) and a number of associated ground-stone artifacts. The unit also yielded two palettes. Excavation to a depth of 60 cm below the surface did not expose an obvious floor. A large number of masonry stones were present throughout the unit, indicating collapse of the walls. Each 10-cm arbitrary level contained a few sherds, a few lithics, and some charcoal. A mano came from the 30-cm to 40-cm level, and a small hearth 50 cm to 60 cm in size was present in the southeastern corner. A few of the recovered sherds were burnt. Artifacts continued into the 60-cm to 70-cm level. The last level was heavily churned from extensive juniper root disturbance.

Unlike Cholla House, Slope House did not have evidence of prepared floors, burnt artifacts, or burnt

Figure 5.9. Unit 2, Slope House, with mealing bin.

beam fragments. The westernmost portion of the site had few artifacts. The recovered artifact assemblage and the mealing bin feature in the easternmost room of the pueblo suggest a domestic function for the structure. Our excavation of Slope House indicates that it does not appear to have been vacated quickly or burned. Slope House is the only small pueblo excavated by the Tano Origins Project that does not appear to have been destroyed by fire.

ARTIFACT ANALYSES

This section briefly analyzes of the artifacts recovered by archaeological investigations at Lodestar, Cholla House, and Slope House. Comparative notes regarding the Tano Origins Project assemblages and similar data from LA 4624 and LA 4618, two small Coalition period pueblos on the Pajarito Plateau, are also included.

Ceramics

The ceramics recovered at the small sites described in this chapter are discussed by Barkwill Love and Cohen (Chapter 3). The Late Coalition period ceramic assemblages show similarities in ceramic types but significant differences in the frequencies of these types. The two sites in the immediate vicinity of Burnt Corn Pueblo have a higher frequency of decorated sherds than the sites at Lodestar. Decorated types compose about 21 percent of the Cholla House and Slope House assemblages, compared to 6 percent of the assemblage at Lodestar North and 16 percent of the assemblage at Lodestar South. The decorated sherds at all four excavated sites were primarily Santa Fe Black-on-white, with Galisteo Black-on-white making up most of the remainder. These frequencies contrast with the decorated ceramic sherd assemblage at Burnt Corn Pueblo, where the most frequent type is Galisteo Black-on-white. However, in all four of the small sites we investigated, the samples of decorated sherds were small, and many of the sherds came from the surface. At all of the small sites utilitarian wares comprised the majority of ceramics.

Debitage, Cores and Hammerstones

The debitage assemblage recovered at the small sites is dominated by basalt (47.5%), followed by chert (29.4%), chalcedony (12.0%), obsidian (7.3%), and other materials (3.8%). The two Lodestar sites have a significantly greater percentage of basalt debitage (80% at Lodestar North and 64% at Lodestar South) than do the sites in the Burnt Corn community, which have higher percentages of silicates (chert and chalcedony). Cholla House has 61 percent silicates and 33 percent basalt, while Slope House has 62 percent silicates and 24 percent basalt. Obsidian is limited at all four sites (3% to 12%), and exhibits varying degrees of opaqueness. Chert debitage occurs in a variety of colors, ranging from red to pink to white, and a variety of compositions. Additional research is needed to determine the source of the materials, although chert is present in the local gravels and other sources of stone used for tools are located nearby (Chapter 7). The high frequency of basalt at Lodestar reflects the abundance of this resource in the Cerrillos region.

Given the high percentage of basalt, the Tano Origins Project's lithic assemblage might suggest an early Coalition period (Vierra 2002: 102). However, this high percentage may instead reflect proximity to primary local sources. Obsidian is much more common at Los Alamos than in the Galisteo Basin, and this is likely attributable to the proximity of Los Alamos to the Jemez Mountains.

Lithics recorded during surface documentation at Lodestar North indicated that the most common constituent artifacts were basalt flakes. Detailed recording of lithics was not conducted at the other three small sites we investigated but all of these sites exhibit a similar pattern of midden and discarded artifacts (especially lithics) on the east side of the pueblos. Similar findings were reported from Los Alamos (Vierra and others 2002; Schmidt 2006).

Debitage at the small pueblo sites studied by the Tano Origins Project is primarily angular shatter and flakes resulting from primary and secondary stages of core reduction. Secondary flakes made up 71.5 percent of the debitage recovered. The assemblage lacks significant tertiary or pressure flakes. Only 4.1 percent of the debitage was from late stage tool finishing or maintenance. The sample of projectile points found on the surface and during test excavations at all four sites does not appear to correspond with the low number of pressure flakes. The points may have been made off-site, away from the pueblos. Most lithic production at the Lodestar and the Burnt Corn communities appears to have been focused on core reduction, with little or no biface-tool production and maintenance. Most activities at the pueblos that required a sharp cutting edge evidently relied on expedient flake tools with minimal retouch. Cores are rare at the small sites we investigated. Of the three cores we observed, one was chert, one was basalt, and one was siltstone. With only one hammerstone recorded, it appears that lithic reduction and production of tools occurred at a low level at the small sites.

Projectile Points and Other Chipped Stone Tools

Twelve projectile points were recovered during survey and test excavations at Lodestar Ranch, Cholla House, and Slope House. Of these, 9 are obsidian and 3 are chert. Nine of the projectile points are complete, and 3 are fragments, including one base and two distal ends. All of the points in this sample exhibited side-notched hafting styles with straight edge blades. The only other bifacially worked tool we recovered was a distal tip fragment of an obsidian biface, found in Unit 1 at Slope House. The lithic assemblage includes four expedient unifaces, one each of chert, obsidian, chalcedony, and siltstone. In general, finished or formal tools were rare at the small sites we investigated in the Galisteo Basin. Despite the low frequency of obsidian debitage, obsidian was the predominant material for projectile points.

Compared to LA 4624 and LA 4618 at Los Alamos National Laboratory (Vierra and others 2002; Schmidt

2006), the Tano Origins project produced a large sample of projectile points in relation to surface scatter areas and the extent of our excavations. Extensive work at Los Alamos produced 15 points, whereas more limited test excavations and surface survey at the small pueblo sites in the Galisteo Basin produced 13 points. Side-notch hafting and straight blade shape are the predominant type of point in both areas. Average measurements of points from Los Alamos and the Tano Origins Project are similar. Both areas yielded few other formal chipped stone tools.

Ground Stone

Fragments of portable basalt, granite, and limestone ground-stone artifacts are common on the surfaces of all of the small sites. There are also a few bedrock grinding features present. Test excavations yielded a number of fragments, and in some cases well-formed ground-stone tools. Cholla House, in particular, produced a number of formal ground-stone artifacts, including three likely metate fragments, one complete metate, and two well-formed two-handed manos. The manos were found at a depth of 70 cm, lying next to a presumed hatch cover. The manos were scorched on their undersides, and it is likely that they were on top of the roof when the pueblo burned and collapsed. The test units excavated at Lodestar and Unit 2 at Slope House also had a few pieces of ground stone. Together, this evidence suggests that carefully prepared ground-stone tools are common in small pueblos in the Galisteo Basin. Two granite pigment palettes were recovered from Unit 1 at Slope House.

Turquoise

A small part of the lithic assemblage of the Tano Origins Project consisted of turquoise beads and unmodified pieces of turquoise. Several small pieces of turquoise were recorded during investigations at Lodestar North, Lodestar South, and Slope House. However, the majority of turquoise (58 of 69 pieces) came from a single test unit at Cholla House. There we found 25 pieces of turquoise in situ and another 18 pieces of turquoise in the screening of fill. This concentration may represent the remains of a container stored in the supporting beams of the pueblo that fell as the burning roof collapsed into the room. Smaller amounts of turquoise found at the other sites included two beads. The rest of the turquoise occurred as small pieces. Significant amounts of turquoise, especially at Cholla House, and the proximity of the communities we investigated to sources in the Cerrillos Hills may mean that the local population participated in the extraction of turquoise or manufacture of finished beads. This inference is also supported by finds of unworked turquoise at Burnt Corn Pueblo (Chapter 4). The argument has been made that Classic period communities in the western Galisteo Basin, particularly San Marcos, dominated the turquoise trade (see Snead and others 2004). Turquoise at Coalition period sites in the Galisteo Basin may push this activity further into the past.

Bone Tools and Ornaments

Work at the four small sites in the Galisteo Basin recovered eight bone tools. Two of these bone tools came from just above the burnt floor at Lodestar North, and both of these were likely awls. Six bone artifacts were recovered from the lower levels of Unit 1 at Cholla House. Most of these were also awls, in good condition. One bone bead came from Slope House.

Pendants

A single pendant of steatite was recovered in Unit 1 of Slope House. This pendant was roughly oval in shape with a drilled hole.

DISCUSSION AND CONCLUSION

The goal of investigating small Late Coalition period pueblos in the Galisteo Basin was to obtain the comparative information needed to better understand the role and occupational history of the much larger Burnt Corn Pueblo. Of particular interest was how the small sites articulated with the Burnt Corn community and whether or not the small sites had short occupation spans and sudden termination by fire, as was the case at Burnt Corn Pueblo. This comparison was made more robust by examining other small Coalition period sites in the Galisteo Basin and on the Pajarito Plateau.

Our evidence supports Lang's argument (1977a: 23) that there was substantial variation in construction techniques used in small pueblos during the Pindi phase. Walls varied from pure adobe to elaborate shaped stone masonry. In general, there was not a "blueprint" or set of standards for individual families or small groups of families to follow. Design and construction appear to have been idiosyncratic and were likely determined primarily by topographic setting and available resources. Archaeologists working at Los Alamos have identified a temporal sequence of construction methods ranging from unshaped stone masonry mixed with adobe to shaped stones set in mortar (Schmidt 2006: 41). More excavation needs to be done in the Galisteo Basin to determine if this pattern holds there. At present, the diversity of masonry styles associated with the briefly occupied Burnt Corn Pueblo (Chapter 4) suggests that the temporal sequence of construction techniques found on the Pajarito Plateau may not have occurred in the Galisteo Basin.

However, site organization at small Pindi phase pueblos does indicate some shared design principles. Most buildings were oriented in a linear fashion just east of north. The small sites at Los Alamos, Lodestar, and in the vicinity of Burnt Corn Pueblo all had a high density of surface artifacts and middens directly east of the pueblo. This layout reflects the "front" orientation of the pueblo, and the area of greatest activity. The Waldo Site and Slope House were exceptions, as they were oriented to topographic features rather than using the more common east-of-north alignment. The extensive excavations of pueblos at Los Alamos revealed that larger pueblos with two or more parallel rows of rooms shared a similar organization wherein west, or rear, rooms were used for storage and east, or front, rooms were used for habitation. Some larger Coalition period pueblos also had public spaces and kiva structures placed in the front of communities. The limited scale of testing at Lodestar and Burnt Corn did not permit us to determine if this pattern pertains in the Galisteo Basin.

All small sites investigated thus far seem to have had short occupation spans, as evidenced by shallow middens, low artifact densities, and the lack of obvious reconstruction episodes. However brief these occupations may have been, extensive surface scatters at Cholla House, Slope House, and Lodestar North, indicate that these sites were not ephemeral. Seasonal patterns of occupation may be indicated, or perhaps a relatively mobile settlement strategy. The Arroyo Sin Nombre Community discussed by Munson and Head (Chapter 7) is a loose cluster of small structures that may represent a seasonal farming community associated with Burnt Corn Pueblo, and this provides a relevant point of comparison.

The manner of site abandonment or termination of occupation at small pueblos is of considerable interest because of the conflagration that ended the occupation of Burnt Corn Pueblo. The preliminary investigation of small pueblos at Lodestar Ranch and in the immediate vicinity of Burnt Corn Pueblo discussed in this chapter revealed some persuasive evidence that fire was a common end to Late Coalition period buildings in this region. Of the five small pueblos investigated by the Tano Origins Project, three were likely burned with a number of usable and even valuable artifacts inside. The excavations at Feature 3 at Lodestar South were less conclusive, and burning there was limited to a burnt clay lining of an interior wall of a possible ramada structure. But our excavation at Lodestar South may have extended along the back wall of the pueblo rather than inside it, and thus not provided information about burning within the pueblo. Slope House alone exhibited no obvious evidence of burning.

Evidence that contemporary small sites in the region were also burned is variable. The Waldo Site shows no evidence of burning, although burned rock, corn, and adobe were noted on the surface of LA 9146, a small pueblo located in its vicinity (site form, NHMPD).

At Los Alamos, an Early or Middle Coalition period site (LA 4624) had evidence of fire, but the excavators thought it had also been salvaged for beams and masonry. Together with a lack of valuable artifacts recovered inside the rooms, this evidence does not suggest that an unexpected fire ended occupation of the pueblo. One Late Coalition period pueblo (LA 4618) at Los Alamos, however, does conform to the patterns of conflagration that we observed in our excavations: a fire destroyed the building and a number of artifacts or valuable items were left in the pueblo.

Although preliminary, the investigations of small Late Coalition period sites in the Galisteo Basin support the interpretation that the abandonment of the Burnt Corn Pueblo community was likely associated with violence and burning of pueblos. The interpretation of data obtained from these sites adds important dimensions to understanding the region at this time. Analyses of small sites will prove to be an important approach to understanding the abandonment of individual communities and regions during the turbulent periods that occurred in the later prehistory of the Southwest.

CHAPTER SIX

The Burnt Corn Pueblo Landscape

Gregory Greene and Phillip Leckman

Archaeological survey was an integral part of the Tano Origins Project. In the 2000 and 2006 seasons, we surveyed 200 ha in the Burnt Corn community core, finding 47 sites and 95 isolated occurrences. Some of the survey data we collected have been analyzed elsewhere (particularly in Snead 2008a), but the rich body of information about the organization of community landscapes in the Coalition and Classic periods provides additional opportunities for new approaches. As we surveyed the Burnt Corn landscape, we were inspired by Alfonso Ortiz, who quoted a Tewa prayer that affirms, "Within and around the earth, within and around the hills, within and around the mountains, your authority returns to you" (Ortiz 1969: 13). We pondered ways to bring that perspective to bear on our archaeological perception of the land.

As described by Carl Sauer (1925: 26, 46), landscape is a unique, temporally contingent space shaped by the interactions of human culture with a particular natural environment. Archaeological investigation into these interactions has converged on two major foci. On the one hand, analysts have followed Willey's (1953: 1) emphasis on the ecological and economic factors shaping human patterns on the landscape, examining variables such as the locations of favored lithic resources, the potential for agriculture, or the availability of water. On the other hand, especially in recent years, investigators have stressed the phenomenological aspects of landscape: things heard, sensed, and experienced. Many researchers have portrayed these two perspectives as oppositional and largely exclusive ways of viewing landscape (Tilley 1994: 8–10, Thomas 2001: 169–170).

Belying this pessimistic viewpoint, however, an increasing number of archaeologists treat these two approaches to landscape as different parts of a single whole, as equally valid and important dimensions of the complex web of meanings and significances that humans assign to their natural surroundings. Conceptualized in these terms, landscape becomes what Anschuetz and others (2001: 160–164) call a "unifying concept for contrasting perspectives," thereby providing a multipurpose venue for exploring and evaluating data drawn from a diverse assortment of theoretical and methodological research strategies (Whittlesey 1998: 27). Rather than being subject to conflicting and exclusive perspectives, the ecological, economical, and ideational aspects of landscape are incorporated into a richer, more complete examination of the way humans understand and interact with their environment.

A tripartite organizing principle for landscape studies provides a useful device for organizing data drawn from a variety of quantitative, experiential, and ideational sources (Anschuetz and others 2001: 177–181). This principle considers (1) human-environment interactions in terms of *settlement ecology* and other economic and ecological variables, (2) investigations of *ritual landscapes* based on cosmologically or spatially driven interpretations of ritual patterns, and (3) *ethnic landscapes* derived from culturally specific patterns of land use and landscape knowledge. This integrative landscape perspective is echoed by Snead (2008), whose treatment of late-prehistoric Puebloan landscapes of the northern Rio Grande Valley is further subdivided into landscapes of *provision*, related to agriculture; land tenure or other dimensions of subsistence; *identity*, concerning cultural and natural landscape features linked to ideology and meaning within a society; *movement,* related to mobility and travel between sites and other landscape features; and *competition*, or the direct or indirect evidence on the landscape for the contention, violent or otherwise, between and among human communities.

While all four of the dimensions of landscape identified by Snead are addressed here to some degree, in this chapter we are primarily concerned with landscapes of identity and competition as these relate to the establishment, defense, and maintenance of the Burnt Corn community during the Late Coalition period. In the first part of the chapter, we consider the social dimensions of spatial patterning within the community, including the location of Burnt Corn Pueblo relative to local landforms, the spatial proximity of documented structures within the community to each other, and the intervisibility between sites. We are interested in what these variables tell us about integration and defensibility. The second half of the chapter analyzes a particular class of archaeological phenomena, grinding slicks or ground slick boulders, exploring the significance of these features as physical markers of Puebloan cosmologies and sacred landscapes. This analysis establishes explicit links between the economic activities of the community's prehistoric residents and the inferred cosmological principles that informed their world view, echoing a number of recent studies that examine the connection between community organization and cosmology in the northern Rio Grande region (Fowles 2004, 2009; Snead 2008a). Our analysis reveals that the placement and use of outwardly mundane aspects of Burnt Corn Pueblo life, like the grinding slicks considered here, are invested with meaning within Puebloan conceptions of space, cosmology, and identity. The grinding slicks provide physical reminders of the overarching systems of cosmic order within which the Burnt Corn community was situated. In many respects, they are as much a testament to community integration and cohesion as are the aspects of social organization considered in the first part of the chapter.

APPROACHING COMMUNITY DYNAMICS WITH GEOGRAPHIC INFORMATION SYSTEMS

The Pindi phase archaeological remains documented by the Tano Origins Project in the Cañada de la Cueva drainage were occupied for a generation or less at the end of the thirteenth century. This discrete occupation provides a promising opportunity for exploring the intra- and extra-community dynamics of a single Puebloan community in the Galisteo Basin during a turbulent and, as yet, poorly understood era (Snead 2006: 1). We used a Geographic Information Systems (GIS) project to analyze these dynamics. This analysis investigates agricultural intensification, land use, and movement, but is ultimately focused on the spatial integration of Burnt Corn Pueblo and other identified structures in the community.

We are interested in what this integration tells us about community defense and organization. The primary data used in the analysis are the documented locations of surface architecture associated with the Cañada's Pindi phase occupation, including two large pueblos and seventeen smaller room blocks or other structures that may represent field houses or farmsteads (Snead 2008a: 56).

The analysis has three major components. First, we examine the physical placement of Burnt Corn Pueblo and other structures relative to local landforms and consider this in terms of slope, access and other landscape characteristics linked to defensibility in previous studies (Haas and Creamer 1993; Kvamme 1993; Wilcox 1979; Wilcox and Holmlund 2007; Wilcox, Robertson and Wood 2001). Second, we investigate intervisibility and lines of sight between Burnt Corn Pueblo and other community structures, again considering these data in terms of defensibility. Finally, we examine routes of access within the community by modeling potential least-cost paths and patterns of movement between and among individual sites, and by estimating the amount of time it would have taken for people to move from site to site.

Defensibility along the Cañada de la Cueva

Sites, features, and artifacts dating before and after the occupation of Burnt Corn Pueblo have been documented throughout the Cañada de la Cueva survey area (Fig. 6.1). Late Coalition period sites with surface architecture are concentrated exclusively in the narrow drainages surrounding Burnt Corn Pueblo (LA 359) and Pueblo Escondido (LA 358) (Fig. 6.2). These sites consist of room blocks and small structures represented by stone masonry foundations.

It is unclear whether the settlement pattern we documented in the area surrounding Burnt Corn Pueblo is typical of the region during the Late Coalition period. The broader cultural landscape may more closely resemble the settlement pattern associated with the Petroglyph Hill area, where there are a few dispersed structures and loose residential clusters, such as those found along the Arroyo Sin Nombre floodplain (Chapter 7). However, the concentration of structural sites along the Cañada de la Cueva and its tributaries in the immediate vicinity of Burnt Corn Pueblo, and the complete absence of structures from surveyed mesa top areas to the north, south, and east, remains striking, especially in light of the fairly

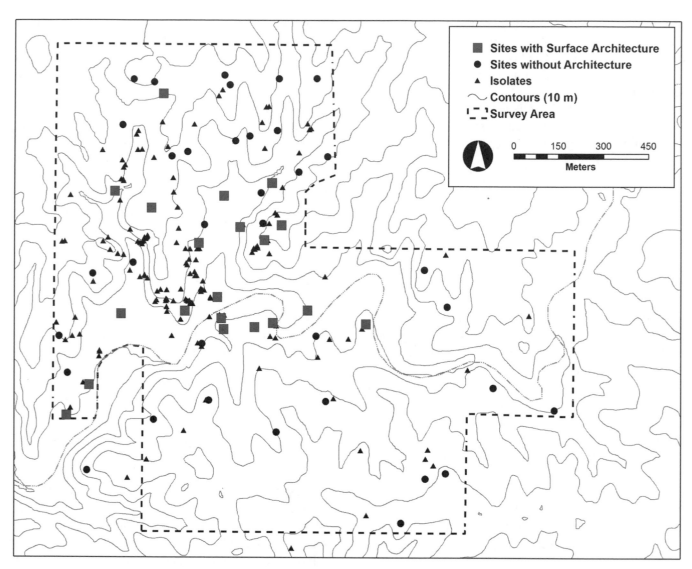

Figure 6.1. Documented archaeological sites and isolates in the Cañada de la Cueva study area.

abundant non-structural remains documented across these mesa tops. As Snead suggested (2008a:56), the association of architectural sites with the Cañada de la Cueva, and their absence from adjacent surveyed areas, is likely related to an agricultural strategy centered on floodwater farming on the abundant arable land along the drainage bottom.

Although located in proximity to the floodplain, many of the structures in the Burnt Corn community exhibit characteristics that suggest placement with defensibility in mind. According to Haas and Creamer's seminal consideration of warfare and violence among the Kayenta Anasazi, defensively-positioned sites should exhibit a number of specific characteristics (Haas and Creamer 1993:26). In addition to a clear line of sight to neighboring

allied settlements and potential routes of access, defensible sites should be elevated above the surrounding terrain, ideally in locations with limited access. Proximity to reliable water sources or arable land is generally desirable (Haas and Creamer 1993:30-36), so when access to these resources was sacrificed in favor of a more open viewshed or a less accessible location, it is likely that a site's position was chosen with defense in mind.

As quantified by Kvamme (1993:175-176) in his ground-breaking GIS-based predictive model for defensive site location based on Haas and Creamer's observations, potentially defensive sites should be located on relatively level ground that grades rapidly into steep slopes in at least three directions. Burnt Corn Pueblo clearly meets these criteria (Fig. 6.3), occupying an

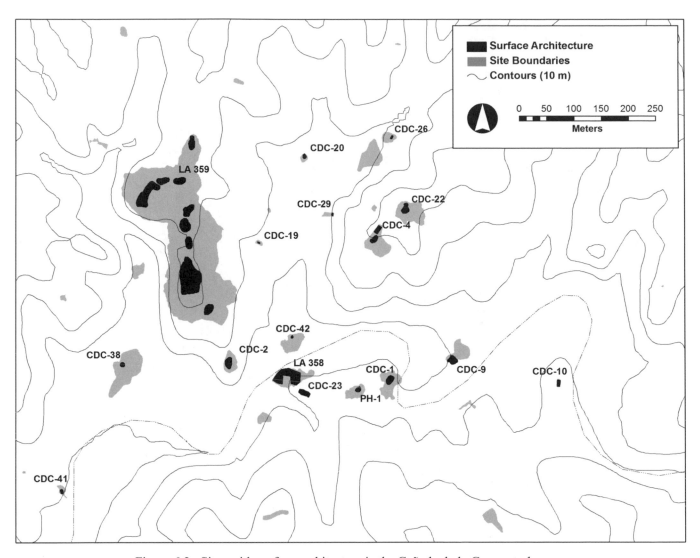

Figure 6.2. Sites with surface architecture in the Cañada de la Cueva study area.

excellent defensive position. The site's ridgetop location is fairly level around the pueblo itself, but the topography drops off rapidly to the northeast, south, and west. In these directions, slopes of more than 20 percent fall abruptly to the cañada floor; to the west, this drop is more than 20 meters. The approach to Burnt Corn Pueblo from the east is somewhat gentler but still represents a considerable slope, and the long ascent from the drainage floor would have given the pueblo's occupants ample time to react to any threat approaching from that direction. Finally, there is a relatively level approach along the ridgeline from the north but this meets a narrow choke point at the northern end of the pueblo with steep drops on either side. The roughly 20-m span across this choke point could have been easily monitored and protected, and indeed, the relatively isolated northern

room block of the pueblo may have been used for this purpose (Snead 2008a: 92).

The topographic placement of Burnt Corn Pueblo strongly suggests the site was located with defense in mind, and it is interesting that many of the other structural sites in the community are similarly located in defensible positions. The three small room blocks located atop the steep-sided mesa to the east of the pueblo are situated in a defensible setting comparable to Burnt Corn Pueblo, and they command an excellent vantage point over the surrounding terrain. Many of the smaller structures located along the lower terraces immediately above the cañada floodplain appear to be located in defensible elevated positions. They are not protected by slopes as long or as steep as those surrounding Burnt Corn Pueblo or the small mesatop room

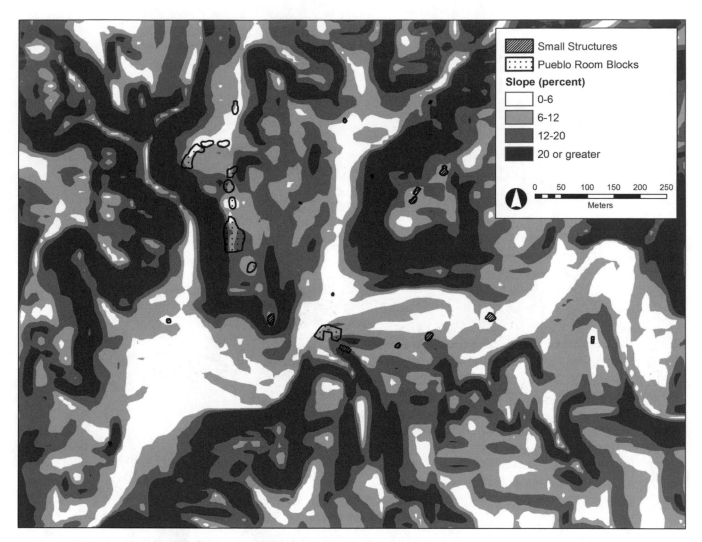

Figure 6.3. Distribution of surface architecture in the Burnt Corn community in relation to local slopes and landforms.

blocks, but as Figure 6.3 illustrates, many of the flood-plain structures are nonetheless situated in relatively elevated settings adjacent to fairly steep slopes. These settings would have protected against flooding as well as violence. Given the concern for defense exhibited by the people who built Burnt Corn Pueblo, it does not surprise us to find that defensibility was also considered when contemporaneous farmsteads were established.

Community Intervisibility

Intervisibility is a measure of the ability of an observer at one location to perceive other locations, and vice versa. As such, intervisibility is frequently used by archaeologists to argue for the existence of intersite signaling systems linked to mutual protection and defense

(Doolittle 1998; Fowles 2004; Haas 1990; Haas and Creamer 1993; Kvamme 1993: Swanson 2003; Wilcox and Holmlund 2007; Wilcox, Robinson, and Wood 2001). Clear lines of sight between settlements deemed to be allied is a key component of many arguments for defensive site location (Haas and Creamer 1993: 26, 30-36; Wilcox and Holmlund 2007: 19). The presence of clear sight lines across large swathes of territory, especially potential routes of access for potential enemies, is an important aspect of defensibility. In recent years, the intervisibility of important locations within a community has also been interpreted as a force for community integration and maintenance (Bernardini 1998; Graves and Van Keuren 2003; Moore 1996).

Early intervisibility analyses frequently required the development of project-specific methods for directly

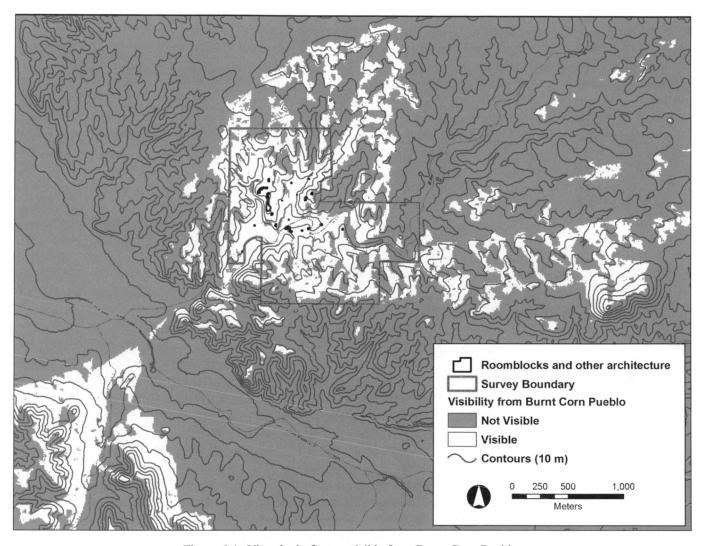

Figure 6.4. Viewshed of areas visible from Burnt Corn Pueblo.

modeling line-of-sight between sites (Kvamme 1993: 177-180). Intervisibility in current GIS analyses, however, is typically modeled in terms of viewsheds, defined as elevation-based calculations of visibility from a particular location or locations with continuous coverage corresponding to the extent of a base elevation dataset (Connolly and Lake 2006). The Burnt Corn community visibility analysis employs a modified digital elevation model (DEM) that accounts for surface architecture by adding 2.5 m to the ground surface at the locations of prehistoric structures. This adjustment is based on the average height of roofs at excavated Coalition and Classic period sites (Creamer 1993:18–19). The resulting viewshed is modeled from the perspective of observers, with a 1.5 m viewing height, standing atop the room blocks at Burnt Corn Pueblo. Visibility is thus mapped

not from a single point, a reductive prospect for a site as large as Burnt Corn, but calculated collectively for the roofs of the pueblo as a whole, a more realistic proxy for a village in which rooftops were likely a focus of the community's economic and social activity.

The viewshed illustrated in Figure 6.4 demonstrates that a person standing on top of Burnt Corn Pueblo would have been able to see virtually the entire Burnt Corn community. To the south and west, visible areas extend to the tops of the ridgelines running just beyond the current survey boundaries. To the north, visibility is somewhat spotty but it extends well beyond the community, affording decent coverage along tributaries of the cañada and across the northern mesa tops in many areas. The most extensive visibility exists to the southwest, where portions of the Galisteo Creek terraces and

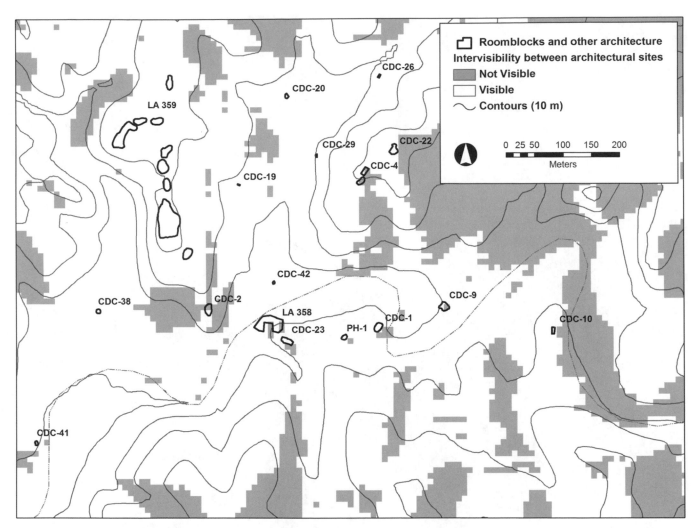

Figure 6.5. Viewshed of intervisibility between room blocks, small sites, and other structures in the immediate vicinity of Burnt Corn Pueblo. Sites with architecture are labeled.

adjacent slopes are visible along the gap formed by the cañada, and to the east, where western-facing slopes are visible for more than 3 kilometers before visibility terminates at Petroglyph Hill, likely a significant cosmological landmark for the community's residents (Chapter 7; Snead 2008a: 93).

If attention is focused on the central portion of the community (Fig. 6.5), the results indicate that all documented Coalition-period structures in the community would have been at least partially visible from the pueblo. Although contemporary forest cover in the project vicinity is probably significantly more dense than it would have been while the community was occupied (Allen 1998), these intervisibility results generally mirror observations made in the field.

In sum, these results suggest that Burnt Corn Pueblo's location afforded clear lines of sight to all potentially contemporaneous sites in its vicinity, as well as providing a reasonable vantage point for monitoring approaches to the community from the southwest, northeast, and east. Sight lines to the south, west and north were less optimal, but appear to be the best available for the immediate area. Visibility from the hilltop sites to the east, for instance, was not markedly different than that at Burnt Corn Pueblo. In general, the advantages of locations within the Cañada de la Cueva, with proximity to arable land and water, appear to have outweighed the somewhat reduced visibility of the setting. But it also appears that being seen from the pueblo may have factored strongly in decisions about where to locate other room blocks and farmsteads. All sites with architecture are located within the portion of the survey area with the fewest gaps or hidden cul-de-sacs. We think that defensibility based on topography and intervisibility likely played key roles in determining how the Burnt Corn community was laid out.

Community Access and Connectivity

Movement and ease of travel between sites provides a means of assessing the degree to which sites were interconnected, and this dimension may have played a role in determining where sites were located. The primary variable employed in this analysis is the time required to travel from one location to another, modeled using an algorithm adapted from the work of Waldo Tobler (1993). Unlike the isotropic Euclidean distance measures frequently used in archaeology (for example, Wilcox 1996), Tobler's Hiking Function incorporates slope, rate of speed, and bearing to estimate the time necessary to travel across a specific landscape in a particular direction.

An isochronic contour calculated to model travel time from the outskirts of LA 359 reveals that the Burnt Corn community is very tightly clustered (Fig. 6.6). With the exception of the small room blocks atop the ridge to the east of Burnt Corn Pueblo, virtually every site with Coalition-period surface architecture in the survey area can be reached within five minutes of walking at a rate of four km per hour.

Anisotropic distance measurements based on Tobler's algorithm were used to calculate least cost paths, or routes of minimum effort, between two or more points. Figure 6.7 illustrates least-cost paths from the pueblo to several outlying sites with surface architecture (CDC 4, 9, 22, and 46), and to two artifact scatters near the edges of the study area which may have been associated with possible routes out of the Cañada de la Cueva drainage. The modeled paths run along drainage bottoms, lending support to the notion that they likely served as the fastest and easiest routes across the community. Measuring the proximity of several site and feature classes to the cost paths (Table 6.1) reveals that substantial percentages of both Coalition period structural sites and isolates occur in proximity to presumed paths across drainage bottoms, usually on terraces overlooking the drainages themselves.

In sum, documented structures in the Burnt Corn community were tightly integrated, in part because many

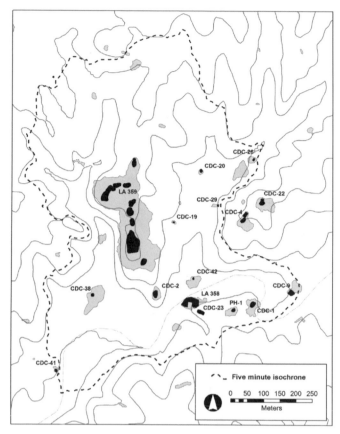

Figure 6.6. An isochronic contour illustrating sites and locations within a 5-minute walk from Burnt Corn Pueblo. Sites with architecture are labeled.

Table 6.1. Percentage of Features within a Specified Distance of Modeled Cost Paths

Distance to Cost Path	Sites (%)	Isolates (%)	Structures (%)
50 meters	27.08	41.21	47.06
100 meters	52.08	56.36	64.71

of them were located immediately adjacent to easily traversable drainage-bottom routes through the cañada. This is not surprising. However, the results of the cost-distance-model complement our findings regarding defensibility and intervisibility, and provide another clue as to why so many field houses and farmsteads were tightly clustered around Burnt Corn Pueblo rather than distributed more evenly along the arable portions of the cañada. Although a defensible topographic setting

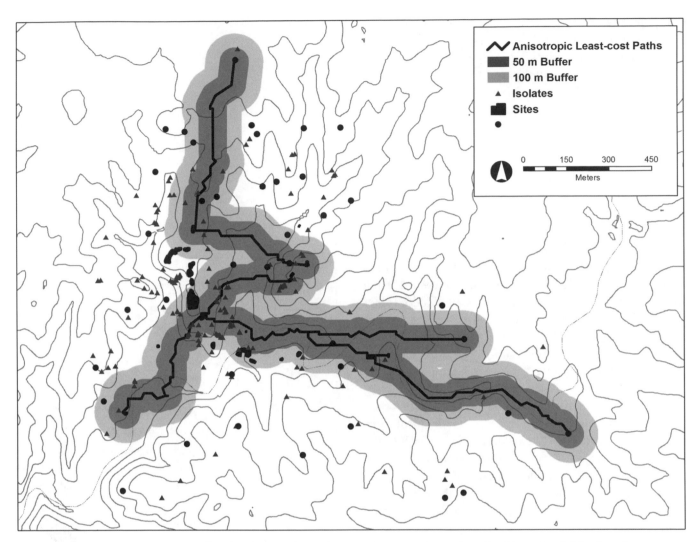

Figure 6.7. Least-cost travel paths along drainage bottoms between Burnt Corn Pueblo and neighboring sites.

and a good vantage point over the landscape are major considerations if a perceived threat of violence exists, the advantages of both would be compounded if sites are aggregated in proximity to each other. If small sites were located near a large, elevated, highly defensible site like Burnt Corn Pueblo, the advantages of integration would be even greater. Threats spotted from an elevated vantage point could have been rapidly relayed by signal or messenger to residents of outlying sites. These people could have swiftly fled to the relative safety afforded by the pueblo's size, enclosed-plaza architecture and elevated position, both to take advantage of its position as a refuge and to rally for defense of the community.

The potential for mutual defense and nearby refuge is not the only plausible reason for the proximity of these sites to each other. Easy access to level, arable land and

dependable floodwaters, and other ecological factors such as the colder microclimates and shorter growing seasons along north-facing slopes, may also have influenced where fields and farmsteads were located. The Cañada de la Cueva may have been shielded somewhat from bad weather, and represented one of the larger zones of relatively flat, arable land along the north side of Galisteo Creek.

Our understanding of the Burnt Corn community's spatial organization, particularly downstream towards the Cañada de la Cueva's confluence with the Galisteo Creek, is constrained by limited archaeological survey data. The fact remains, however, that other well-documented areas with the same advantages, including the Arroyo Sin Nombre floodplain a few kilometers to the east (Chapter 7), were not exploited with the same intensity as the area around Burnt Corn Pueblo. Many factors, including aspects of belief, identity, and cosmology may have contributed to the decision about where the community was established. Given the ultimate violent fate of Burnt Corn Pueblo, it seems likely that the group of late-Coalition period migrants who "placed" the new settlement also took into account the highly defensible elevations offering excellent vantage points over the surrounding landscape.

GRINDING SLICKS AND THE BURNT CORN RITUAL LANDSCAPE

Grinding slicks, typically considered a manifestation of agriculture, food preparation, or other subsistence activities, provide a cogent case study for understanding the role that diverse cultural features play in constituting landscapes. Commonly found in the vicinity of pueblos, grinding slicks are defined here as boulders or bedrock outcrops that bear evidence for human-created pecking, grinding, or polishing. Although experimental archaeology and residue analysis have been used to study grinding slicks, as has their association with portable grinding tools such as manos and metates, considerably less attention has been paid to their spatial and geographical attributes. Grinding slicks vary widely in size, shape, and composition, but these characteristics have unknown significance. We know little about the methods ancient people used to select a proper location for a grinding slick, or why certain stones were chosen in favor of others. There is considerable diversity in the slope and aspect of grinding slicks relative to features in the surrounding landscape, and these also may have played key roles in determining which locations were selected for use.

One rarely-considered aspect of grinding slicks in Pueblo landscapes is their potential cosmological significance. In Pueblo cosmologies, many different elements of the landscape are considered to be components of a sacred topography, and the "functional" role of grinding slicks does not necessarily exclude this type of significance. In the remainder of this chapter, we explore the possibility that grinding slicks in the Burnt Corn community played a role in ritual practice embedded within the landscape. We analyze more than 500 grinding slicks surrounding the pueblo to investigate the orientation and location of these features relative to the locations of shrines, topographic features, and cardinal directions. To make an empirical case, our study uses a GIS approach that emphasizes complex spatial relationships.

Grinding Slicks at Burnt Corn Pueblo

Stones and boulders bearing smoothed or polished surfaces resulting from repeated linear grinding are ubiquitous in the Burnt Corn landscape. These features are most common around the outskirts of Burnt Corn Pueblo and in the vicinity of the small structures located along the Cañada de la Cueva. During the recording process, certain stones were observed to be ground while other stones were not, despite similar size, shape, material composition, and proximity to the Burnt Corn Pueblo. During our fieldwork to document individual grinding slicks, we noticed that looking laterally along the grinding surface of some grinding slicks led the eyes directly to distant but visibly prominent and distinguishable features on the landscape (for a similar revelation, see Snead 2008b). Most notable among these landscape features were Petroglyph Hill, the Cerrillos Hills, and Cerro Pelón. Nearby landcape features including a petroglyph panel, "cupuled" boulders, agricultural fields, and water sources were also highlighted by the view looking along grinding slicks (Figs. 6.8, 6.9, 6.10).

To investigate the potential significance of this observed correlation between the orientation of grinding slicks and the topographic features of the Galisteo Basin landscape, we researched ethnographic descriptions of the role of space and place in Puebloan cosmologies; most notably that presented by Tewa anthropologist Alfonso Ortiz in his 1969 book, *The Tewa World: Space, Time, Being and Becoming in a Pueblo Society*. Significant differences may exist between the world-views of Ortiz's twentieth-century Ohkeh Owingeh informants and the thirteenth-century inhabitants of Burnt Corn Pueblo, but Ortiz's work illuminates several key concepts that can be viewed as part of an overarching Puebloan sense of landscape that the prehistoric residents of Burnt Corn likely shared. Similar pan-Puebloan concepts are drawn from Snead and Preucel's (1999) examination of Keres sacred landscapes (see also Snead 2008a: 82–85).

By way of comparison, we examined several archaeological discussions of grinding slicks in Puebloan contexts believed to be ancestral to the modern Tewa and Tiwa of north-central New Mexico. Although typically brief, the references to grinding slicks in these studies suggest intriguing links between the placement, creation, and maintenance of grinding slicks and underlying aspects of Ancestral Pueblo spirituality. Our investigation correspondingly focused on identifying and quantifying

Figure 6.8. Petroglyph Hill and a prominent rock outcrop viewed from a grinding slick.

Figure 6.9. Lone, Captain Davis, and Ortiz Mountains viewed from a grinding slick.

Figure 6.10. Cerro Pelon and Los Cobreros Mesa viewed from a grinding slick.

correlations between grinding slick orientation and significant features within the viewable landscape.

The Tewa World

As outlined by Ortiz (1969: 176), the conceptual and symbolic basis of Tewa social behavior is governed by human and spiritual associations with key geographical points in the Tewa world. This world contains a set of reference points, presented by a series of tetrads, or groups of four (Ortiz 1969: 18). As described by Ortiz's Ohkeh Owingeh informants, these nested tetrads include:

1. The Outermost (First) Tetrad represents the limits of the Tewa spiritual world, which is bounded by four sacred mountains.
2. The Second Tetrad represents sacred *Tsin,* or flat-topped hills. These hills are particular to each Tewa pueblo and are defined by the *Towa e,* the native political officials.
3. The Third Tetrad represents the principal directional shrines, located in the four cardinal directions. The shrines are particular to each village and mark the symbolic boundaries of the village.
4. The Innermost (Final) Tetrad represents a series of shrines within each village, with the most important being the plaza shrines that define and consecrate the pueblo (see also Snead and Preucel 1999: 179). A central shrine, or "mother earth navel," typically marks the sacred center of the village.

There is considerable evidence that the organization of the Burnt Corn landscape reflects principles similar to those described by Ortiz. Figure 6.11 shows the important regional features in relation to Burnt Corn Pueblo and the Galisteo Basin, including several points in the wider regional geography included in the Tewa tetrads. Figure 6.12 shows the location of important local features throughout the Burnt Corn community. Although many of these cultural features have been discussed by Snead (2008a), the grinding slicks have not previously been the focus of analysis.

Grinding Slicks

Landscape analysis of grinding slicks was pioneered in the Southwest by Kurt Anschuetz, who defined them as "ground slick boulders" and notes that they typically consist of "boulders with large oblong ground facets averaging roughly 16 by 8 cm" (1998: 339–340). Dozens of grinding slicks were documented in the course of his fieldwork in ancestral Tewa territory along the Rio Chama drainage. He considers these features to be an informal class of shrines, possibly used for repeated tool-sharpening that became ritualized over time. Anschuetz notes that they "commonly occur in small clusters on boulders enclosing the villages' physical limits" (Anschuetz 1998: 340). Similarly, Severin Fowles, drawing on his work in the vicinity of the ancestral Northern Tiwa village of T'aitöna (Pot Creek Pueblo), writes "[g]round slick boulders are assumed to have functioned in ritual contexts as shrines, and their common association with cupule boulders provides some measure of support for this assumption" (Fowles 2004: 537–541). A more recent article documents spatial relationships between grinding slicks and cupule boulders in his study area (Fowles 2009: 461).

These two studies highlight variables that are important in relating grinding slicks to other elements of the cultural landscape, including spatial distribution, feature size, and the relationship between slicks and cupuled boulders. Figure 6.13 shows the location of the grinding slicks and six cupuled boulders surrounding Burnt Corn Pueblo. The average dimensions for grinding facets located in the Burnt Corn community are approximately 15 cm by 29 cm, nearly twice as large as those recorded by Anschuetz (1998: 339–340) in the Rio Chama drainage (Fig. 6.14). A comparison of the Burnt Corn and Rio Chama study areas indicates the ubiquity of these features across the northern Pueblo world and suggests possible ritual associations.

Analytical Methodology

We developed systematic procedures to analyze the 500-plus grinding slicks surrounding Burnt Corn Pueblo using the variables of slope, aspect, and the length and width of each grinding facet. Metates were not included in our analysis because their present position may have been different from their position during their time of use.

We recorded the length and width of each grinding slick using a metric-ruled measuring tape. The slope and aspect were determined using a gravity-based clinometer and a compass. Slope indicates the degree of inclination of each slick, and was measured lengthwise, from the highest point to the lowest point. Aspect measures the

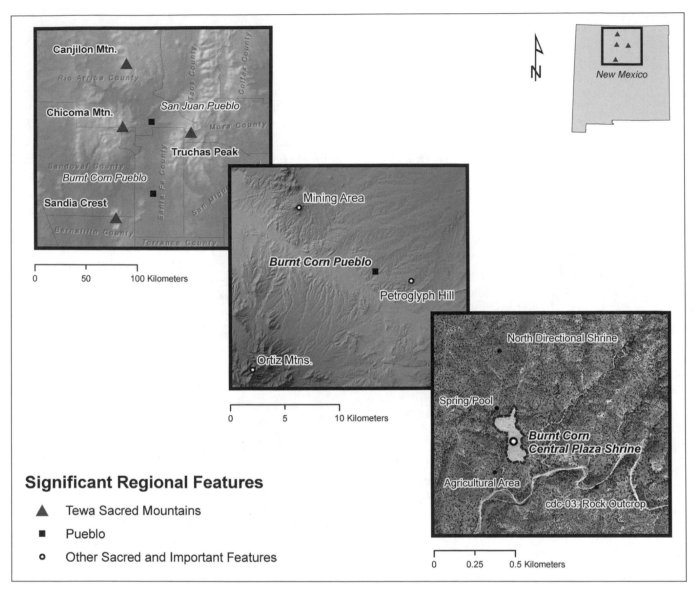

Figure 6.11. Important regional topographic features in
relation to Burnt Corn Pueblo and the Galisteo Basin.

true north azimuth (North = 0°/360°) along the length of each slick, with the lower end of the slick determining the direction. Length and width measurements were recorded for the span of visible wear patterns on each grinding facet.

We assumed each grinding stroke was made in a downward motion, starting at the highest point of the facet, carrying on to the lowest, and then retracting back to the highest. We also assumed that if grinding took place on grinding slicks situated on a hillside, the person grinding would not be looking uphill while working,

but rather downhill. Therefore, when our field measurements recorded an azimuth facing uphill, we converted that into the back azimuth by adding 180 degrees so that the azimuth was oriented downhill. The person grinding, then, would be looking *outward* upon the landscape.

The qualitative aspects of the analysis involved observations to document grinding quality, using a rating system with a scale from 1 to 5 (Fig. 6.15). Facets with more finely ground surfaces received a higher number, and those with rougher or more ephemeral ground surfaces received a lower number. All facets rated 3 or

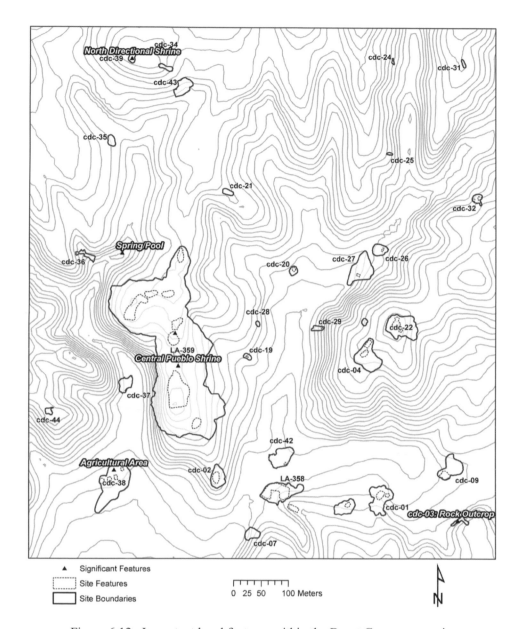

Figure 6.12. Important local features within the Burnt Corn community.

higher were photographed. We made exceptions for stones having naturally smoother surfaces. However, most of the grinding slicks surrounding the Burnt Corn community were rough granite, with lumpy or knobby natural cortex that reflected heavy weathering. Depending on the type of stone, we assumed that the more finely ground a slick was and the more repeatedly it had been used, the greater the importance that particular feature held. We assumed that smaller gaps between the ground portions of individual facets represented more finely ground slicks, taking into consideration the composition of the stone's natural surface, or cortex, in comparison to the modified surface.

In our analysis, we decided to emphasize the most heavily ground features, those with ratings of 4 to 5. The surfaces of slicks with a 1 or 2 rating were typically too rough and inconsistent to determine a length versus a width, or to observe the general trending of the slick aspect. Slicks rated 3 were more amenable for analysis but excluded due to time constraints. The resulting body of analyzed data consists of 274 facets, slightly more than half the original total.

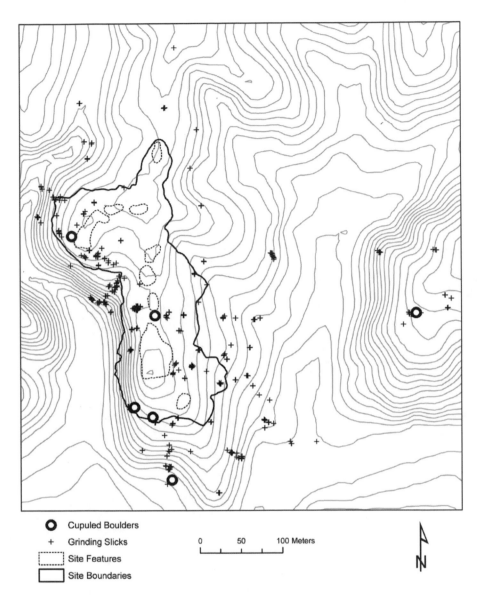

Figure 6.13. Grinding slick and cupuled boulder locations in the vicinity of Burnt Corn Pueblo.

Spatial Analysis

The GIS approach used two basic geoprocessing techniques to analyze the collected data. First, a hill aspect analysis measured the aspect (true-north azimuthal direction) of the hill on which each grinding slick was situated. Determining hill aspect allowed for comparison with the grinding slick aspect. Table 6.2 quantifies the number of grinding slicks situated on the hill surrounding Burnt Corn, categorized by cardinal direction.

Second, a viewshed analysis determined the viewable area from slick locations. Initially, we performed viewshed calculations for individual slicks, but after several iterations, it became obvious that processing time had to be reduced. Thus, we grouped the grinding slicks according to similar hill aspect, and then by geographically similar clusters. Each group was assigned a unique number and visibility was calculated from the groups rather than from individual slicks. By grouping the slicks in this manner, the number of calculations dropped from 274 (one for each individual facet) to 68 (one for each group). In the final analysis, there were 55 groups of slicks rated 4 and 13 groups of slicks rated 5.

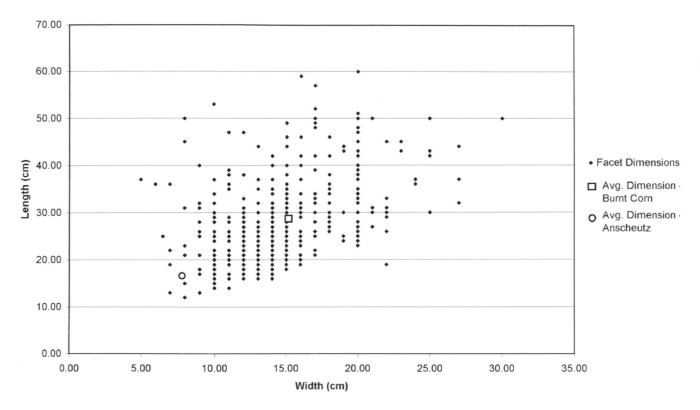

Figure 6.14. Burnt Corn grinding slick facet dimensions compared to average facet dimensions in the Rio Chama drainage.

Table 6.2. Number and Direction of Grinding Slicks from Burnt Corn Pueblo

Hill Aspect	Facet Count
East	122
Northeast	2
Northwest	81
South	83
Southeast	47
Southwest	86
West	80
Total	501

The viewshed analysis was completed in fewer than 30 hours of computational time. We were concerned about the effect of grouping the grinding slicks to facilitate the analysis, so we considered the potential drawbacks to analyzing the vantage point of these groups rather than individual slicks. We note that when performing a viewshed analysis of an individual facet, only the landscape features visible from that particular location would be included in the final calculation. Minor local obstructions obviously affected the view, so slicks located 5 m apart from each other could have entirely different views of the landscape. When analyzing the viewshed of an entire group, *all* landscape features visible from *any* location within the group would be included in the final calculation. However, until elevation data at better than 10 m resolution become readily available, a 5 m distance interval between slicks is virtually negligible. Therefore, this issue has only minute applicability to the analysis of this data.

To determine which landscape features were most highly visible from *all* grinding slick groups, and, by extension, the most commonly viewed and possibly preferred landscape features, a weighted overlay calculation was derived by superimposing each viewshed on top of another, "merging" them into a final viewshed. We gave the visible areas of each viewshed a value of 1 and the nonvisible areas a value of 0. The most highly visible landscape features from all slicks rated 4 and all slicks rated 5 are illustrated in Figures 6.16 and 6.17. From

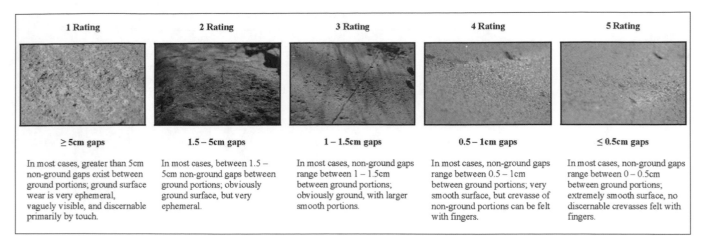

1 Rating	2 Rating	3 Rating	4 Rating	5 Rating
≥ 5cm gaps	1.5 – 5cm gaps	1 – 1.5cm gaps	0.5 – 1cm gaps	≤ 0.5cm gaps
In most cases, greater than 5cm non-ground gaps exist between ground portions; ground surface wear is very ephemeral, vaguely visible, and discernable primarily by touch.	In most cases, between 1.5 – 5cm non-ground gaps between ground portions; obviously ground surface, but very ephemeral.	In most cases, non-ground gaps range between 1 – 1.5cm between ground portions; obviously ground, with larger smooth portions.	In most cases, non-ground gaps range between 0.5 – 1cm between ground portions; very smooth surface, but crevasse of non-ground portions can be felt with fingers.	In most cases, non-ground gaps range between 0 – 0.5cm between ground portions; extremely smooth surface, no discernable crevasses felt with fingers.

Figure 6.15. The grinding slick rating system.

slicks rated 4, Captain Davis Mountain and Lone Mountain are the most highly visible (viewable from 35 to 55 slick groupings), while Captain Davis Mountain, Lone Mountain, and the eastern half of the Ortiz Mountains are the most highly visible from slicks rated 5 (viewable from 10 to 13 slick groupings). The Mining Area is the least visible from all 4 and 5 rated slicks.

To elucidate the relationship between grinding slick groups and horizon features in the GIS analysis, we wrote a program that drew lines radiating outward from the grinding slicks in the direction of the slick aspect. Each line continues for a distance of 40 km; a distance that encompasses the span of the entire GIS dataset. When interpreted through the plan view of a two-dimensional map, these lines serve as guides, showing the features each grinding slick "line-of-sight" intersects. The azimuthal directions of the grinding slicks are illustrated in Figures 6.18 and 6.19.

In our analysis, for a particular grinding slick to correlate with a landscape feature, the feature must have a line passing through it, and be visible from the corresponding slick. Therefore, the lines are compared with their proximity to significant features *and* to the viewable areas, as determined by the group-generated viewshed. To compensate for possible human error in recording the actual grinding slick aspect, an arbitrary tolerance level of ±1° was applied to all slick aspect lines. The effect of this 1 degree tolerance level on the lines radiating outward from the grinding slicks is a line that resembles more of a "pie slice," with the end of the line being wider. This adjustment results in the possibility that a greater number of features will be encompassed as distance from the origin point increases. However, we think the error tolerance is acceptable for the purpose of our analysis. At a distance of 1.5 km, there is approximately 17 m of widening; while at a 40 km distance there is approximately 700 m of widening. We also made an effort to sort potentially significant features of the landscape surrounding the Cañada de la Cueva in terms of their "line-of-sight" distance from Burnt Corn Pueblo (Fig. 6.20). Landscapes contain a variety of features with potential ritual significance to ancestral Puebloans, including mountains, lakes, springs, hunting grounds, agricultural fields, and mineral resources (Snead and Preucel 1999: 176). We used the shrine identified in Burnt Corn's central plaza as central point for these categories, and defined a radius of zero to 1,500 m for the first distance interval because we think this is the distance easily traversed within a community.

This initial zone enclosed virtually all of the identified archaeological manifestations directly associated with the Burnt Corn community, including residential sites, probable agricultural field locations, the water resources represented by the Cañada de la Cueva and its tributaries, and, most importantly, a set of what appear to be shrines and rock art panels located at the outskirts of the community. If these features are considered in terms of the contemporary Puebloan conceptual landscapes, the shrines might be equated with the directional shrines that distinguish the symbolic boundaries of the community, and the shrine in Burnt Corn's plaza might be considered one of the series of shrines within the community that define and consecrate the pueblo and its significant features in the immediate vicinity. The

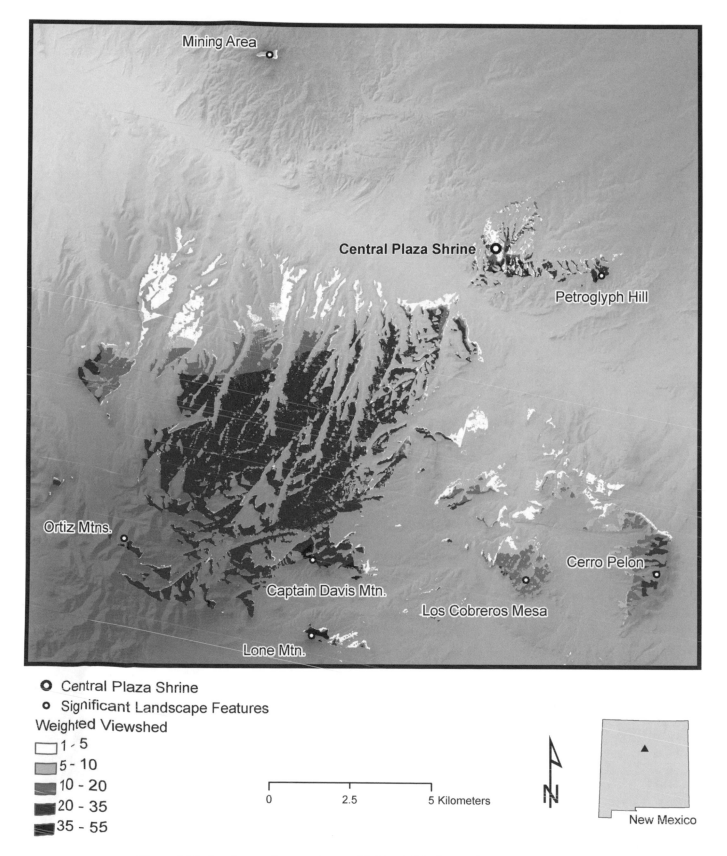

Figure 6.16. Landscape features that are highly visible from grinding slicks rated 4.

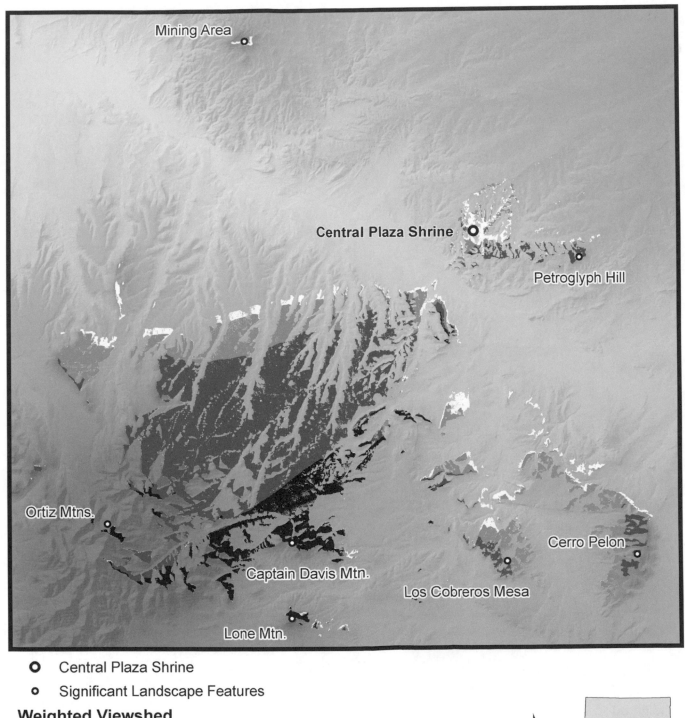

Figure 6.17. Landscape features that are highly visible from grinding slicks rated 5.

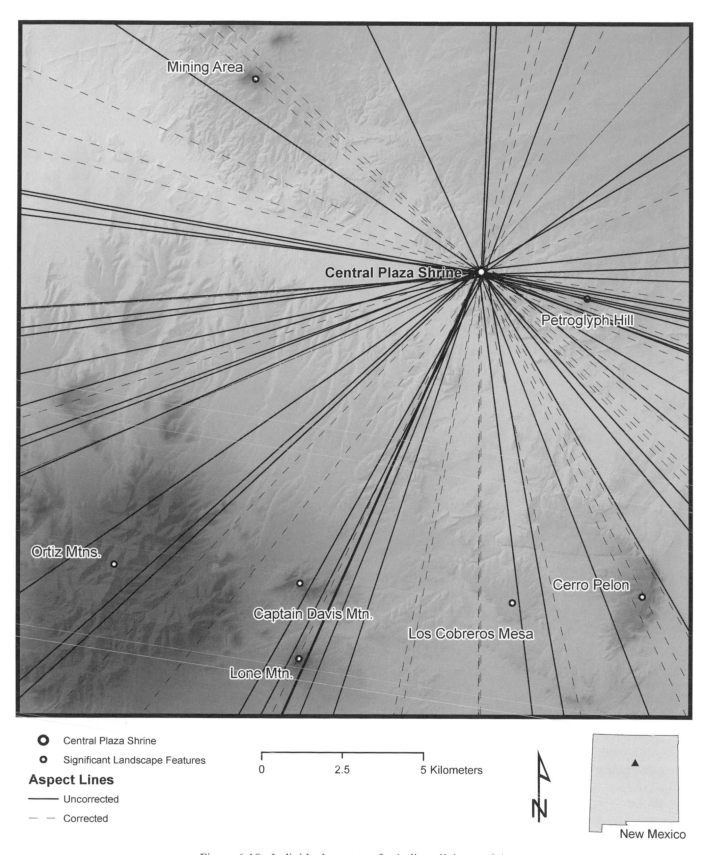

Figure 6.18. Individual aspects of grinding slicks rated 4.

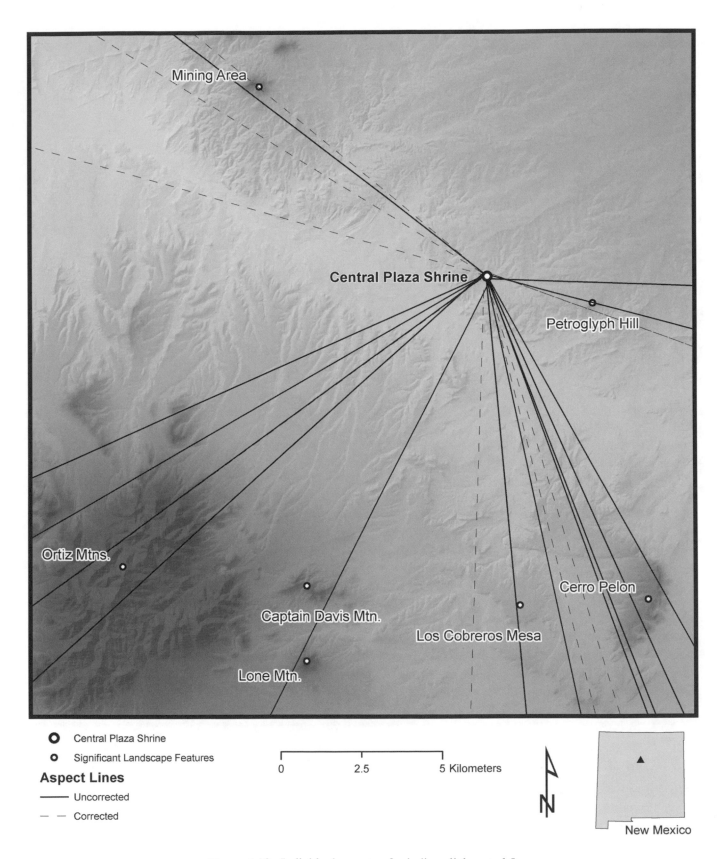

Figure 6.19. Individual aspects of grinding slicks rated 5.

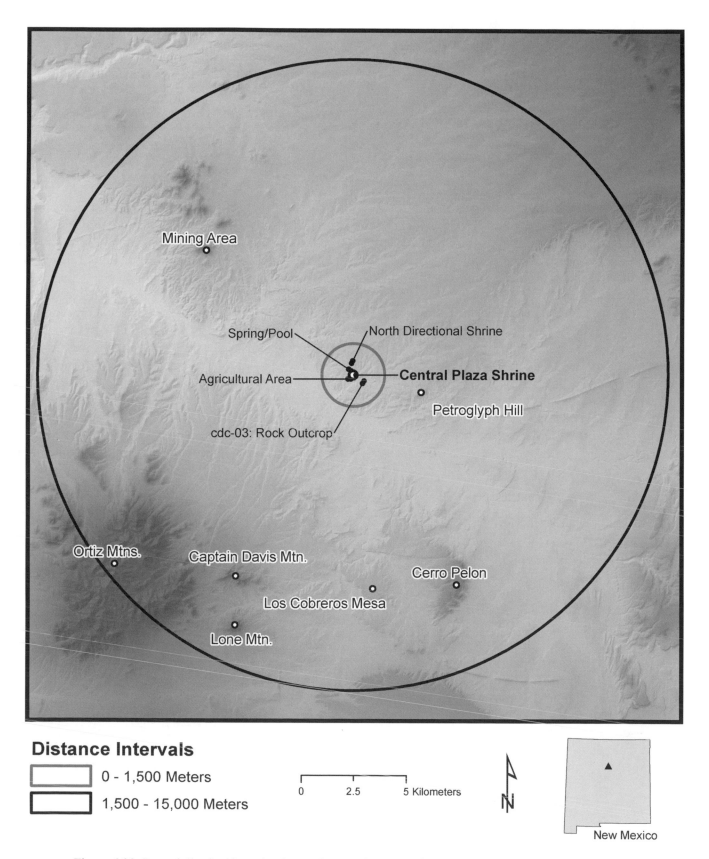

Distance Intervals

☐ 0 - 1,500 Meters

☐ 1,500 - 15,000 Meters

Figure 6.20. Potentially significant landscape features in terms of their distance from Burnt Corn Pueblo.

water catchments identified along the drainage that runs immediately to the west of Burnt Corn Pueblo also represent features with potential ceremonial significance located within the first distance interval. In many respects, the features identified within this interval are similar to those contained within the two innermost Tetrads outlined by Ortiz.

The second distance interval extended from 1.5 km to 15 km, and encapsulated a number of potentially important features, including Petroglyph Hill and its wealth of rock art, the turquoise mining area in the Cerrillos Hills, and the prominent peaks of the Ortiz Mountains. Interestingly, this division also incorporated Los Cobreros Mesa, Cerro Pelon, and other nearby "flat-topped hills," inviting analogy to the Second Tetrad discussed by Ortiz.

The third and final distance interval extended from 15 km and beyond. This outer interval is less well-defined than the other divisions, but it includes Sandia Crest to the southwest, and the three peaks identified by Ortiz (1969) and J. P. Harrington (1916) as the sacred boundaries of the historic Tewa spiritual world. As such, this distance interval could be equated with Ortiz's First Tetrad. These distant features were not included in this analysis.

Results

Table 6.3 summarizes the correlations between grinding slick aspect and significant landscape features surrounding Burnt Corn Pueblo. Positive correlations are most pronounced in Interval 2, between 1.5 km and 15 km distance from the central plaza shrine of Burnt Corn Pueblo (Snead 2008a). Significant features in this interval include Petroglyph Hill to the east, the lead and turquoise mining area in the Cerrillos Hills to the west, and the Ortiz Mountains, Captain Davis Mountain, Lone Mountain, Los Cobreros Mesa, and Cerro Pelon to the south of the community. These landscape features are potentially analogous to the village-specific "flat-topped hills" discussed by Ortiz.

The data show that correlations between grinding slick aspect and landscape features increase as distance increases. In Interval 2 grinding slicks rated 4 increased to 56.3 percent correlation, and slicks rated 5 jumped to 91.3 percent correlation. The slicks rated 5 were almost entirely associated with significant landscape features in the second distance interval, whereas slicks rated 4 were less associated with these same features. This observation

Table 6.3. Positive Correlations between Aspect and Landscape Features for Grinding Slicks Rated 4 and 5 in the Vicinity of Burnt Corn Pueblo

Slick Rating	n	Interval 1		Interval 2	
		n	%	n	%
4	87	29	33.33	49	56.32
5	23	6	26.09	21	91.30

suggests that slicks receiving the most use had a greater tie to features just beyond the community limits, and perhaps held higher significance within the Tano world, whether for food processing, weapon or tool sharpening, ceremonial purposes, or other grinding activity.

The results of this analysis suggest a tie between the stones chosen for grinding activities and the features in the surrounding landscape. From this, several factors become apparent as to why some stones were *not* chosen. Perhaps the length or slope of the rock surface was oriented in such a way as to direct the landscape view to undesirable or insignificant features. Further analysis should be conducted to investigate these assumptions.

Studies of grinding slicks elsewhere in the Galisteo Basin may confirm these results, and help further explain the ritual concepts underlying ancestral Puebloan notions of cosmology and landscape. Patterns of grinding slick orientation and distribution observed during the Petroglyph Hill survey are similar to those in the Burnt Corn community, and those features provide data for future analysis (Chapter 7). If episodes of insecurity or perceived outside threat occurred during the habitation of the Burnt Corn community, the ties of meaning and belief that joined people to the land would have helped generate a stronger cohesion amongst the inhabitants. Studies like this help unveil some of the practices by which the community's occupants solidified and reinforced this bond.

CONCLUSION

Although the two dimensions of the Burnt Corn community landscape presented here might seem substantially different, we think they are related. On one hand, the threat of violence exerted a considerable influence on the community's location and layout, pushing its residents to locate their major settlement in a highly defensible location with excellent lines of sight, and encouraging them to locate their farmsteads and fields in proximity to this refuge. On the other hand, the grinding-slick boulders scattered across the community landscape share commonalities of orientation that suggest their placement, creation, and use were governed by underlying cosmological principles tied to prominent landmarks on the Burnt Corn horizon. The concept of landscape incorporates many dimensions, including a cosmological and sacred domain and a domain focused on the day-to-day requirements of subsistence and resource procurement. No single dimension of the landscape necessarily takes precedence, and no single explanation accounts for every trace of past landscape interactions. In explaining *why* the Burnt Corn community existed and *what* it was, Snead (2008a) places as much emphasis on the economic concerns of soil, water, and provision as he does on the Puebloan concepts of the proper placement of a village relative to hills, bodies of water, and other features of the natural world. In this chapter, we have struck the same balance, providing new insights into a community held together as much by a shared identity manifested in ritual practice as by a mutual defense against the threat of violence and strife.

CHAPTER SEVEN

Surveying Petroglyph Hill: Cultural Landscapes of the Galisteo Basin

Marit K. Munson and Genevieve Head

Opportunities to conduct fieldwork in areas near Burnt Corn Pueblo developed over the course of the project. This work greatly expanded the geographic and archaeological context of the research program, and helped build bridges with local landowners and the public and private institutions that manage much of the open land in the Galisteo Basin. Our survey of a tract of land around Petroglyph Hill dramatically enhanced our understanding of the cultural landscape. Petroglyph Hill is situated within protected open space managed by Santa Fe County. The archaeological sites within this open space are important cultural resources maintained for the public benefit, and they are threatened by the pressure of development. Our research thus contributed information important in managing the Galisteo Basin, as well providing new information about the ancient past.

The toponym "Petroglyph Hill" does not appear on any official maps of the Galisteo Basin, and apparently came into the local vocabulary only in the last few decades. Nonetheless, the distinctive double-peaked outcrop looms large in the natural and social landscape of the region. In recent times, the view from the top has drawn hikers, picnicers and partiers from Santa Fe, a mixed group of nature lovers, petroglyph afficionados, and vandals. A century ago, it was local ranch hands and townspeople who left their marks, building fences and rough stone walls and inscribing pictures, names, and dates on the volcanic rock. Even then, the rocks already bore witness to centuries of visits by ancient peoples, visits that started during the Archaic period and extended through the Coalition and Classic periods.

This long span of use is due in part to Petroglyph Hill's topographic prominence. The twin summits are visible from some distant locations, and their peaks offer commanding views of the surrounding ridges, arroyos, and plains. The prominence of the hill is also reflected in the different cultural landscapes within which this singular landmark was, and still is, embedded. Investigation of Petroglyph Hill thus offers unique insights into the configuration of space and place beyond the pueblo villages that are so often the focus of archaeological attention. In this chapter, we focus on the changing landscapes of Petroglyph Hill during the Coalition and Classic periods.

TOPOGRAPHY

Petroglyph Hill perches just north of the Galisteo Creek, almost 30 km south of Santa Fe and west of the historic village of Galisteo (Fig. 7.1). The prevailing NE-SW orientation of the terrain reflects the volcanic origins of the topography, which is interdigitated with colluvium that has eroded from the southern end of the Rocky Mountains for eons, and the overlying remnants of ancient lakes. The southeastern slopes of Petroglyph Hill drain into an intermittent tributary of the Galisteo Creek that we have designated Arroyo Sin Nombre. Three active springs occur in this drainage. A long ridge forms the south side of Arroyo Sin Nombre that mirrors the orientation of Petroglyph Hill to the north, and the two landforms squeeze the watercourse between steep secondary ridges and the mouths of smaller runoff drainages. Further south the bed of the Arroyo Sin Nombre widens into a broad floodplain, and the southern ridge ends immediately above the Galisteo Creek in a prominence called the Cerrito de la Gotera (Snow 1994).

This terrain must have been attractive to ancient farmers and foragers. The numerous southeast-facing slopes catch the winter sun and provide good views over much of the Galisteo Basin. Breaks in the ridge give easy access to the springs in Arroyo Sin Nombre. The broad floodplain and small benches in Arroyo

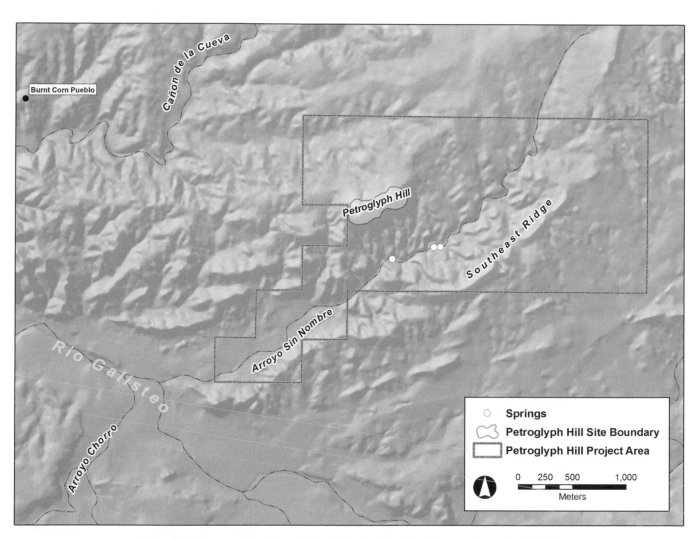

Figure 7.1. Survey area in relation to Burnt Corn Pueblo and Petroglyph Hill.

Sin Nombre provide deep soils with good agricultural potential. Raw materials for tool stone are also available. Concentrated deposits of well-silicified petrified wood, including large logs, are found near La Gotera, and there are pavements of flakes that attest to the use of lithic resources. In addition to the springs, the Galisteo Creek afforded a semi-permanent water source. The valley of this primary watercourse also served as a route for travelers entering or leaving the Galisteo Basin, perhaps guided by the rocky knob of La Gotera.

Visitors to the top of Petroglyph Hill gain panoramic views over numerous archaeological sites and topographic features. Burnt Corn Pueblo, the largest Coalition period site in the area, is 3.25 km to the northwest. During its occupation, with smoke from cooking fires and its two-story height, the village would have been a dominant feature in the mid-distance. Less visible after its destruction, Burnt Corn's location would nonetheless have remained a focal point of the landscape even as its cultural significance shifted from an inhabited place to a place of memory (Anschuetz 2005; Snead 2008a).

Over time, and as other villages gained prominence in the social topography of the Galisteo Basin, Petroglyph Hill became a less direct vantage point. Despite the sweeping vistas from the hill, distance and topography preclude direct views of major Classic period sites. The closest neighbors, San Marcos and San Lazaro pueblos, are situated in low drainages that would have made them difficult to see, save perhaps for smoke rising from cooking fires. Similarly, the Classic villages of Shé, Colorado, and Largo in the heart of the basin further south and east were never clearly visible, but anyone with knowledge of the Basin's landscape would have been able to identify the mesas that rise above them. Distinctive topographic features such as the sharp line of Creston Dike (also known as Comanche Gap) (Schaafsma 1992b), the bald crown of Cerro Pelón, the Sangre de Cristo and Ortiz mountains, and the broad expanses of grassland between them all were important landmarks visible from Petroglyph Hill.

Despite these lofty views of the Galisteo Basin and beyond, views *toward* the twin peaks are much less striking. Approaching Petroglyph Hill from the northwest, for example, one climbs gently sloping land dissected by small drainages; from this direction, the twin hilltops are visible as mere bumps on the horizon. From the south, on the broad floodplain of Arroyo Sin Nombre, Petroglyph Hill is obscured by intermediate terrain and cannot be seen at all. From this location it is necessary to climb the southeastern ridge bounding Arroyo Sin Nombre to recognize Petroglyph Hill's conical peaks as prominent features. If one moves back 15 or 20 km, however, Petroglyph Hill emerges from the landscape again, not dominating the horizon but appearing as a low, darker form against the distant slopes behind it. It is thus a mid-distance landmark. Once one knows where to look, it is a distinctive and persistent, albeit subtle, feature.

Petroglyph Hill and its companion feature, La Gotera, would have provided triangulation points for travelers and landscape markers for the distant observer. For those living close by, these geologic features pinpointed a specific place in the broad landscape of the Galisteo Basin and surrounding region, anchoring not just the physical and visual topography, but the social and cultural topography as well.

THE TANO ORIGINS PROJECT AND PETROGLYPH HILL

There were two components to the Tano Origins Project investigations of Petroglyph Hill: a pedestrian survey that focused on documenting and understanding the cultural landscape surrounding Petroglyph Hill (directed by Head), and a rock art study that focused on documenting petroglyphs and archaeological features on the hill itself (directed by Munson). The project began in 2004 as a joint effort of Santa Fe County, George Mason University, and Trent University. Major funding was provided by the National Science Foundation, with additional support from the Arizona Archaeological

and Historical Society and Santa Fe County. Laboratory space was provided by the Museum of Indian Arts and Culture/Laboratory of Anthropology. During two seasons of fieldwork and subsequent investigations, the pedestrian survey covered almost 560 ha on County land within 2 km around Petroglyph Hill. Ultimately 184 prehistoric and historic-era sites and 292 isolated occurrences were recorded (Fig 7.2). Documentation of the site of Petroglyph Hill, which took place during the 2004 field season, identified 1,865 petroglyphs, as well as a small number of features and a very light artifact scatter. Collectively this work represents a distinctive sample of archaeological evidence from the cultural hinterlands of the Galisteo Basin.

THE ARCHAEOLOGICAL LANDSCAPE AROUND PETROGLYPH HILL

Past human activity in the Petroglyph Hill area can be seen through several categories of archaeological evidence collected by the survey: assemblage size, feature type and diversity, and structure size and character. We recorded 210 separate components, with physically and culturally distinct occupations, at 184 sites. These were dated using chronologically diagnostic artifacts present on the surface. Ceramics were identified to type and ware when possible, using the ceramic manual developed by the National Park Service Intermountain Region for inventory surveys of Bandelier National Monument and Pecos National Historical Park (McKenna and Miles 1987; Eininger and others 1996) and the field ceramic manual developed and distributed by the Museum of New Mexico (Wilson 2007). Ceramic cross-dating is a ubiquitous technique in survey archaeology but one that remains problematic. Assigning reliable dates for sites in the Pueblo period, for instance, requires ceramic sequences that are rigorously cross-dated and which meet normative assumptions about the production and circulation of pottery. Our adoption of this approach thus does not imply certainty about the dates of specific sites, only that these are the best "fit" within the broader chronological framework.

Prehistoric components dominate archaeological sites in the landscape surrounding Petroglyph Hill (n = 174, 83%) with most of these (n = 117, 67%) ascribed to the Ancestral Pueblo era. A much smaller number (n = 5, 3%) can be confidently placed in the Archaic period. There were 52 components (30%) that could not

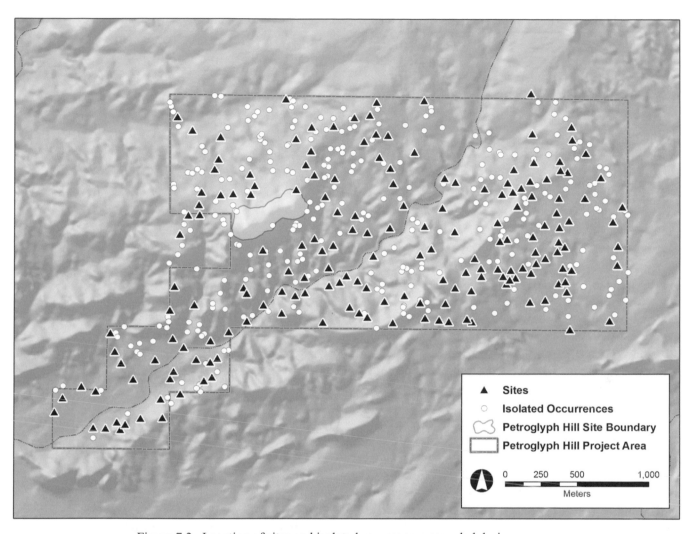

Figure 7.2. Location of sites and isolated occurrences recorded during survey.

be dated beyond identifying them as prehistoric. Due to the focus of the Tano Origins Project, most of the following discussion emphasizes the Ancestral Pueblo era.

Most Ancestral Pueblo components have artifact assemblages with fewer than 100 artifacts (n = 94; 80%), and the majority of those (n = 72; 77%) contain fewer than 40 artifacts. The small assemblage sizes suggest brief episodes of use, indicating that most locations were visited only once or a very few times. This is supported by the fact that scatters without features are also the most common type of site component (n = 70; 60%). Of the components *with* features (n = 40; 35%), only 18 have multiple feature types and only 4 of these have more than two feature types.

Thermal features represented by soil stains and hearths were the most common non-structural feature

types, suggesting camping or food processing activities. Rock concentrations and rock alignments that may have been used for small-scale agriculture are the next most frequent feature types. The ephemeral nature of rock features suggest infrequent use and possibly lack of maintenance after construction. Isolated petroglyphs were recorded in several cases, and grinding features were present both as isolates and in association with sites.

There are no village sites in the immediate vicinity of Petroglyph Hill. Instead, what we find are enigmatic alignments of stone representing simple structures. These are typically a single course in height, only occasionally forming four walls or even a corner. Such alignments are generally thought to have been foundations for roofs made of brush or other perishable materials.

Table 7.1. Time Period and Type of Dated Puebloan Sites Recorded by the Petroglyph Hill Survey

Time period	Sites with structures	Sites with features	Sites with artifact scatters	Total
Coalition	4	11	7	22
Early Coalition	2	5	6	
Late Coalition				
Pindi phase	2	4	0	
Galisteo phase	0	2	1	
Coalition and Classic	6	2	10	18
Pindi phase to Classic	2	2	3	
Galisteo phase to Classic	4	0	7	
Classic	3	16	26	45
Totals	13	29	43	85

It is also possible that they were once more substantial masonry structures that were robbed for stones by later inhabitants to use elsewhere (Head and Snead 1992; Snead 2008a) Some structures are represented by low mounds with building stone, others by cleared areas in outcrops of broken rock, but none were larger than two rooms. Most can be found in or near the broad floodplain of Arroyo Sin Nombre, or on the ridge forming its eastern flank.

Overall, the generally small size of recorded sites and structures, the limited diversity of features, and the small number of artifacts in the assemblages indicate that the area was used by limited numbers of people engaged in subsistence pursuits who did not live here permanently and who did not spend a great deal of time when they were here. It seems evident that in the Ancestral Pueblo era, at least, very few people ever called this area "home."

There are some interesting differences over time in this episodic pattern of land use (Table 7.1). Especially relevant for the Tano Origins Project are differences between the Coalition and Classic periods. Figure 7.3 shows the location of sites with structures coded by time period and phase. The earlier structures, those dated to the Santa Fe (A.D. 1150-1250) and Pindi (A.D. 1250-1300) phases of the Coalition period, are all found in the lowlands along the course of Arroyo Sin Nombre and near its mouth. Structures dated to the Late Coalition Galisteo phase (A.D. 1300-1325) and the Classic period (post-A.D. 1325) occur in the lowland areas and on top of the long ridge southeast of Arroyo Sin Nombre, an area that had not been previously exploited.

Table 7.2. Assemblage Sizes at Sites with Structures by Time Period

Time Period	Fewer than 50 artifacts	50 or more artifacts	Total
Coalition	1	3	4
Coalition and Classic	2	4	6
Classic	3	0	3
Totals	6	7	13

Changes in the length of occupation and probable function of structural sites from the Coalition to the Classic periods can be seen in variable assemblage sizes (Table 7.2). All but one of the Coalition period structural sites have over 100 artifacts, while none of the Classic period structural sites have more than 50 artifacts. We interpret this to mean that there were longer occupations in the earlier period, and that the structures were perhaps used as temporary residences. The small numbers of artifacts associated with the Classic period structures suggest these sites were only temporarily used.

Differences in land use between the Coalition and Classic periods are also apparent in the general kinds of sites recorded during the survey. Structures are more common on Coalition sites (n = 4; 18%) than on Classic sites (n = 3; 7%). Artifact scatters make up only one third (n = 7; 32%) of Coalition sites, while they account for over half (n = 26; 58%) of Classic sites. The higher relative frequency of Coalition structures and the larger assemblage sizes suggest people stayed long enough on

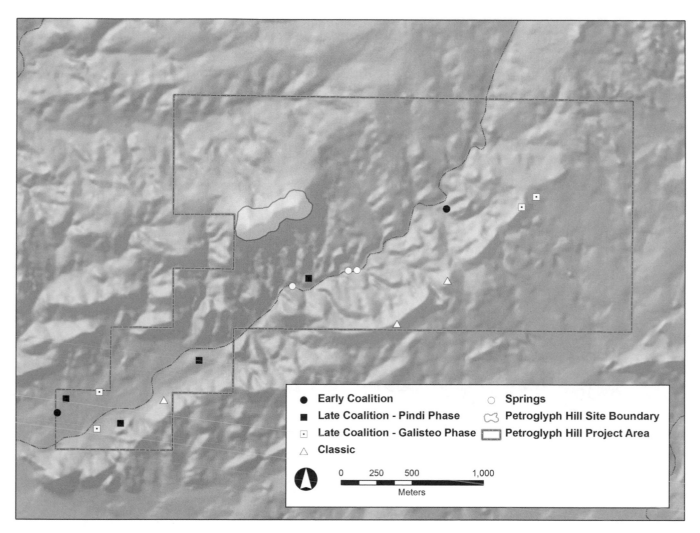

Early Coalition   ○ **Springs**
■ **Late Coalition - Pindi Phase**   ⌇ **Petroglyph Hill Site Boundary**
▫ **Late Coalition - Galisteo Phase** ⬜ **Petroglyph Hill Project Area**
△ **Classic**

0   250   500   1,000
Meters

Figure 7.3. Location of structures by period and phase.

their visits, or returned often enough, to require fairly durable shelters and to leave behind relatively large numbers of artifacts. The preponderance of small scatters from the Classic period suggests short term, intermittent, and casual use of the Petroglyph Hill surroundings.

It is likely that some of the structures from the Coalition period represent small farming communities. The cluster of Coalition period sites along the Arroyo Sin Nombre floodplains probably represents just such a group, exploiting the deep soils at that location. Ambiguity in the ceramic dating makes it possible that this community was an early settlement, preceding Burnt Corn Pueblo; however, the ephemeral character of the architecture, low density artifact scatters, and other associations discussed below make it likely that habitation of these sites was seasonal. Given that Burnt Corn

Pueblo lies 3.25 km to the northwest, we think that these sites may be associated with the occupation of that site. Small settlements, occupied during the summer months during the agricultural season, have been widely used by Pueblo people and are well documented at Zuni (Rothschild and others 1993).

Petroglyph Hill is farther from Classic period villages than it is to Burnt Corn Pueblo. The closest Classic period village, San Lazaro, is 5.5 km away, making it a longer walk for seasonal activities than a trip from Burnt Corn Pueblo. This may help to explain the relatively small size of Classic period sites recorded by our survey. A similar pattern of smaller, more ephemeral manifestations at greater distances from a central pueblo was identified during an inventory survey at Pecos National Historical Park (Powell 2002: 247). In

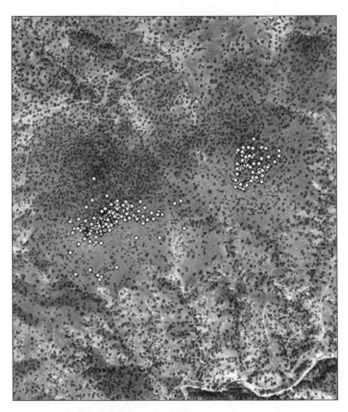

Figure 7.4. Location of petroglyphs
on Petroglyph Hill.

the case of Petroglyph Hill, it is likely that residents of San Lazaro, and perhaps San Marcos and Galisteo Pueblo, used the region for subsistence tasks but that they came infrequently and briefly.

The location of later sites also suggests a different pattern of activity. Many are located along the ridge south of Arroyo Sin Nombre, where there are significant viewsheds. The implication is that Classic period users of the Petroglyph Hill area had a greater need to see or to be seen. If the relatively light artifact scatters associated with these sites are also considered, there is a possibility that they served, at least in part, as lookouts.

There is also a notable disjunction in the occupation of structures dating to the Early Coalition (Santa Fe phase) and the Classic period occupation. Though Late Coalition structural sites occupied during the Pindi and Galisteo phases may have been used or reused in the Classic period, the two Santa Fe phase structures were not revisited. This tendency is also evident in the artifact scatters, with a relatively small number of sites containing both diagnostic black-on-white and glaze-ware ceramics.

This pattern of avoidance of an area during certain periods has been documented elsewhere in the region, and is particularly evident at Burnt Corn Pueblo, where there is virtually no overlap between the Coalition period and Classic period landscapes (Snead 2008a). There is also no evidence of re-occupation at other Coalition sites studied by the Tano Origins Project, such as Manzanares (Chapter 2) and the Lodestar sites (Chapter 5). Whether this pattern reflects a radical shift in land use practices or a cultural preference in site selection is unclear. It does seem distinct, however, since surveys in adjacent regions such as the Pajarito Plateau suggest a more complicated pattern of site reuse over time (Powers and Orcutt 1999).

Recording Petroglyph Hill

The Petroglyph Hill rock art site (LA 148,959) was recorded in June of 2004 (Munson 2005a), using standard techniques that emphasize dating and context-related information for the rock art (Munson 2002: 85–104). For recording purposes, the petroglyph panels were grouped into 170 locales, or clusters of panels in proximity to one another. The inventory of the site documented 734 panels, with a total of 1,865 petroglyphs. There are no pictographs or any signs of pigment added to any of the petroglyphs; this is not unusual for rock art sites with a dark substrate, such as the heavily patinated porphyritic andesite of Petroglyph Hill.

The distribution of rock art on Petroglyph Hill generally maps the availability of suitable rock surfaces, with petroglyphs scattered across both summits (Fig. 7.4). The majority of the rock art (80%) is concentrated on the larger peak to the west, with a lighter scatter across the smaller peak to the east. We think this is due to the quality of the rock surfaces on the larger peak, where the south and southwest sides encompass sloping bedrock outcrops and small near-vertical cliff faces surrounded by large boulders (Fig. 7.5). The top of the western peak has relatively flat sheets of exposed bedrock, divided by natural joints into squared-off blocks scattered with small boulders, and these surfaces also host considerable rock art.

The outcrops of the eastern peak, which are smaller and more fragmentary, contain fewer petroglyphs than are found on rock faces of the western peak. As with the western peak, most petroglyphs are concentrated on the more substantial outcrops of the south-facing slope. The talus slopes at the base of both peaks, and the saddle between them, are dotted with a small number of petroglyphs scattered across jumbled boulders. In contrast, the northern- and northwestern-facing slopes of both summits have only a smattering of small boulders, with correspondingly fewer petroglyphs than found elsewhere on Petroglyph Hill.

Dating of Petroglyphs

The dating of the rock art at Petroglyph Hill was accomplished through standard relative dating methods relying most heavily on technique, subject matter, iconography, and style (Keyser 2001). Some recorded petroglyphs fit solidly into styles associated with the Archaic, Coalition, and Classic periods (Schaafsma 1992a), while other petroglyphs depict historic subject matter, such as hearts, brands, watches, and written inscriptions. These broad classifications were combined with a subjective assessment of relative age observed during fieldwork, which took into account placement within a panel, relative patination, and weathering. Although these dating methods do not allow for great precision, combining multiple sources of information makes it possible to develop a general picture of the temporal and cultural affiliation of the rock art at this location.

The most reliable distinction in dating rock art at Petroglyph Hill is differentiating between prehistoric and historic petroglyphs. Petroglyphs made with metal tools, with scratched techniques, or with historic subject matter constitute a surprising 40 percent of the assemblage (762 of 1,865 elements). There is considerable discussion among rock art recorders working in the Galisteo Basin about the dating of fine-line scratched petroglyphs. Such petroglyphs are difficult to see in the field and virtually invisible in photographs. Careful recording of petroglyphs at the Galisteo Dike suggests that they are ubiquitous at that site (Brody 2007), and scratched petroglyphs are probably more common throughout the Galisteo Basin than previously recognized. The temporal and cultural affiliation of these images is not clear, although the Petroglyph Hill recording generally accepted scratched images as historic (see Munson 2005a). Historic rock art elements at Petroglyph Hill take a wide range of forms, from Spanish and English inscriptions to a carefully pecked image of a windmill.

There are numerous examples of Classic Puebloan-style petroglyphs that involve the chiseling technique believed to indicate the use of metal tools. These images may be evidence for continued Puebloan use of

Figure 7.5. Cliff face with petroglyphs on south side of Petroglyph Hill (Locale 43). Photograph by Marit K. Munson.

Petroglyph Hill during the historic period. Alternatively, these Puebloan-style petroglyphs could be copies of earlier images, made by non-Puebloans associated with the town of Galisteo or local ranches.

The majority of the remaining 60 percent of recorded elements at Petroglyph Hill (1,103 out of 1,865) are believed to be prehistoric in age. The Archaic period is represented by a single complex panel and ten isolated elements showing complete repatination and stylistically typical curvilinear meanders that are consistent with early dates (Schaafsma 1992a).

The majority of the prehistoric images are consistent with Ancestral Pueblo rock art styles in the Rio Grande Valley (Schaafsma 1992a). These prehistoric images include depictions of animals such as deer and deer tracks, canids, a badger, birds and bird tracks, and numerous snakes and horned serpents. There are also representations of lizards and a few dragonflies.

Geometric designs are dominated by simple spirals, circles and concentric circles, zigzags, and meandering lines; more complicated geometrics include terraced designs and patterns that resemble motifs from pottery or textiles.

Human figures are depicted in both naturalistic form and a "boxy" rectilinear style (Munson 2002). Some are shown as fluteplayers, shield bearers, or individuals with bows and arrows. Faces are relatively common, usually with only minor elaboration beyond basic facial features. The detailed human figures that are so prominent at other Rio Grande rock art sites, such as the "masks" that are so often discussed as possible katsina representations (Saville 2001; Schaafsma 1992a; Schaafsma and Schaafsma 1974) or the elaborate warrior figures and shield bearers of Creston (Schaafsma 1992b), are absent at Petroglyph Hill.

The relative lack of elaboration and detail of images at Petroglyph Hill makes temporal distinctions between Coalition and Classic rock art difficult. For the purposes of this study, only a small number of elements were considered diagnostic of the Coalition period, including hunters with bows, deer tracks, and naturalistic quadrupeds such as canids or deer. These constitute fewer than about 3 percent of the prehistoric elements at Petroglyph Hill. An equally small number of elements were considered diagnostic of the Classic period, including horned serpents, badgers, dragonflies, four-pointed stars, shields and shield bearers, and terraced designs. Petroglyphs dating to this period occur in somewhat greater frequency, constituting 9 percent of the prehistoric images.

The remaining prehistoric images cannot be definitively dated to a specific time period, although patination and superpositioning support dates in the Coalition or Classic periods. Unfortunately, the continuity of some naturalistic images through both periods (Munson 2002) means that the distinctive Classic Rio Grande style images are more likely to be identified conclusively than those from the Coalition period. Given these methodological constraints, the numbers reported here probably substantially underestimate the true proportion of Coalition elements at Petroglyph Hill.

In addition, the surprisingly low number of identifiably Classic Rio Grande elements suggests that the Pueblo IV presence on Petroglyph Hill was relatively light. In an assemblage of such substantial size, one would expect a greater number of the warriors, star beings, elaborate humans, horned serpents, and various

animals indicative of the Classic Rio Grande style (Schaafsma 1992a; 2000). The relative absence of these Classic period icons suggests that Puebloan use of Petroglyph Hill in the fourteenth century and later was minor compared to sites like Creston or those associated with Pueblo villages such as San Cristobal or Pueblo Blanco.

In sum, all of the major time periods of Galisteo Basin prehistory and history are represented in the rock art at Petroglyph Hill. Approximately 60 percent of the elements are prehistoric. Although there are a few Archaic elements, most of the prehistoric petroglyphs date to the Coalition or Classic periods. In addition, the site includes a substantial historic component that reflects at least 120 years of historic ranching and other land use in the basin.

The temporal range and quantity of petroglyphs suggests that the site was visited infrequently prior to the Coalition period. It was during the Coalition period that Petroglyph Hill received its most intensive, though still moderate, prehistoric use. The intensity of use dropped during the Classic period, and remained light through the mid-1900s. The usage patterns shifted around 1960, after which there was an increase in graffiti and vandalism (Munson 2005b).

Evidence of Use

During the survey and site documentation of Petroglyph Hill, we sought evidence for how petroglyphs were created and how the vicinity was used. Most of the artifacts located, however, were small and inconspicuous. It is clear that recent visitors have effectively cleared the site of readily visible artifacts, particularly on the most heavily visited areas of the west summit.

Lithics included five complete or partial projectile points, several biface fragments, a core, and a variety of flakes, flake fragments, and debitage in a wide range of material types. Despite the presence of several grinding slicks, only a single mano fragment was located. Two tiny turquoise fragments surfaced in an anthill on the west hill; one showed signs of working.

No hammerstones were noted during the survey, although they were surely used to create the prehistoric petroglyphs (Moore 1994). It is possible that each individual artist carried his or her own hammerstone, removing it when done, but this does not appear to have been the practice at other sites in the region. The rock art site associated with San Cristobal, for instance, has literally dozens of hammerstones visible on the surface.

Figure 7.6. Rough stone wall incorporating Pueblo IV petroglyph. Photograph by Marit K. Munson.

Petroglyph Hill consists of smaller boulders and steeper slopes than the San Cristobal site, making it likely that any tools left behind were lost in the cracks and crevices among the fragmented outcrops. The extensive collection of artifacts by site visitors during the historic period might also be a factor, although the relatively non-descript nature of hammerstones makes them a less obvious target for most casual collectors than arrowheads or other more distinctive types of lithics

Few ceramics remain on Petroglyph Hill, although both Coalition and Classic period wares and types are represented. The Coalition period and very early Classic period are represented by five Santa Fe Black-on-white sherds, a probable Wiyo Black-on-white sherd, and six sherds of Glaze A. Classic ceramics included a single Glaze B or C sherd and 20 sherds from a single Glaze C bowl, probably Espinosa Glaze Polychrome (A.D. 1425-1490). The small number of sherds at the site is almost certainly due to twentieth-century collectors picking up readily visible artifacts. The majority of the ceramics were found on the smaller eastern peak, which receives less modern visitation, and most of the sherds there were quite small, no more than 2 cm to 3 cm along their greatest dimension. In all, the artifact assemblage is consistent with mid- to low-intensity generalized use during the Coalition and early Classic periods, along with steady use in the historic period, including long-term collecting.

Archaeological features documented on Petroglyph Hill were almost entirely grinding surfaces or rock alignments. The latter take the form of flat cleared areas, loosely encircled by rough stone walls. None of these areas are completely enclosed, and it is not clear whether the rocks were moved in order to create the open space or to construct low enclosures.

Some of the rock features on the western summit of Petroglyph Hill may have served as shrines. For example, a rough stone wall on the western peak incorporates an in-situ Classic style petroglyph of a human figure (Fig. 7.6), suggesting that the feature dates to some time before the 1600s. Dates for most of the rock features are uncertain, though, as most of these features now incorporate historic materials such as wire and fence posts. These additions make it difficult to confirm which features, other than the extensive rock art, are prehistoric and which are historic in date.

Figure 7.7. Pueblo III style rock art (Locale 7). Photograph by Marit K. Munson.

Density, Scale, and Use of Space

Despite the large number of petroglyphs present on the two hills, the scale of the panels and of the individual elements within them tends to be quite small. The majority of the panels are less than one-square meter in size, with five or fewer elements per panel. Although some of this can be ascribed to the ready availability of small boulders compared to substantial cliff faces, even relatively large panels on the cliffs typically consist of a few elements surrounded by considerable open space. As a result, there is little superpositioning in the rock art at Petroglyph Hill. Although some panels have densely packed elements, most are relatively small individual images that seldom overlap each other.

Despite the low rate of superpositioning, it is sometimes possible to infer the relative order of production of elements based on the use of space. For example, one long flat panel (Fig. 7.7), located at the top of the western peak, is covered with 25 elements, all placed with minimal superpositioning. The smaller and more peripheral petroglyphs were probably made after the panel was mostly filled by the more central elements; similarly, some elements, such as rows of repeated triangles, appear to be copies of previously existing petroglyphs.

These additions over time hint at the accretional nature of the rock art at Petroglyph Hill, suggesting that the images visible today were created through repeated visits to the site.

The process of creating petroglyphs over time is also suggested by the presence of numerous petroglyphs that were laid out but never completed. The majority of the elements at Petroglyph Hill were produced with a pecking technique, using a hammerstone to remove the layer of dark desert varnish from the rhyolitic boulders and outcrops. Even in relatively sloppy petroglyphs, the individual dints produced by pecking are usually close enough together to form a more-or-less solid line. However, some elements at Petroglyph Hill were created with very sparse pecking that produces a light dotted pattern. This sparse pecking seems to have been the pattern that the creators intended to follow later when pecking a thicker, more substantial line. For example, one spiral petroglyph consists of solidly pecked lines towards the center of the spiral, with sparse dotting continuing the spiral line outwards (Fig. 7.8). Other examples include a panel where multiple images were laid out but never filled in (Fig. 7.9).

It is not clear how common such "incomplete" petroglyphs are in the Northern Rio Grande, as they have not previously been reported in the literature. Working

Figure 7.8. Partly finished spiral petroglyph, with dotted guidelines (Locale 43). Photograph by Marit K. Munson.

Figure 7.9. Panel with a human figure and long-tailed animal (at left) that were roughed in but never completed (Locale 123). Photograph by Marit K. Munson.

on petroglyphs over multiple sessions may have been a strategy for spreading out the labor needed to create the images over time, or it might reflect time constraints on an individual session of producing the rock art.

Orientation, Visibility, and Views

Almost a third of the rock art at Petroglyph Hill is oriented facing upwards, on a horizontal surface such as bedrock, or the top of boulders. These horizontal panels are interesting because of their implications for what the creator of the petroglyphs saw while they were working on the image. The most substantial horizontal surfaces are on the top of the western peak, primarily along the top of the outcrops that fall away to the south and west.

For example, one panel located on the western side of the peak forms a small horizontal platform perched at the edge of the hill (Fig. 7.10). The talus slope drops away abruptly below the panel, emphasizing its prominence and the dramatic views out over the Galisteo River drainage towards the Ortiz Mountains. At the same time, the panel's location means that the rock art itself is completely invisible from all directions, except on the immediate approach across the western summit. This implies that the visibility of the imagery from afar was not a significant factor in the placement or production of the rock art. Instead, it is reasonable to assume that the view formed an important part of the experience

of an individual adding to or using the panel. This artist-focused rock art forms a distinct contrast with the scale and position of rock art at sites such as Creston, for which Schaafsma (1992b) has argued that visibility of the petroglyphs themselves was one of the primary factors in the rock art's production.

About two-thirds of the rock art at Petroglyph Hill is on vertical or inclined surfaces. These tend to be oriented primarily to the southeast, with numerous panels also facing to the east, south, and southwest. This reflects the general topography of the peaks and the available rock surfaces; at the same time, it means that most of the rock art at Petroglyph Hill faces outwards, towards the steeper slopes on the hill's south side. In other Galisteo Basin rock art sites, such as Creston, a similar placement of petroglyphs has been interpreted as an attempt to communicate with individuals approaching the site from a distance (Schaafsma 1992a). At Petroglyph Hill, however, the scale of the images, combined with the slope and size of the hill, makes it nearly impossible to see any of the rock art from a distance.

The limited visibility of images at Petroglyph Hill from afar is also a factor of patterns of access to the site. Although it is possible to climb up the talus slopes to the outcrops on the southern and eastern faces of the hill, these steep slopes require some effort to negotiate. It is much easier to follow the gentler slope on the western side up to the saddle between the peaks before

Figure 7.10. Petroglyph platform overlooking the Ortiz Mountains (Locale 19). Photograph by Marit K. Munson.

turning to follow the ridges to either summit. This is the route that is taken by nearly all contemporary visitors, judging by the informal trails that have been trampled into the dirt.

The result of this approach from the saddle is that most of the rock art is not visible until one is literally on top of it, in the case of the hilltop panels, or until one has climbed down to stand immediately in front of the panels on the slopes. The difficulty in viewing the images from the mid-distance is exacerbated by the fragmented nature of the hill's outcrops and boulders, which results in a complicated jumble of panels.

In short, the size and visibility of individual petroglyphs and rock art panels at Petroglyph Hill are strictly limited. This suggests that the hill itself was the focus of attention, rather than any local attribute at a smaller scale. Viewed from the surrounding area, it is the dual peaks that are prominent and that draw attention , not the existence of the petroglyphs (Fig. 7.11).

CULTURAL LANDSCAPES

The prehistoric sites in the area surrounding Petroglyph Hill reflect use of the land for subsistence, but embedded within the evidence of prosaic pursuits are hints of the cultural landscapes of Pueblo peoples. Integrating information from the survey and documentation of Petroglyph Hill and its surrounding area provides useful insights into these landscapes and how they changed over time.

Coalition Period

It is apparent from our evidence that during the Coalition period households or individuals, probably from the Burnt Corn community, established small farmsteads along the course of Arroyo Sin Nombre. In the uplands surrounding Petroglyph Hill, they probably obtained wild resources, leaving behind artifact scatters and sites with enigmatic rock features, both with and without ground stone.

Pueblo people during the Coalition period also established reference points in the landscape as a means of anchoring themselves in culturally meaningful space. This occurred at different scales. Isolated petroglyphs indicate locales of individual significance. A shrine referencing the summit of La Gotera is probably associated with the Arroyo Sin Nombre farming community as a whole. Petroglyph Hill, as the locally dominant landform, would have attracted visitors from a wider region.

The relevance of specific landscape features for larger groups of people does not necessarily imply collective action. The absence of large activity areas atop Petroglyph Hill and the difficulty in seeing the petroglyphs from any great distance indicate that the site was artist-focused, rather than oriented to the outside world (Brody 1989; Munson in press). Combined with the low-intensity but consistent use of the site over time, this suggests that the petroglyphs were a way to create permanent marks that translated into a relationship of artist and topography; that is, to transform intriguing physical space into a culturally significant place (Arsenault 2004; Snead 2008a: 97–99).

The significance of Petroglyph Hill in the Coalition cultural landscape is additionally suggested by the presence of grinding features that reference place, and they very likely functioned in the same system of visual anchoring through individual practice as do those in the nearby Burnt Corn landscape analyzed in Chapter 6 (see

Figure 7.11. Petroglyph Hill, viewed from the southeast. Photograph by Genevieve Head.

also Snead 2008b). As such they make an interesting comparison, worth discussing in greater detail.

During the Petroglyph Hill survey we differentiated horizontal "grinding slicks," or ground areas made on horizontal substrate, from "oblique ground surfaces." Oblique ground surfaces usually consist of a boulder or bedrock with an upper face that is at least ten degrees off horizontal, most often over 20 degrees. Some portion of this face shows evidence of grinding, often quite intense, that left heavy wear. The relatively steep angle of the ground faces of these features suggests that foodstuffs were not processed on them, as the steep angle would make it difficult to recover the ground product. Tool sharpening, or possibly grinding pollen, are more likely activities. Most were ground in such a way as to create an oblong ground surface with a long axis and it is this long axis that is used to judge the orientation of the feature.

Of the 18 grinding features recorded, 8 were oblique. They have diverse associations, with orientations that

suggest differences with the Burnt Corn sample. For instance, two oblique ground surfaces are associated with structural sites on the Arroyo Sin Nombre floodplain. One is on a small boulder atop a low rise in the flood plain, and the associated oblique ground surface orients the user toward a prominence on the near horizon that is directly in line with Burnt Corn Pueblo (Fig. 7.12). The second oblique ground feature is a large boulder on a ridge immediately across Arroyo Sin Nombre from Petroglyph Hill. This boulder has an oblique ground surface whose long axis points straight toward Petroglyph Hill (Fig. 7.13).

Interestingly, neither Petroglyph Hill nor Burnt Corn Pueblo are visible to sites on the floodplain. The farmers or users of these sites had convenient access to the agricultural land in the Arroyo Sin Nombre floodplain and to the tool stone along the eastern ridge of the drainage, and they could see down to the Galisteo Creek, but they could not see the closest village. The location of

Figure 7.12. Grinding surface in foreground orients the viewer toward Petroglyph Hill, which is out of sight beyond the escarpment in the background. Photograph by Genevieve Head.

these structural sites offered advantages such as arable land, and perhaps access to the Galisteo Creek, that outweighed isolation. In this light the apparent referencing of significant places via grinding features implies an effort to signify connections between elements of the landscape even when they were not actually visible.

This brief analysis is obviously not systematic, but implies some interesting differences with the Burnt Corn grinding slicks discussed by Greene and Leckman (Chapter 6). The dramatically lower density of these features logically relates to the greater distance from Burnt Corn pueblo. Orientation, however, may also relate to the proximity of a settlement. What Greene and Leckman identify as referencing landscape features on the horizon may, at Petroglyph Hill, be reversed, and in at least one case the point of reference may be Burnt Corn

itself. Thus we have not the perspective of the village looking out, but of the landscape looking back.

The degree of visibility and inter-visibility of grinding features, settlements, and rock art panels is an issue that merits greater attention in archaeological studies of the Coalition period. In contrast with the growing body of work on Classic period rock art sites and features (Brody 1989, 2007; Brody and Brody 2006; Mich 2000; Munson 2007; Schaafsma 1990, 1992b; Smith 2002), the implications of these relationships in the Coalition landscape have, with a few exceptions (Munson 2005a, in press; Snead 2008a), been largely neglected. This is perhaps because of the small scale and lack of drama in Coalition rock art and grinding features; nevertheless, the act of marking the landscape has important implications for the transformation of space into place.

Classic Period

During the Classic period, the cultural focus of the area shifted away from Burnt Corn Pueblo and the vicinity of Petroglyph Hill. Connections between the Petroglyph Hill landscape and the large village of San Lazaro can be inferred both due to relative proximity (5.5 km) and topographic orientation. A direct route between the two areas is provided by Arroyo Sin Nombre and, on the other side of the Galisteo Creek, by Arroyo Chorro. In contrast to views of the Coalition landscape, however, neither San Lazaro nor the other nearby Classic villages are visible from Petroglyph Hill, a fact that suggests a somewhat different relationship between the large Classic pueblos and the rock art site.

Survey data also show that Classic period residents of the Galisteo Basin did not spend as much time in the broad floodplain of Arroyo Sin Nombre as their Coalition predecessors. They continued to make use of resources in the area, an activity represented by simple artifact scatters rather than more substantial occupations. At the same time, the construction of structures on the ridge top provided both shelter and wide views, aspects that were perhaps less desirable during the Coalition period in comparison to agricultural land. Watchfulness, vigilance, and long range views are thus associated with the Classic period occupation in contrast with a more symbolic representation of such connections in the earlier period.

An interest in landscape views is also reflected in the Classic-period rock art at Petroglyph Hill, which continued to attract Ancestral Pueblo visitors. As with the

Coalition period, Classic use of the hill centered on the artists and their experiences, rather than communication with outsiders. What is odd about this pattern of use is that it is strikingly different from that of most other documented rock art sites from the Classic period. At Petroglyph Hill, all panels, whether Coalition or Classic, are small in size and show little superpositioning. Other Classic-period Galisteo Basin sites, however, are known for large-scale, densely packed images. These include the 8.5-m long serpent at Pueblo Blanco, the 1.5-m to 2-m tall warrior figures at Creston, and giant horned serpents and grimacing faces at Pueblo San Cristobal (Schaafsma 1992a), among others. These images are famous not just for their size, but for their skillful rendering; they are pecked with clear, solid lines that have crisp edges and a remarkable level of detail. In addition, many of these prominent sites have a substantial amount of rock art. At Creston, a total of 5,000 elements were recorded, with the vast majority dating to the Classic period (Brody and Brody 2006).

In contrast, Classic-period rock art is present in relatively low quantities at Petroglyph Hill (Munson 2005a). Although difficulties with dating make an exact figure impossible, the entire site has only 1,103 prehistoric elements, out of a total of 1,865 elements. The production of rock art at Petroglyph Hill in the Classic period was light enough, in the end, that historic residents of the town of Galisteo had ample space to create substantial additions to the rock art three centuries later.

In addition, the prehistoric images at Petroglyph Hill are often sketchy in appearance, with lines that are rough and diffuse. Solidly pecked areas often include gaps that allow the original patinated surface to show. This gives the Petroglyph Hill rock art a less finished look, similar to petroglyphs at La Cieneguilla and other sites (Kurota 2006; Steed 1976). Such images were created with less attention to detail than many of the large images at Creston, San Cristobal, and other well-known sites.

Recent fieldwork in the Galisteo Basin provides additional documentation of considerable variation in size, iconography, and placement of rock art images within and among major rock art sites (Brody 2007), as well as in smaller panels scattered throughout the basin (Kurota 2006). The contrast between Classic-period rock art at the prominent sites and that of Petroglyph Hill suggests that the sites may have had different purposes, functions, and patterns of use (Munson in press).

Rock art at sites in proximity to large Classic-period pueblos was likely produced by village residents,

Figure 7.13. Oblique ground surface oriented toward Petroglyph Hill. Photograph by Genevieve Head.

presumably for purposes tied to local concerns. At sites such as San Cristobal, evidence suggests that proximate rock art was made by members of different religious societies or other sodalities on behalf of the village as a whole, and with the villagers' knowledge (Munson, in press).

In contrast, the rock art sites away from villages, such as Petroglyph Hill, were less directly linked to specific pueblos, and probably not limited to the use of specific groups. The images were of more general interest, and the hill was likely used by the inhabitants of multiple Galisteo Basin villages at different times. The sketchy nature and small scale of Classic rock art at Petroglyph Hill implies a lack of concern with visibility of the final product at a distance, suggesting that visitors would need to be aware of the site's location, or perhaps drawn to the conical peaks of the hill. Residents of San Lazaro and other Classic villages would not have known when the site was in use unless they happened to be nearby.

Figure 7.14. Historic petroglyph of a bear, signed "by JSA." Photograph by Marit K. Munson.

The relatively expedient production of rock art at Petroglyph Hill would have required less time of its creators. Classic-period use of the hill was likely short term and episodic, rather than sustained. The lack of any Classic-period habitations in the immediate vicinity and the expedient, impermanent use of land at this time further support the idea that Classic-period use of Petroglyph Hill was limited in duration.

CONCLUSIONS

The Ancestral Pueblo people living in and using the Petroglyph Hill area in the Coalition and Classic periods anchored their activities through reference to three dominant features of the physical landscape: the topographic prominence of Petroglyph Hill, the abundance of both raw materials and agricultural land along Arroyo Sin Nombre, and the natural travel corridor formed by

the Galisteo Creek. Yet despite the enduring nature of the physical features, it is the differing ways in which Coalition-period and Classic-period inhabitants used, lived on, and saw the land that raises significant questions for the Tano Origins Project.

When Burnt Corn Pueblo and the surrounding community were established, the prominent twin peaks of Petroglyph Hill on the eastern horizon would surely have drawn the pueblo's inhabitants to the hill, and this topography probably played a role in the siting of the pueblo (Snead 2008a: 107, 125). In fact, the special interest that the pueblo's residents took in Petroglyph Hill is suggested by an oblique grinding surface at the south end of the Burnt Corn community that aligns the user with both Petroglyph Hill and a small, locally prominent outcrop located in the near distance called "Black Rock" (Snead 2008b: 93). The outcrop, which has a smattering of rock art at its top, has a distinctive flat triangular shape that creates a strong visual similarity with the appearance of Petroglyph Hill as seen from Burnt Corn Pueblo, and with the shape of the small boulder that constitutes the grinding surface.

Making the trip to Petroglyph Hill in A.D. 1290 would have been a worthwhile effort, for the view from the top encompasses the entirety of the Burnt Corn community, overlooking not only the pueblo itself, but also the smaller settlements dotted along the drainages. The views in the other directions, especially to the east and south, open up broader landscapes that are neither visible from the Burnt Corn community nor from Arroyo Sin Nombre, where structures are primarily located at lower elevations. In a practical sense, Petroglyph Hill would have provided a visual link among the many sites associated with the Coalition inhabitants of the area.

In a more symbolic sense, though, Petroglyph Hill represents an important transition in Coalition views of the Galisteo Basin landscape. Whether the hill served as a shrine, the site of small-scale or private religious ritual, or, most simply, a beautiful place to catch the breezes and survey the world, the steady accretion of petroglyphs over time would have literally marked the transformation of interesting physical geography into a culturally significant place. The rock art at Petroglyph Hill is visible evidence that the Coalition-period inhabitants of the Burnt Corn Community were making themselves at home; regardless of their communities or landscapes of origin, they were settling into the Galisteo Basin and doing what humans do wherever they go: making sense of the landscape.

A trip to Petroglyph Hill in the A.D. 1350s might have been very different from the one taken in A.D. 1290. The Galisteo Basin pueblos of the Classic period, built following the violent events of the late-thirteenth and early-fourteenth centuries, were constructed within landscapes that were already populated with meaning. Thus, while the Coalition-period residents of the Galisteo Basin had to orient themselves by making sense of new landscapes, the Classic-period Galisteans faced the task of making sense of familiar landscapes that had taken on new and presumably distressing significance (Snead 2008b). Although one response to the destruction of Burnt Corn Pueblo in the A.D. 1300s might well have been to abandon the area, the Classic-period Puebloans remained in the western Galisteo Basin, where they established new communities or joined the population of existing villages. From a Petroglyph Hill-centered view, this meant a withdrawal from the immediate area because the landmark is not visible from any of the closest Classic-period pueblos, such as San Lazaro, San Marcos and Galisteo Pueblo, and those villages are not visible from Petroglyph Hill.

Nonetheless, the Classic-period inhabitants of the Galisteo Basin continued to visit the area sporadically, building small structures on the ridges above Arroyo Sin Nombre and climbing the slopes of Petroglyph Hill to take in the view and add their contribution to the growing palimpsest of images. Over time, as the images built up, the process of making petroglyphs required each visitor to engage with the previous inhabitants of that space, responding to existing marks in space (Luis and Garcia Diez 2008). Did Classic Puebloans recognize Coalition-era petroglyphs as images created by human agency? Did they speak of them as reminders of time immemorial, as the Zuni do today when talking about their ancestors' markings (Young 1988)?

What exactly these individuals made of the world spread out below them is unknown, but the prospect from the peaks provokes intriguing, though highly speculative, questions about motivations and knowledge of the past. The stunning view from the horizontal panel in Locale 19, at the top of the western peak, looks out towards Burnt Corn Pueblo (Fig. 7.10), an observation made more poignant by the dominance of Classic style petroglyphs on the panel. These petroglyphs imply that Classic-period Puebloans were making rock art while looking out over the remains of Burnt Corn Pueblo's destruction. To what degree were the artists aware of those past events? Had Burnt Corn Pueblo become a part of the cultural landscape, a location kept alive in memory? If, as Snead (2004, 2008a) has suggested, the trauma sustained at Burnt Corn Pueblo translated into long-term avoidance after the village's destruction, is it possible that Classic-period Puebloans sought views of the location from afar? Perhaps the Classic inhabitants of the Galisteo Basin merely appreciated the views of the mountains and the cool updrafts rising off the hill, as we do today.

Regardless of what drew Ancestral Pueblo people to Petroglyph Hill, it is clear that the hill's topography was incorporated into the cultural landscapes of the Galisteo Basin over multiple centuries. Ancestral Pueblo understandings of the landscape shifted and changed over time, from marking the land as it became home in the Coalition period to negotiating a more complex landscape and a new order in the Classic period, built on a violent past. Throughout these changes and despite the meanings associated with it, Petroglyph Hill remained a prominent physical and cultural feature, an important geographic and symbolic anchor for the Burnt Corn community and for the later inhabitants of the broader Galisteo Basin (Fig. 7.14).

CHAPTER EIGHT

Conflagration and Conflict

James E. Snead and Mark W. Allen

It was only fifteen years ago that Lawrence Keeley published *War Before Civilization* (1996) and forever changed the archaeology of conflict. His claim that archaeologists have pacified the past by downplaying the evidence of prehistoric and traditional warfare was provocative, and considerable ink has been spilled on the topic since. It is not a stretch to label this reevaluation of the role of conflict as a paradigm shift. A number of important archaeological publications about conflict soon followed, including Arkush and Allen (2006), Haas (2001), Lambert (2002), LeBlanc (1999), Martin and Frayer (1997), Milner (1999), Rice and LeBlanc (2001a), and three edited volumes that represent a single, extended argument (Chacon and Mendoza 2007a, 2007b; Chacon and Dye 2008).

Notably, some Southwestern archaeologists were ahead of Keeley's catalyst. Since the late 1980s research on the nature and context of conflict in the precolumbian American Southwest has produced considerable information (Lambert 2002; for influential harbingers, see Mackey and Green 1979; Watson and others 1980; Woodbury 1959). Large-scale approaches to conflict in the Southwest as a culture area (LeBlanc 1997, 1999, 2000; Turner and Turner 1999; Wilcox and Haas 1994) share space with detailed examinations of warfare and other forms of conflict as manifest in specific "regional" pasts (Billman and others 2000; Chenault and Motsinger 2000; Haas and Creamer 1993; Kuckelman 2002; Kuckelman and others 2000; Lowell 2007; Rice and LeBlanc 2001b; Schaafsma 2000; Wilcox and others 2001). In his important synthesis *Prehistoric Warfare in the American Southwest,* Steven LeBlanc (1999: 24) describes the progression of this work as "an evolution from initially just admitting to the existence of Southwestern warfare to the recognition that it was important in some areas, to the realization that it had broad relevance, and finally, to the actual demonstration that it was possible to examine it in terms of why it happened, who it happened to, and how it worked."

In recent years there have been systematic attempts to integrate research on conflict in Ancestral Pueblo populations with the global archaeological literature on the subject. This is increasingly common on a theoretical level (Lekson 2002; Solometo 2006; Wilcox and others 2006). From our perspective, however, the interest in adopting diverse interpretive approaches is rarely paralleled by concern for the *empirical* basis on which such studies are based (Allen and Arkush 2006: 7). A concern for evidence necessitates a clear focus on research design. With the exception of the work of Julie Solometo and David Wilcox, few of the recently published research projects in the Southwest have adopted the study of conflict as an explicit topic for investigation.

Looking at the empirical evidence for conflict requires a focus on material signatures and their social correlates. As we move from discussion about the presence of conflict in the Puebloan past to a discussion of its character, the use of trait lists as generic indicators of categories of conflict such as "war" (for example, Vencl 1984) is approaching its useful end. The detailed evidence available in the Southwestern archaeological record means that subtle patterns can be discerned, ultimately allowing us to approach conflict in its social and cultural complexity. In some instances, fine-grained evidence of site formation processes has supported the development of counter-arguments to conflict-based interpretations of the Puebloan past. In these counter-arguments, complex ritual practices of closure and decommission account for archaeological patterns rather than overt violence (Adams and LaMotta 2006: 60). This progression is implicitly a Southwestern manifestation of a broader movement within archaeology to approach evidence for "destruction" with greater interpretive flexibility (Stevanovic 1997; Zuckerman 2007).

An important step that needs to be taken in studies of past warfare is fuller consideration of ethnographic sources on traditional warfare (Allen and Arkush 2006:7). Unfortunately, cultural anthropologists seldom paid attention to the empirical details of conflict, violence, and war in their research. Nevertheless, careful use of ethnography as well as historic documents can be fruitful. Paul Roscoe (2008, 2009), for instance, has made substantial contributions to the study of small-scale society warfare through fieldwork and analyses of historical data from New Guinea. Theoretical and comparative analyses of warfare are better represented in cultural anthropology (Kelly 2000; Otterbein 1994, 2004) but these tend to lack specific details. Nonetheless, they offer large comparative samples and models for further testing. We think Southwestern archaeologists should use both ethnographic data and comparative studies to better understand warfare in the Precolumbian periods.

The work of the Tano Origins Project between 2000 and 2007 provided the opportunity to look at an apparent example of conflict in the Southwestern past at a variety of scales and through different categories of evidence. Our original research design was structured to evaluate migration as a possible source of conflict within the population of the Galisteo Basin in the late thirteenth century A.D. As the project evolved, however, it became apparent that our ability to address conflict had outstripped our ability to address the movement of peoples, so our intent to integrate these two areas of concern will require more time, analysis, and thought. In the meantime, as archaeologists we are advised to pay attention to what is revealed in our data, and the archaeology of Burnt Corn Pueblo and its landscape reveals compelling information about conflict in the Tano past.

Before we turn to the evidence from Burnt Corn Pueblo, it is important to discuss what we mean by "conflict." It is a notoriously loose term, potentially incorporating everything from passive subversion to thermonuclear war (Crown and others 1996: 200). Our interest is in conflict that, regardless of underlying causality, results in violent interaction between human social groups. We have few preconceptions about the nature of this violence except that it results in overt action incorporating force. To a certain extent our approach mirrors David Webster's definition of war as "planned confrontations between organized groups of combatants who share, or believe they share, common interests" (Webster 2000: 72). It is not yet clear that "war" would be the most

appropriate characterization for the Ancestral Pueblo context, but the explicit focus on group confrontation is relevant. We do not deny that other forms of conflict involving violence were present in the precolumbian Southwest (Martin 1997). The evidence we muster for conflict in the Burnt Corn case, however, is anchored at the group level. We are also conscious of the risk of teleology in our approach, that is, that our definition of conflict makes the discovery of conflict inevitable, but think that the empirical evidence makes its own, powerful case.

REVIEWING CONFLICT IN THE COALITION PERIOD

There has been remarkably little discussion of conflict during the Coalition period in the northern Rio Grande. Besides the traditional reluctance to incorporate violence into interpretations of the Ancestral Pueblo past, there are two additional factors at play: paradigms that prioritize cooperation over competition and an overly mechanistic approach to the empirical signature of conflict. These perspectives have structured the archaeological vision of this critical era in ways that have excluded alternatives.

Material evidence for conflict in the archaeological record of the northern Rio Grande has been known for more than a century. A. V. Kidder, for instance, noted that some of the structures of apparent Coalition period date that underlie the Classic period Pueblo at Pecos had been destroyed by fire:

> Pueblo construction involves so little readily inflammable material that it appears most unlikely that extensive conflagrations could be accidental. So I imagine that enemies, presumably from the east, had fired this part of the town. No other building of the Black-on-white phase buildings that we dug on the *mesilla* had been burned and, short of much more excavation, there is no way of telling how general this disaster had been (Kidder 1958: 58).

With the exception of Kidder and a few other scholars (for example, Hibben 1937), archaeologists were reluctant to address the implications that burned sites had for interpretations of the Pueblo past. For much of the twentieth century the prevailing themes of archaeological research for the Coalition period concerned local adaptation and population mobility. Framed in terms of the ecological paradigm dominant in the 1970s, the era between A.D. 1150 and A.D. 1325 was one in which small groups of farmers moved through a landscape of relative scarcity. Interaction among these groups played a secondary role to the demands of subsistence and climatic variability. Changing patterns of archaeological evidence for the period were interpreted as reflecting different adaptive strategies or perhaps inmigration of new populations (Biella 1979: 142; Dickson 1979: 44; Dutton 1964; Lang 1977b). Cooperation, rather than competition, was the expected social "norm," manifest in the influential model of settlement put forward by Rosalind Hunter-Anderson (1979). Her suggestion that "conflict avoidance" had been a major factor in shifting settlements on the Pajarito Plateau was widely influential.

Conflict emerged in interpretations of the Coalition period in the 1980s, as archaeologists employed a more exacting approach to the archaeological record and developed more complex models of Ancestral Pueblo society. A thorough review of the archaeology of the era identified evidence of conflict in several archaeological districts, particularly the Chama (Crown and others 1996: 193). Judith Habicht-Mauche's (1993: 90) "complex tribe" model suggested that "intensified competition and conflict over limited and widely dispersed land and other natural resources" played a role in the Coalition-Classic transition in the region. The most substantive discussion of conflict was provided by Mike Walsh (1998), whose study of lithic procurement on the Pajarito Plateau identified patterns of competition and exclusion that intensified during the Coalition period (1998).

None of these studies were designed to address competition and conflict through multiple lines of archaeological evidence. Data, in fact, have proven to be a central challenge to *incorporating* conflict into interpretations of ancestral Pueblo society in the region, in part because the bar for postulating violence has been set high. Thus despite evidence of apparently significant structural fires at Pindi phase Pueblo Largo, transformations at the settlement through time are described as resulting from "slow change" (Dutton 1953: 351). A similar argument made for Pueblo Alamo is summarized by Allen (1973: 14),

Judging from the tree ring dates mentioned and the complex of pottery present, the settlement was finally abandoned sometime near the close of the thirteenth century. It is not thought that it saw an end through an overwhelming attack of enemies.

Some burning of rooms was evident, but such evidence is not always indicative of enemy action. Although some portable artifacts such as metates were found upon the floors within the rooms, one does not gain the impression that the site was hastily abandoned. For example, no crushed vessels were found beneath burned roofs, nor were any remains found indicating the death of any of the residents while defending the pueblo against attack.

The implications of this argument are that when the complete suite of characteristics pertaining to conflict are absent, including massive burning, destruction deposits, obvious casualties, and piles of weapons, some other interpretation is more reliable.

From this brief summary we conclude that conflict has yet to be seriously evaluated as a fundamental element of Coalition period society in the northern Rio Grande. Although this is also true for the subsequent Classic period, with the notable exception of Polly Schaafsma's study of the iconography of warfare in rock art (2000), it is a particular loss for our understanding of the thirteenth century. It increasingly clear that conflict played a central role in the "abandonment" of the Colorado Plateau (Lipe 1995: 158), and in the wake of the work by Walsh (1998) and others (Fowles and others 2007; Snead 2008a) we are increasingly cognizant of the fundamental role of competition in local dynamics *within* the northern Rio Grande. Addressing this question becomes an essential step in moving beyond our preconceptions and viewing Ancestral Pueblo society from a nuanced, cultural perspective.

CONFLICT IN THE COALITION GALISTEO AT MULTIPLE SCALES

A key component of an effective research design for investigating the archaeology of conflict is incorporation of the unique perspectives provided by different vantage points. Here we consider the views from the Galisteo region, the Burnt Corn Pueblo and Lodestar communities, and the individual constituent sites that we have investigated.

Regional Scale

To begin at the broadest scale available through our research, we find there is considerable evidence for conflict during the thirteenth and early fourteenth centuries A.D. in the Galisteo Basin and its immediate surroundings. Despite the relatively few excavations that have been conducted on sites dating to this era, evidence for destruction by fire is widespread. The list of excavated sites for which there is *no* known evidence for burning (Colina Verde, Waldo, LA 3333) is shorter than the list of those sites where some degree of destruction by fire is evident (Burnt Corn, Cholla House, Lodestar North, Lodestar South, Manzanares, Pueblo Largo, Pueblo Alamo). Evidence for fire is also present at Pindi phase sites in the Galisteo Basin that have not been excavated, such as the small room block at LA 9146 (Chapter 5). Burning at the sites excavated by the Tano Origins Project is widespread, and apparently systematic. Our review of the literature indicates that even though earlier investigators had an aversion to recognizing violence, the fact that most of the sites they excavated burned to the ground is compelling evidence of major catastrophes.

There are several indicators of conflict during the Pindi phase in the Galisteo Basin in addition to fire damage. Settlement location, in particular, reflects a perception of threat. The positioning of Burnt Corn Pueblo away from the hypothesized principle route of travel along the Galisteo Creek, and its ridgetop location, represent a defensive posture. This pattern is shared by Pueblo Largo, located on a mesa rim far up a tributary drainage. In the case of Burnt Corn Pueblo, the isolation of the site is also intriguing. The relative scarcity of Pindi phase sites in the western Galisteo Basin, away from Burnt Corn Pueblo, may indicate the existence of a buffer zone surrounding the settlement (Snead 2004). Such zones imply conflict or potential conflict over resources as they reflect delineated ownership of land (LeBlanc 2006). The lack of thorough survey in the area around Lodestar means that we cannot yet compare this locality with Burnt Corn Pueblo with respect to site positioning relative to neighbors. However, the relatively dispersed nature of this small community signifies a different orientation than that of the more tightly-clustered Burnt Corn community.

Community instability is another aspect of the Galisteo Basin settlement pattern during the Pindi phase that we think reflects conflict. Evidence from many of the Pindi phase sites that have been excavated, including those studied by Hammack (1971) during his work at Waldo, reveals short occupation spans. Wall or roof repairs, structural modifications, and multiple floors are rare, and middens tend to be relatively shallow.

Elsewhere in the northern Rio Grande similar settlement patterns have been considered to reflect a mobile farming strategy in which residences are moved frequently to take advantage of climate and soil conditions. We argue, however, that instability can be a response to threats, with frequent shifts of residence compelled by changing perceptions of risk or overt warfare.

Discontinuity of settlements over time is an aspect of this instability. We think temporal changes in settlement location provide important information about conflict. It has been noted that many prominent Classic period pueblos are "new foundations," built in locations away from earlier communities (Biella 1979: 143; Kohler 1993: 3). This pattern is evident in the Galisteo Basin as well. Richard Lang (1977a: 389) found no real evidence for a Pindi phase occupation underlying the Classic settlement at San Cristobal, and all of the room blocks at San Marcos with black-on-white ceramics are also associated with Classic period glaze wares (Reed 1954: 324; Ramenofsky and others 2009). There is at present no evidence for a Coalition occupation beneath Pueblo Blanco (Creamer and others 1993). Of the major Classic period Galisteo Basin sites, only San Lazaro has substantive evidence for thirteenth century origins (Jan Orcutt, personal communication, 2000). Indeed, even when the Galisteo Basin was home to thousands of people in the Classic period, large swaths of the countryside that had been populated in previous centuries were comparatively empty. This discontinuity is difficult to account for in ecological terms because the resources that once made such areas habitable would eventually have recovered from overuse, as is implied by cyclical settlement or long-term settlement continuity elsewhere in the northern Rio Grande (see Ruscavage-Barz 1999). We suggest that a better explanation for settlement discontinuity is intentional avoidance of previous settlement locations by new populations or new aggregations of people.

Community Scale

The Lodestar and Burnt Corn community landscapes that have been central to this project reflect a concern for conflict. They are, however, organized in different ways, and each provides insight into perceptions about threats in Pindi phase Galisteo society at large.

The Lodestar Community was a relatively dispersed series of residences approximately half a kilometer in length (Fig. 5.1). The five "farmsteads" presently known in this community are notably intervisible, a pattern evident when they were first recorded (Jager 1995). Their positions along the edges of steep terraces overlooking agricultural land underscore defensive considerations. Limited survey in the Lodestar area hampers further analysis. While it is likely that the community was originally somewhat larger than our present definition, we do not think it was much different in character.

A concern for intervisibility also structures the Burnt Corn community. GIS analysis indicates that the small farmsteads and field houses along the Cañada de la Cueva were visible from Burnt Corn Pueblo, and generally within a five-minute walk (Chapter 6). However, the three small structures located atop an adjacent ridge in an ideal "lookout" position are an exception to this pattern. The defensive position of Burnt Corn Pueblo on a ridgetop is enhanced by the organization of the settlement. Routes into the community center from the north and south were "blocked" by outlying structures, and the sites at the southern end of the ridge would have overlooked the Cañada de la Cueva and the route leading to the Galisteo Creek.

Overall, the Burnt Corn community was organized as a highly articulated defensive system. Cross-culturally, this pattern accords well with the clustered "security communities" noted by Roscoe (2009) among small-scale societies in New Guinea. His work clearly established that site clustering of this type is primarily for defense. From a Southwestern perspective, the Burnt Corn landscape resembles the landscapes associated with historic pueblos during times of conflict. The outlying sites, in particular, resemble the "guard pueblos" known ethnographically at Hopi (Connelly 1979: 540; Snead 2008a; Snead and others 2004). In this model, groups seeking to join a settled community are assigned land at tactically vulnerable places in the landscape to serve as guards against hostile intruders. The new residents thus lived in marginal, exposed areas, where they performed an essential guarding function in times of danger. The outlying structures at Burnt Corn are good candidates for such a system. The guard pueblo pattern may also explain the location of Pueblo Escondido (LA 358), the second largest structure in the Cañada de la Cueva. It is within a few hundred meters of Burnt Corn Pueblo but is situated on a low bench just above the valley bottom with limited visibility in most directions. Nonetheless, Pueblo Escondido is ideally positioned to block traffic moving up and down the Cañada de la Cueva, and thus closely matches the profile for a guard pueblo.

The reorganization of settlement following the Pindi phase is evident in the Burnt Corn and Lodestar community landscapes, and in the Galisteo Basin as a whole. The most obvious aspect of this reorganization is the end of occupation at all of the residential sites we examined, none of which appear to have been inhabited past A.D. 1310. These sites were never resettled. Local occupations that followed the destruction of Burnt Corn Pueblo and other sites at the end of the Pindi phase were ephemeral and located outside the environs of the former community center (Snead 2008a, Chapter 5). This change in the location of settlements occurred despite the fact that the population of the Galisteo Basin increased over the fourteenth century. The lack of reoccupation of relatively optimal environments for farming and related activities is difficult to account for without some dramatic transformation.

In evaluating the reorganization of settlement, it is important to understand that the Pindi Phase inhabitants had clearly built to stay. The landscape of identity associated with Burnt Corn Pueblo includes shrines and sacred topography that defined a lived place in a thoroughly Puebloan mode (Fig. 8.1; Snead 2008a). The elaborate spatial sensibility described in Greene and Leckman's analysis of grinding slicks created landmarks that would have been visible and understood for generations (Chapter 6). Such an emphasis on placemaking clearly was not a short-term settlement strategy,

An emphasis on place in a risky time is as much a part of the Petroglyph Hill landscape as it is of the nearby communities. As Munson and Head discuss (Chapter 7), the establishment of landmarks at various scales was an important element at Petroglyph Hill, as was the discontinuity of settlement following the Pindi phase. They provocatively argue that the shift in site location away from the arroyo bottoms towards higher ground during the Classic period is a response to a "need to see or to be seen." A similar pattern is evident in the Burnt Corn landscape after the destruction of Burnt Corn Pueblo. The people who continued to use the area were far from home and help, and whether they were growing corn or gathering piñon nuts, they appear to have kept a close eye on their surroundings.

Site Scale

The most detailed scale of archaeological evidence collected by the Tano Origins Project provides the clearest evidence of conflict in the Galisteo Basin during the Pindi phase. Our work at Burnt Corn Pueblo (Chapter 4) and at smaller sites in the Burnt Corn and Lodestar

Figure 8.1. Cupuled boulder shrine in the landscape of Burnt Corn Pueblo. Photograph by James Snead.

communities (Chapter 5) provides a body of data that indicates sudden and overwhelming destruction.

To sum up the discussion in Chapter 4, all of the nine structures that made up Burnt Corn Pueblo were burned to the ground at some point early in the 1300s, in our estimate approximately A.D. 1310. The probability of a low fuel load on the ridgetop, the wide dispersion of these structures, and the apparent presence of fire both within rooms and on the surface of the roofs argue against a forest fire or accidental burning. The alternative scenario that the burning was a tactic to eliminate insect infestations or to destroy contaminated food supplies is unconvincing when one considers the calamitous impact such an event would inevitably have had on the occupants of the community and the degree of unnecessary work involved. In the face of some sort of biological challenge the simplest response would have been to move, as indeed appears to have happened constantly in the Pueblo world. The nature of the burning

at Burnt Corn Pueblo, resulting in the collapse of roofs and upper walls in at least four of the excavated units, shows that the process was systematic and thorough. In our estimation, this fire resulted from a comparatively drastic measure that would only have been undertaken under dire circumstances.

The limited contents of the rooms at Burnt Corn Pueblo provide fodder for multiple interpretations. One interpretation of the empty corn storage room exposed in Structure 7 of Unit 2, and the sealed features in Structure 2 of Unit 6, was that the inhabitants had time to prepare for the conflagration. From this perspective those who left the pueblo before or during the burning were able to take some of the dried corn with them. This linkage is circumstantial, however, and we think it is also possible that the storage room had been cleared to receive a new crop of corn. The presence of grinding stones on the roofs as well as usable items cached in ceilings also argues against a completely orderly "evacuation."

The pattern of destruction in the Burnt Corn community was not limited to Burnt Corn Pueblo. The burning of nearby Cholla House was equally systematic and more convincingly sudden, because its owners did not have time to remove a stashed collection of turquoise, bone tools and two well-formed large manos that were likely sitting side-by-side on the roof next to a hatch entrance. These items fell on top of small-diameter burning beams that had collapsed onto the prepared clay floor. Other burning beams subsequently fell as the roof continued to burn and the upper adobe walls collapsed inward, sealing the room. This pattern is echoed by that exposed at Lodestar where burning clearly took place in at least two, and probably all three, excavated structures. Valuable artifacts and functional tools were left inside the burnt rooms. The same arguments against accidental fire or forest fire that apply to Burnt Corn Pueblo are equally applicable to these additional cases.

The low number of artifacts recovered from Burnt Corn Pueblo makes comparison of assemblages difficult, but lithics documented at the smaller sites suggest several arguments. Although numerous obsidian projectile points were found on the surface and on the floor of some of the small structures, recovered faunal remains did not include the large animals that might be hunted with such weapons. The debitage in these structures did not contain evidence for the production of finished bifaces or projectile points, as tertiary flakes were rare. While this is hardly conclusive evidence of attacks it is a pattern that may be meaningful. The caches of projectile points may have been stored by the inhabitants for use in defense of their pueblo. Study of the faunal and artifact assemblages from other Coalition sites in the region is needed to answer these questions.

The Burnt Corn and Lodestar communities also experienced comparatively brief occupations. Shallow middens were ubiquitous at these locations. The only evidence for reconstruction comes from the Burnt Corn plaza pueblo, but given the short span indicated by tree-ring dates at the site, this does not contradict a length of occupation of a single generation. These circumstances are profoundly different from those just a few decades later, when many Galisteo communities survived for hundreds of years.

The post-destruction history of Burnt Corn Pueblo and the Lodestar settlements is remarkably similar. In all cases, after the conflagrations there were no attempts to rebuild. The excavation evidence from Burnt Corn Pueblo, particularly the absence of burned "primary" roof beams, suggests the possibility of post-fire salvage of building materials. Some of the collapse of the upper walls may be due to this process. There is no suggestion of other forms of salvage, nor is there convincing evidence of ritual caches in the post-destruction era. From the available evidence, it appears that all of these structures remained unused but visible until they were gradually hidden by time and vegetation.

CRITIQUE

Some evidence produced by this study might be considered to conflict with our argument regarding conflict. Here we review this evidence in anticipation of a critique, and to expand the discussion about studying warfare through archaeological evidence.

First, identifying "defensibility" in the landscape is not a straightforward process. As Snead (2008a) has argued elsewhere, the siting of a place like Burnt Corn Pueblo was done in response to several needs, of which a potential response to hostile neighbors is one. Sites atop remote buttes and pinnacles identified in various parts of Arizona are obviously defensive (Haas and Creamer 1993; Solometo 2006; Welch and Bostwick 2001). However, such topographic features are scarce in the Galisteo Basin. We think locations on ridgetops, mesa edges or isolated hillocks, such as the topographic settings of Burnt Corn Pueblo, Pueblo Largo, and Colina Verde, are nonetheless fairly straightforward cases of defensible positioning, particularly when they are separated from farming land.

Not all Pindi phase pueblos, however, are defensive in this way. Manzanares, for instance, is situated on a flat river terrace. Lodestar North is bounded by a mesa edge to the east, but can be approached across flat, open terrain to the west. We thus do not argue that all Pindi phase sites are situated in topographically defensible locations.

Isolation, elevation and slopes, however, are not the only indices of defensibility (LeBlanc 1999:56-8). Large communities or more organized settlements have less to fear than smaller or less integrated sites. Recent ethnographic research by Roscoe (2008, 2009) on traditional warfare in New Guinea illustrates that larger communities and other "security groups" were a strong deterrent to attack. Similarly, the largest fortified settlement in a regional analysis of Maori fortifications was minimally protected by earthworks, clearly relying on large numbers of warriors for security (Allen 1994).

Manzanares was substantially larger than Burnt Corn Pueblo, and it may be that its larger population made a more classically defensible site location unnecessary. Smaller settlements, such as Lodestar, are the anomaly in this scenario, although what appears to be intervisibility between the different sites indicates a high level of integration (noted by Jager 1995).

Intervisibility between communities, frequently associated with high levels of competition, does not appear to have been emphasized in the Galisteo Basin during the Pindi phase, although we have not tested the hypothesis directly. It has been suggested that some of the hilltop shrines may have served as signaling stations (David Wilcox, personal communication 2000), and Petroglyph Hill is visible from throughout the Basin, including part of the Lodestar Community (Fig. 8.2). No direct evidence for pyro-communication has been recorded, however, and the issue of site contemporeneity would have to be further resolved to adequately test this hypothesis.

Brief occupations, such as those at the Burnt Corn and Lodestar communities, were not universal in the Pindi phase Galisteo Basin. Tree-ring dates from Colina Verde suggest that it was inhabited for more than a century. Our argument that high mobility and frequent abandonments may have been a product of competition and conflict does not account for the communities that were occupied for longer time spans. One reason for settlement longevity in times of conflict could be that some communities fared well under such conditions, either by projecting enough deterrent to avoid aggression or by being successful aggressors themselves.

Figure 8.2. Room block in the Lodestar community, with Petroglyph Hill on the eastern horizon. Photograph by James Snead.

All of these factors are derived from the fact that we are not yet able to fully characterize Coalition period settlement in the Galisteo Basin. Survey data for this period remain scarce, and this is a district in the northern Rio Grande region where relatively large but unrecorded pueblos are still being discovered (Gary Hein, personal communication, 2006). Overall the picture is one of diversity, a point made by Lang (1977a: 23) a generation ago, and it is likely that the data will resist broad, interpretive statements for some time to come.

It is important to recognize that the chronology underpinning our analysis remains incomplete. The contemporaneity of Burnt Corn Pueblo and Manzanares is supported by tree-ring dates (Chapter 2). Until further absolute dates are obtained, assigning other sites to the Pindi phase is reliant on cross-dating. This attribution is generally supported by ongoing ceramic analyses (Chapter 3), but some inter-site variation in ceramics may be chronological in nature. Even so, this phase encompasses perhaps two generations, which while precise for archaeology, can mask significant change.

For example, if Cholla House and Burnt Corn Pueblo were exact contemporaries, it would support our interpretation that they represent a clustered community of farmsteads organized around a central community house. It would also support the contention that these two places were burned in a single cataclysm. If, however, they were built 20 years apart, a different scenario might apply. In that case, an early Burnt Corn community cluster of farmsteads without a center would have closely resembled the Lodestar community. The destruction of Cholla House might thus have preceded that of Burnt Corn Pueblo, supplying a motive for the construction of a defensible community center as the remaining population aggregated in an ostensibly safer place. The ultimate burning of the community house would then have been the end of a multistage process of destruction, consolidation, and annihilation.

More precise chronologies for the Burnt Corn farmsteads and Lodestar would allow us to further evaluate these scenarios, and the presence of preserved wood at these sites make better chronological control possible to achieve. However, whether they burned at roughly the same time or at intervals throughout a few decades, the overall picture remains the same: a significant degree of conflict was a hallmark of the Pindi phase. Either a single cataclysm or a generation of strife would represent a distinct pattern in the Pueblo history of the northern Rio Grande, one in which violence played a particularly pernicious role.

DISCUSSION

In our evaluation, the empirical evidence for the destruction of Burnt Corn Pueblo and the Lodestar community demonstrates the presence of violent conflict within Pindi phase society in the Galisteo Basin. Indications of conflict are present at all of the scales engaged by our analysis. The next step is to evaluate just what sort of conflict these patterns represent, and this presents interpretive challenges, not the least of which is that to our knowledge this is a relatively distinct case in the Southwestern archaeological record.

There are, however, a few relevant empirical cases, some of which allow us to eliminate specific scenarios. It is clear that the Galisteo Basin in the late thirteenth century A.D. was not characterized by extreme conflict such as is manifest in the archaeological record of the Kayenta (Haas and Creamer 1993) and Chevelon (Solometo 2006) regions. Both cases feature groups of people "taking deliberate and extreme measures to move into remote, inaccessible, and highly defensible locations" (Haas and Creamer 1993: 134). In the Chevelon case this resulted in redoubts built on high pinnacles that can barely be reached today (Solometo 2006). The response of the inhabitants of the Pindi phase Galisteo Basin to the threat of conflict does not reflect such desperation. There is no sense of extreme fear in the layout, organization, or construction of the sites investigated in the region. Maybe there should have been, if our interpretations are correct. Perhaps the inhabitants of Lodestar or Burnt Corn simply underestimated their own vulnerability.

Sites studied by the Tano Origins Project also lack another characteristic often considered standard in examples of Ancestral Pueblo warfare: large numbers of human casualties. The most infamous examples of this pattern are Castle Rock Pueblo (Kuckelman 2002) and Cowboy Wash (Billman and others 2000) both of which attracted considerable recent attention (Turner and Turner 1999; White 1992). It seems evident that the horrific character of the discoveries in these locations

set up a false series of expectations for the pattern of conflict within Ancestral Pueblo society and that, ironically, the absence of evidence for anthropophagy and other forms of extreme processing of human remains is considered by some to indicate the absence of conflict all together.

The closest case study of which we are aware is provided by evidence from the El Morro Valley (LeBlanc 2001; Watson and others 1980). LeBlanc describes the Scribe S site, constructed in the mid-1200s, as having been built in a relatively defensible position, demonstrating little central planning, and occupied only briefly prior to being completely burned. Following the destruction event, settlement in the valley was radically reorganized as the population constructed large, plaza-oriented pueblos (Watson and others 1980: 217).

What happened at Scribe S is as difficult to narrow down as what happened at Burnt Corn Pueblo and Lodestar, but LeBlanc (2001: 30) notes that expectations of a raiding pattern of warfare based on cross-cultural models of tribal societies fail to capture the full range of possibilities evident in the ethnographic literature. Scribe S thus points again to our own complex expectations for human conflict in past settings. When combined with preconceptions that populations in conflict must take refuge atop remote pinnacles and leave piles of dead bodies behind, it is clear to us that leaving the "pacified past" behind is only the first step in developing a clear-eyed approach to the archaeology of conflict in Pueblo history.

If one current trend is to expect ultra-violence in Pueblo warfare, another trend is to interpret evidence for site destruction as indicating ritual processes rather than conflict. This position derives from the archaeological literature on the so-called "decommissioning" of structures (Cameron 1990; Schlanger and Wilshusen 1993; Wilshusen 1986). To simplify, this proposition suggests that targeted destruction by fire was a ritual practice used in particular settings throughout Pueblo history. Recent data, including what appears to be selective burnings of kiva roofs at Castle Rock (Kuckelman 2002: 238) and the co-occurrence of burnt features and ritual deposits at Homol'ovi (Walker and Lucero 2000), have been used to build a broader theoretical argument that rejects the correlation between destruction and warfare (Adams and LaMotta 2006).

We are thus potentially faced with two levels of critique when interpreting the destruction of Burnt Corn Pueblo as an episode of conflict. First, apparently moderate levels of violence introduce ambiguity to the issue and, second, that attributing the destruction to ritual practices is more in keeping with Puebloan tradition than wholesale violence. In response to the first argument, we counter that the implications of "missing" data pertaining to conflict at Burnt Corn Pueblo and Lodestar, in particular the absence of apparent human fatalities, are irrelevant to an interpretation of conflict. A simple answer would be that our sampling of the different sites was insufficient to rule out the possibility that human remains are actually present, and that further excavation might produce the evidence for a "massacre" along the lines of the Castle Rock case. Formation processes might also be in play, because any human remains left in the open areas of these communities would have been dispersed by scavengers. This scavenging may have similar to that which appears to have occurred at the Crow Creek Site in South Dakota, where the significance of the light scattering of human remains across the site noted during excavations in the 1950s could be understood only after the discovery of a mass grave in the 1970s (Bamforth 1994; Kivett and Jensen 1976; Zimmerman and Whitten 1980).

On a deeper level, we find it unreasonable to expect that whatever transpired at Burnt Corn Pueblo should have produced extensive casualties. It is often extremely difficult to put a population "to the sword" even if that is the desired outcome (Gordon 1953), and the presence of numerous casualties should be the anomaly, rather than their absence. What happened in southwestern Colorado in the twelfth and thirteenth centuries was horrific, but not typical. Nevertheless, ethnographic examples show tremendous variability in mortality rates in traditional warfare, ranging from fairly low level casualties to extremely high levels of mortality, at least on occasion (Keeley 1996, Roscoe 2008). Even hunter-gatherers sometimes experienced the massacre of an entire community (Burch 2005). Cross-culturally, one of the primary goals of a serious attack was to catch the enemy unwary and asleep.

We also think that the sheer scale of the destructive events identified by the Tano Origins Project is, at present, unprecedented in the Southwestern archaeological record. Nearly all the burning events described by archaeologists focus either on features within settlements, such as pit houses and kivas, or on particular monumental structures such as Salmon Ruin (Irwin-Williams 1972). Elaborate decommissioning practices such as those described by Severin Fowles (2004: 621) for kivas at T'aitöna (Pot Creek Pueblo, LA 260) did not

clearly extend to rooms with domestic function (Fowles, personal communication, 2008), and this observation seems to be generally true for the thirteenth and fourteenth centuries across the Southwest.

Rice (1999: 76–78) points out that associations between fire and conflict consist of widespread burning, destruction of entire structures, and artifact assemblages left in place. When such episodes are clustered in time and space it is particularly difficult to view them as any event other than conflict. His logic provides a parsimonious explanation of what we have observed among the Pindi phase Galisteo Basin sites. For instance, we know of no example where the destruction of a pueblo was accompanied by the burning of associated farmsteads *and* other communities nearby. Even ethnographic descriptions of the destruction of villages do not imply such a scale of devastation (Malotki 2002).

Despite what we see as a poor fit between a decommissioning model and our evidence as a whole, the fate of Burnt Corn Pueblo remains a challenge. Notwithstanding the extensive burning characterizing nearly all our excavated sites, the relatively clean character of the Burnt Corn rooms and potential evidence for an orderly departure are distinct from the broken artifacts and general mayhem of Lodestar. Nearby Cholla House, however, can reasonably be interpreted as a farmstead put to the torch. We do not know if Cholla House burned the same day as Burnt Corn Pueblo, but that may have happened.

Perhaps the most glaring reason to suspect violence at Burnt Corn Pueblo is the seemingly catastrophic loss of the new harvest in the flames. The willing destruction of such a wealth of corn with knowledge of the human catastrophe that would have likely followed is difficult to envision. Even in ethnographic cases where communal strife and correlative accusations of witchcraft provoked drastic responses, such as the fissioning of villages, wholesale destruction seems to have involved outside forces. Elsewhere, Snead has drawn from Hopi sources to suggest "Orayvi events" and "Awatovi events" as models for site abandonment (2008b), and it should be noted that the obliteration of a village in the latter case was conducted by torch-wielding assailants.

Rather than treating destruction or decommission as an "either-or" scenario, we contend that variable manifestations of conflict are to be expected in the realistically competitive context that our evidence suggests existed in the Pindi phase Galisteo Basin. Viewed without abstraction, war or other forms of overt conflict have stages, phases, and forms that may be difficult to label. Mervyn

Meggitt's (1977) classic ethnographic treatment of warfare in New Guinea, *Blood is Their Argument* (1977), describes a series of complex encounters between Mae Enga groups that involve everything from assassination to raids, ceremonial battles, and full-scale war.

It is thus possible to imagine that both Lodestar and Burnt Corn Pueblo were destroyed at roughly the same time but in different ways. The key to such diverse responses is the broader context of the conflict that we are convinced was a fundamental element of Pueblo society in the Galisteo Basin during this era (Snead 2008a). Here we follow David Wilcox and his colleagues (2006: 222) in suggesting that the local population "acted on principle, politically defining what they thought their interests were, and thus sometimes finding themselves in conflict either internally or externally with their neighbors."

We do not expect the series of events that led to the obliteration of these communities to have been simple or reducible to a straightforward cause and effect. On the contrary, there would have been an unpredictable and evolving catastrophe for the people of the Galisteo Basin. For archaeologists, addressing these issues in the Pindi phase allows us to address "the trajectories and cultural dynamics through which patterns evolve" (Plog 2003: 185). But for those who lived in the region in A.D. 1300, the circumstances were altogether more tragic.

FUTURE RESEARCH

Future research for the Tano Origins Project will lead in various directions. We are convinced that the matter of origins is essential to understanding the turmoil of the Pindi phase. By environmental measures, the end of the A.D. 1200s was a relatively good time to live in the Galisteo Basin. If resource shortage is thus an unconvincing explanation for the conflict we see in the archaeological record, some socio-political causality related to the movement of population may be more plausible. In light of increasing skepticism over traditional means of identifying populations, as discussed by Barkwill Love and Cohen (Chapter 3), better ways to think about this process are required.

Closer attention to archaeological theory, detailed ethnographic analogies, and ethnological syntheses of conflict and warfare will help us to understand the ebb and flow of people across the Galisteo Basin, and more effort to mine the archives of Southwestern museums and research centers for useful data will help to broaden the empirical sample. Current research has identified several examples of catastrophic burning from sites within or just outside the Galisteo Basin in the 150 years following the Pindi phase, and this may yield useful insights into broader patterning (Snead 2007). What appear to be multiple burnings at the early thirteenth-century site of Pueblo Alamo (Chapter 2) are well-documented in site files, implying that deeper study will pay dividends. This approach should also involve collections research, both to evaluate "signatures" that may be evident in the Burnt Corn and Lodestar cases, and to contribute to broader studies of artifact patterning in destruction contexts.

Finally, further fieldwork will most certainly refine our interpretations and promote deeper insight. Available evidence suggests that more precise chronology can be obtained through excavation at sites like Cholla House and Lodestar North. A program of survey in the western Galisteo Basin will enable us to better understand the organization of the Lodestar Community, and thus make possible a more thorough comparison with Burnt Corn Pueblo and other sites. For a better "triangulation" on the Pindi phase and associated events, it will be particularly important to conduct excavations at sites elsewhere in the Galisteo Basin to determine whether the processes we have identified within our core study area are truly representative of the basin as a whole or represent a violent anomaly. Considering that the Coalition period in this region continues to be poorly understood, such an effort will contribute to archaeological knowledge on numerous levels.

What seems likely for the immediate future, however, is that our excavations will not include Burnt Corn Pueblo itself. During the past decade we have grown to know this place in the Galisteo landscape, to be familiar with its vistas, and to expect the barking of coyotes from the nearby arroyos after the summer rains. It is a remarkable landscape, but one that is inherently fragile. It is also a place of tragedy, and no one who works there for very long can be unaware of this association. We hope that we have approached Burnt Corn Pueblo and its history with respect, and it is with respect in mind that we leave it be for a time as we pursue the questions that it raises elsewhere.

References

Adams, E. Charles
1991 *The Origin and Development of the Pueblo Katsina Cult*. University of Arizona Press, Tucson.

Adams, E. Charles, and Vincent M. LaMotta
2006 New Perspectives on Ancient Religion: Katsina Ritual and the Archaeological Record. In *Religion in the Prehispanic Southwest*, edited by Christine S. Vanpool, Todd L. Vanpool, and David A. Phillips, Jr., pp. 53–66. Altamira, Lanham, Maryland.

Ahlstrom, Richard V. N.
1989 Tree-Ring Dating of Pindi Pueblo, New Mexico. *Kiva* 54: 361–384.

Alexander, Robert K.
1971 LA 6869: the Wheeler Site. In *Salvage Archaeology in the Galisteo Dam and Reservoir Area, New Mexico*, edited by David W. Kayser and George H. Ewing, pp. 34–94. Laboratory of Anthropology Note 101. Museum of New Mexico, Santa Fe.

Allen, Craig D.
1998 Where Have All the Grasslands Gone? *Quivira Coalition Newsletter* 1(4): 6–9. Santa Fe.

Allen, Joseph W.
1973 *The Pueblo Alamo Project: Salvage at the Junction of U.S. 85 and U.S. 285 South of Santa Fe, New Mexico*. Museum of New Mexico, Research Section, Laboratory of Anthropology Notes 86. Santa Fe.

Allen, Mark W.
1994 *Warfare and Economic Power in Simple Chiefdoms: The Development of Fortified Villages and Polities in Mid-Hawke's Bay, New Zealand*. Ph.D. dissertation, Department of Anthropology, UCLA. University Microfilms, Ann Arbor.
2006 Preliminary Report on Archaeological Investigations at Lodestar Ranch, Cerrillos, New Mexico (with contributions from Greg Greene). Report submitted to the Archaeological Conservancy, Albuquerque.
2007 Archaeological Investigations at Cholla House (CDC–1) and Slope House (CDC–9), Burnt Corn Community, Galisteo Basin, New Mexico (with contributions from Gregory A. Greene). Manuscript in possession of author.

Allen, Mark W., and Elizabeth N. Arkush
2006 Introduction: Archaeology and the Study of War. In *The Archaeology of Warfare: Prehistories of Raiding and Conquest*, edited by Elizabeth N. Arkush and Mark W. Allen, pp. 1–22. University Press of Florida, Gainesville.

Anschuetz, Kurt F.
1998 *Not Waiting for the Rain: Integrated Systems of Water Management by Pre-Columbian Pueblo Farmers in North-Central New Mexico*. Ph.D. dissertation, University of Michigan, Ann Arbor. University Microfilms, Ann Arbor.
2005 Landscapes as Memory: Archaeological History to Learn From and Live By. In *Engaged Anthropology: Research Essays on North American Archaeology, Ethnobotany, and Museology*, edited by Michelle Hegmon and B. Sunday Eiselt, pp. 52–72. Anthropological Papers, University of Michigan Museum of Anthropology 94. University of Michigan, Museum of Anthropology, Ann Arbor.

Anschuetz, Kurt F., Richard H. Wilshusen, and Cherie L. Scheick
2001 An Archaeology of Landscapes: Perspectives and Directions. *Journal of Archaeological Research* 9(2): 157–211.

Anthony, David W.
1990 Migration in Archaeology: The Baby and the Bathwater. *American Anthropologist* 92(4): 895–914.

Arsenault, Daniel
2004 Rock-art, Landscape, Sacred Places: Attitudes in Contemporary Archaeological Theory. In *The Figured Landscapes of Rock-Art: Looking at Pictures in Place*, edited by Christopher Chippindale and George Nash, pp. 69–84. Cambridge University Press, Cambridge.

Bamforth, Douglas B.
1994   Indigenous People, Indigenous Violence: Precontact Warfare on the North American Great Plains. *Man* 29: 95–115.

Bandelier, Adolf F.
1892   *Final Report of Investigations Among the Indians of the Southwestern United States, Carried on Mainly in the Years From 1880 to 1885*, Pt. II. Papers of the Archaeological Institute of America, American Series IV. John Wilson and Son, Cambridge.

Barkwill Love, Lori
2006   Preliminary Ceramic Report: Review of LA 10607 (Manzanares) Collection at the Laboratory of Anthropology, Summer 2006. Manuscript in possession of the authors.

Batten, David C., and Robert Dello-Russo
1992   *A Reevaluation of Some Archaeological Sites in the Galisteo Basin Dam and Reservoir Project Area Santa Fe County, New Mexico.* OCA/UNM Report No. 185–47D. Office of Contract Archaeology, University of New Mexico, Albuquerque. Copies available from Archaeological Records Management Section, New Mexico Historic Preservation Division, NMCRIS 1229, Santa Fe.

Benedict, Ruth
1934   *Patterns of Culture.* Houghton Mifflin, New York.

Bernardini, Wesley
1998   Conflict, Migration, and the Social Environment: Interpreting Architectural Change in Early and Late Pueblo IV Aggregations. In *Migration and Reorganization: the Pueblo IV Period in the American Southwest,"* edited by Katherine A. Spielmann, pp. 91–114. Anthropological Research Papers 51. Arizona State University, Tempe.

Bice, Richard A.
2003   *Indian Mining of Lead for Use in Rio Grande Glaze Paint: Report of the AS–5 Bethsheba Project near Cerrillos, New Mexico.* Albuquerque Archaeological Society, Albuquerque.

Bice, Richard A., Phyllis S. Davis, and William M. Sundt
1998   *The AS–8 Pueblo and the Cañada de las Milpas: A Pueblo III Complex in North Central New Mexico.* Albuquerque Archaeological Society, Albuquerque.

Bice, Richard A., and William M. Sundt
1972   *Prieta Vista: A Small Pueblo III Ruin in North Central New Mexico.* Albuquerque Archaeological Society, Albuquerque.

Biella, Jan
1979   Changing Residence Patterns Among the Anasazi, A.D. 750–1525. In *Archaeological Investigations in Cochiti Reservoir, New Mexico, Volume 4: Adaptive Change in the Northern Rio Grande Valley,* edited by Jan V. Biella and Richard C. Chapman, pp. 103–144. University of New Mexico Office of Contract Archaeology, Albuquerque.

Billman, Brian R., Patricia Lambert, and Banks Leonard
2000   Cannibalism, Warfare, and Drought in the Mesa Verde Region in the Twelfth Century A.D. *American Antiquity* 65(1): 145–178.

Brody, J. J.
1989   Site Use, Pictorial Space, and Subject Matter in Late Prehistoric and Early Historic Rio Grande Pueblo Art. *Journal of Anthropological Research* 45(1): 15–28.

2007   A Preliminary Analysis of the Petroglyphs of the Creston and Galisteo Dikes, Galisteo Basin, New Mexico. Paper presented at the New Mexico Archaeological Council Fall Conference. Albuquerque.

Brody, J. J., and Jean Brody
2006   Petroglyph Recording on the Hogbacks of Creston Dyke ("Comanche Gap," LA 76065) by the Rock Art Recording Field School of the Archaeological Society of New Mexico. In *Southwest Interludes: Papers in Honor of Charlotte J. and Theodore R. Frisbie,"* edited by Regge Wiseman, Thomas C. O'Laughlin, and Cordelia Snow, pp. 35–44. Papers of the Archaeological Society of New Mexico 32. Archaeological Society of New Mexico, Albuquerque.

Burch, Ernest S.
2005   *Alliance and Conflict: The World System of the Iñupiaq Eskimos.* University of Nebraska Press, Lincoln.

Burmeister, Stefan
2000   Archaeology and Migration: Approaches to an Archaeological Proof of Migration. *Current Anthropology* 41(4): 539–567.

Cameron, Catherine M.
1990   Pit Structure Abandonment in the Four Corners Region of the American Southwest: Late Basketmaker III and Pueblo I Periods. *Journal of Field Archaeology* 17: 27–37.

1995   Migration and the Movement of Southwestern Peoples. *Journal of Anthropological Archaeology* 14(2): 104–124.

Cameron, Catherine M., and Steve A. Tomka (editors)
1993   *Abandonment of Settlements and Regions: Ethnoarchaeological and Archaeological Approaches.* Cambridge University Press, Cambridge.

Carlson, Ingrid K., and Timothy A. Kohler
1990   Prolegomenon to the Study of Habitation Site Architecture during the Coalition Period on the

Pajarito Plateau. In *Bandelier Archaeological Excavation Project: Summer 1989 Excavations at Burnt Mesa Pueblo*, edited by Timothy A. Kohler, pp. 7–26. Washington State University Department of Anthropology Reports of Investigations 62. Washington State University Laboratory of Anthropology, Pullman.

Carlson, Roy L.
1970   *White Mountain Redware: A Pottery Tradition of East-Central Arizona and Western New Mexico.* Anthropological Papers of the University of Arizona 19. The University of Arizona Press, Tucson.

Chacon, Richard J., and David H. Dye
2008   *The Taking and Displaying of Human Body Parts as Trophies by Amerindians.* Springer Press, New York.

Chacon, Richard J., and Rubén G. Mendoza (editors)
2007a   *North American Indigenous Warfare and Ritual Violence.* University of Arizona Press, Tucson.
2007b   *Latin American Indigenous Warfare and Ritual Violence.* University of Arizona Press, Tucson.

Chenault, Mark L., and Thomas M. Motsinger
2000   Colonization, Warfare, and Regional Competition: Recent Research into the Basketmaker III Period in the Mesa Verde Region. In *Foundations of Anasazi Culture: The Basketmaker-Pueblo Transition*, edited by Paul F. Reed, pp. 45–65. University of Utah Press, Salt Lake City.

Clark, Jeffery J.
2001   *Tracking Prehistoric Migrations: Pueblo Settlers Among the Tonto Basin Hohokam.* Anthropological Papers of the Unversity of Arizona 65. University of Arizona Press, Tucson.

Connolly, John C.
1979   Hopi Social Organization. In *Southwest,* edited by Alfonso Ortiz, pp. 539–553. Handbook of North American Indians, Vol. 9, William C. Sturtevant, general editor. Smithsonian Institution, Washington, D.C.

Conolly, James,. and Mark Lake
2006   *Geographical Information Systems in Archaeology.* Cambridge University Press, Cambridge.

Cordell, Linda S.
1979a   *Middle Rio Grande Region, New Mexico.* Cultural Resources Overview, Southwestern Region, National Park Service, Santa Fe.
1979b   Prehistory: Eastern Anazazi. In *Southwest,* edited by Alfonso Ortiz, pp. 131–151. Handbook of North American Indians, Vol. 9, William C. Sturtevant, general editor. Smithsonian Institution, Washington, D.C.
1989   Northern and Central Rio Grande. In *Dynamics of Southwest Prehistory*, edited by Linda S. Cordell

and George J. Gumerman, pp. 293–335. Smithsonian Institution Press, Washington, D.C.
1995   Tracing Migration Pathways from the Receiving End. *Journal of Anthropological Archaeology* 14(2): 203–211.
1998   *Before Pecos: Settlement Aggregation at Rowe, New Mexico.* Maxwell Museum of Anthropology Anthropological Papers 6. Albuquerque, New Mexico.

Creamer, Winifred
1993   *The Architecture of Arroyo Hondo Pueblo, New Mexico.* Arroyo Hondo Archaeological Series 7. School of American Research Press, Santa Fe, New Mexico.

Creamer, Winifred, Janna Brown, Thomas Durkin, and Michael Taylor
1993   Draft Final Report: Salvage Excavations and Surface Collections at the Site of Pueblo Blanco (LA 40), Galisteo Basin, New Mexico. Copies available from Archaeological Records Management Section, New Mexico Historic Preservation Division, NMCRIS 4601, Santa Fe.

Crown, Patricia L.
1991   Evaluating the Construction Sequence and Population of Pot Creek Pueblo, Northern New Mexico. *American Antiquity* 56(2): 291–314.

Crown, Patricia L., Janet D. Orcutt, and Timothy A. Kohler
1996   Pueblo Cultures in Transition: The Northern Rio Grande. In *The Prehistoric Pueblo World, A.D. 1150–1350*, edited by Michael A. Adler, pp. 188–204. The University of Arizona Press, Tucson.

Dean, Jeffrey S.
1969   *Chronological Analysis of Tsegi Phase Sites in Northeastern Arizona.* Papers of the Laboratory of Tree-Ring Research 3. University of Arizona Press, Tucson.

Dickson, D. Bruce
1979   *Prehistoric Pueblo Settlement Patterns: The Arroyo Hondo, New Mexico, Site Survey.* Arroyo Hondo Archaeological Series 2. School of American Research, Santa Fe.

Disbrow, Alan E., and Walter C. Stoll
1957   *Geology of the Cerrillos Area, Santa Fe County, New Mexico.* State Bureau of Mines and Mineral Resources Bulletin No. 48. Institute of Mining and Technology, Socorro, New Mexico.

Doleman, William H., and Marie E. Brown
2000   *1998–1999 Class III Survey and Site Revisitation at Galisteo Reservoir, Santa Fe County, New Mexico.* Office of Contract Archaeology, OCA/UNM Report 185–634. University of New Mexico, Albuquerque. Copies available from Archaeological Records Management Section, New Mexico.

Doleman, William H., and Marie E. Brown (*continued*)
    Historic Preservation Division, NMCRIS 64875, Santa Fe.

Doleman, William H., A. Yvonne Oakes, and Allan Dart
    1979   *Archaeological Clearance Investigations Along Seismic Testing Corridors in the Galisteo Basin Area, Santa Fe County, New Mexico, for Teledyne Exploration Company.* Laboratory of Anthropology Notes 148. Museum of New Mexico, Santa Fe.

Doolittle, William E.
    1988   *Pre-Hispanic Occupance in the Valley of Sonora, Mexico: Archaeological Confirmation of Early Spanish Reports.* Anthropological Papers of the University of Arizona 48. University of Arizona Press, Tucson.

Duff, Andrew I.
    1999   Regional Interaction and the Transformation of Western Pueblo Identities, A.D. 1275–1400. Unpublished Ph.D. dissertation, Department of Anthropology, Arizona State University, Tempe.

Duff, Andrew I., and Richard H. Wilshusen
    2000   Prehistoric Population Dynamics in the Northern San Juan Region. *Kiva* 66(1): 167–190.

Dutton, Bertha F.
    1951   The Diggers Complete their Fifth Season of Senior Girl Scout Archaeological Mobile Camps. *El Palacio* 58(11): 354–369.
    1953   Galisteo Basin Again Scene of Archaeological Research. *El Palacio* 60(10): 339–351.
    1955   Report on Senior Girl Scout Archaeological Mobile Camp. *Southwestern Lore* 21(3): 35–41.
    1964   Las Madres in the Light of Anasazi Migrations. *American Antiquity* 29(4): 449–454.
    1980   An Overview of the Galisteo Archaeology. *Transactions of the Illinois State Academy of Science* 72(4): 86–93.

Eckert, Suzanne L.
    2006   Black-on-white to Glaze-on-red: The Adoption of Glaze Technology in the Central Rio Grande Valley. In *The Social Life of Pots: Glaze Wares and Cultural Dynamics in the Southwest, AD 1250-1680*, edited by Suzanne L. Eckert, Judith A. Habicht-Mauche, and Deborah L. Huntley, pp. 163–178. The University of Arizona Press, Tucson.

Eddy, Frank W., Dale R. Lightfoot, Eden A. Welker, Layne L. Wright, and Dolores C. Torres
    1996   Air Photographic Mapping of San Marcos Pueblo. *Journal of Field Archaeology* 23(1): 1–13.

Fewkes, Jesse W.
    1900   Tusayan Migration Traditions. In *Nineteenth Annual Report of the Bureau of American Ethnology*, Pt. 2, pp. 577–633. Washington, D.C.

Ford, Richard I., Albert H. Schroeder, and Stewart L. Peckham
    1972   Three Perspectives on Puebloan Prehistory. In *New Perspectives on the Pueblos*, edited by Alfonso Ortiz, pp. 19–40. University of New Mexico Press, Albuquerque.

Fowler, Andrew P., and John R. Stein
    2001   The Anasazi Great House in Space, Time, and Paradigm. In *Anasazi Regional Organization and the Chaco System*, edited by David E. Doyel, pp. 101–122. Maxwell Museum of Anthropology Anthropological Papers 5, Albuquerque, New Mexico.

Fowler, Don D.
    2000   *A Laboratory for Anthropology: Science and Romanticism in the American Southwest, 1846–1930.* University of New Mexico Press, Albuquerque.

Fowles, Severin M.
    2004   *The Making of Made People: The Prehistoric Evolution of Hierocracy Among the Northern Tiwa of New Mexico.* Ph.D. dissertation, University of Michigan, Ann Arbor. University Microfilms, Ann Arbor.
    2009   The Pueblo Enshrined: Villagescape and Cosmos in the Northern Rio Grande. *American Antiquity* 74(3): 448–466.

Fowles, Severin M., Leah Minc, Samuel Duwe, and David V. Hill
    2007   Clay, Conflict, and Village Aggregation: Compositional Analyses of Pre-Classic Pottery from Taos, New Mexico. *American Antiquity* 72(1): 125–152.

Futch, T. G.
    1997   *The Vista Grande Archaeological Survey in the Ortiz Mine Grant, Santa Fe County, NM.* Report 96–16. American Studies Foundation, Alcalde, New Mexico. Copies available from Archaeological Records Management Section, New Mexico Historic Preservation Division, NMCRIS 52626, Santa Fe.

Futch, T. G., David W. Kayser, Steven R. Dye, David V. Hill, and Gene R. Crouch
    1996   *Archaeological Survey of the William Rossiter 409.16 Acre Tract Along Cunningham Creek Near Arroyo Chorro East of Cerrillos, Santa Fe County, New Mexico.* Report 96–15. American Studies Foundation, Alcalde, New Mexico. Copies available from Archaeological Records Management Section, New Mexico Historic Preservation Division, NMCRIS 52695, Santa Fe.

Gordon, D. H.
    1953   Fire and the Sword: The Techniques of Destruction. *Antiquity* 27: 149–152.

Graves, William M., and Scott Van Keuren
2003   Ancestral Pueblo Villages and the Panoptic Gaze of the Commune. Paper presented at the Complex Society Group Conference, Cotsen Institute of Archaeology, University of California, Los Angeles.

Haas, Jonathan
1990   Warfare and the Evolution of Tribal Polities in the Prehistoric Southwest. In *The Anthropology of War*, edited by Jonathan Haas, pp. 171–189. Cambridge University Press, Cambridge.
2001   Warfare and the Evolution of Culture. In *Archaeology at the Millennium*, edited by Gary M. Feinman and T. Douglas Price, pp. 329–350. Kluwer Academic, New York.

Haas, Jonathan, and Winifred Creamer
1993   *Stress and Warfare Among the Kayenta Anasazi of the Thirteenth Century A.D.* Fieldiana Anthropology No. 21. Field Museum of Natural History, Chicago.

Habicht-Mauche, Judith
1993   *The Pottery From Arroyo Hondo Pueblo, New Mexico.* Arroyo Hondo Archaeological Series 8. School of American Research Press, Santa Fe.
1995   Changing Patterns of Pottery Manufacture and Trade in the Northern Rio Grande Region. In *Ceramic Production in the American Southwest*, edited by Barbara J. Mills and Patricia L. Crown, pp. 167–199. The University of Arizona Press, Tucson.

Habicht-Mauche, Judith A., Stephen T. Glenn, Homer Milford, and A. Russell Flegal
2000   Isotopic Tracing of Prehistoric Rio Grande Glaze-Paint Production and Trade. *Journal of Archaeological Science* 27(8): 709–713.

Haecker, Charles M., and Louanna L. Haecker
1997   Cultural Resource Survey of the 587–Acre Canyon Vista, Ltd., Property, Santa Fe County, New Mexico. Copies available from Archaeological Records Management Section, New Mexico Historic Preservation Division, NMCRIS 58615, Santa Fe.

Hammack, Laurens C.
1971   LA 9147: the Waldo Site. In *Salvage Archaeology in the Galisteo Dam and Reservoir Area, New Mexico*, edited by David W. Kayser and George H. Ewing, pp. 95–137. Laboratory of Anthropology Note 101. Museum of New Mexico, Santa Fe.

Harrington, John P.
1916   The Ethnogeography of the Tewa Indians. In *Twenty-Ninth Annual Report of the Bureau of American Ethnology*, pp. 29–636. Government Printing Office, Washington, D.C.

Haury, Emil W.
1958   Evidence at Point of Pines for a Prehistoric Migration from Northern Arizona. In *Migrations in New World Culture History*, edited by Raymond H. Thompson, pp. 1–8. University of Arizona Bulletin Vol 29, No. 2. Social Science Bulletin No. 27. University of Arizona Press, Tucson.

Head, Genevieve, and James E. Snead
1992   Recycling the Cultural Landscape: Prehistoric Site Reuse on the Pajarito Plateau, New Mexico. Paper presented at the 57th Annual Meeting of the Society for American Archaeology, Pittsburgh.

Hegmon, Michelle
1995   *The Social Dynamics of Pottery Style in the Early Puebloan Southwest.* Occasional Paper 5, Crow Canyon Archaeological Center, Cortez, Colorado.

Herr, Sarah, and Jeffery J. Clark
1997   Patterns in the Pathways: Early Historic Migrations in the Rio Grande Pueblos. *Kiva* 62(4): 365–389.

Hibben, Frank C.
1937   *Excavation of the Riana Ruin and Chama Valley Survey.* The University of New Mexico Bulletin No. 300, Anthropological Series Vol. 2, No. 1. Albuquerque.

Hill, J. Brett
1998   Agricultural Production and Specialization among the Eastern Anasazi during the Pueblo IV Period. In *Migration and Reorganization: the Pueblo IV Period in the American Southwest*, edited by Katherine A. Spielmann, pp. 209–232. Arizona State University Anthropological Research Papers 51. Tempe.

Hill, J. Brett, Jeffery J. Clark, William H. Doelle, and Patrick D. Lyons
2004   Prehistoric Demography in the Southwest: Migration, Coalescence, and Hohokam Population Decline. *American Antiquity* 69(4): 689–716.

Honea, Kenneth
1968   Material Culture: Ceramics. In *The Cochiti Dam Archaeological Salvage Project, Part 1: Report on the 1963 Season*, edited by Charles H. Lange, pp. 111–169. The Museum of New Mexico Press, Santa Fe.
1971   LA 356: La Bolsa Site. In *Salvage Archaeology in the Galisteo Dam and Reservoir Area, New Mexico*, edited by David W. Kayser and George H. Ewing. Laboratory of Anthropology Note 101. Museum of New Mexico, Santa Fe.

Huntley, Deborah L.
2004   *Interaction, Boundaries, and Identities: A Multiscalar Approach to the Organizational Scale of Pueblo IV Zuni Society.* Ph.D. dissertation, Arizona State University, Tempe. University Microfilms, Ann Arbor.
2008   *Ancestral Zuni Glaze-Decorated Pottery: Viewing Pueblo IV Regional Organization through*

Huntley, Deborah L. (*continued*)
    Ceramic Production and Exchange. Anthropological Papers of the University of Arizona 72. University of Arizona Press, Tucson.

Hunter-Anderson, Rosalind
    1979   Explaining Residential Aggregation in the Northern Rio Grande: A Competition Reduction Model. In *Archaeological Investigations in Cochiti Reservoir, New Mexico, Vol. 4: Adaptive Change in the Northern Rio Grande Valley*, edited by Jan V. Biella and Richard C. Chapman, pp. 169–175. Office of Contract Archaeology, Department of Anthropology, University of New Mexico, Albuquerque.

Irwin-Williams, Cynthia (editor).
    1972   The *Structure of Chacoan Society in the Northern Southwest: Investigations at the Salmon Site–1972.* Eastern New Mexico University Contributions in Anthropology Vol. 4, No. 3. Eastern New Mexico University and The San Juan County Museum Association, San Juan Archaeological Research Center and Library, Portales.

Jager, Tamara
    1995   *Archaeological Survey of Proposed Improvements to NM Highway 14, Santa Fe County, New Mexico.* SWCA Archaeological Reports 94–131. SWCA Inc. Environmental Consultants, Albuquerque, New Mexico.

Kayser, David W., and George H. Ewing (editors)
    1971   *Salvage Archaeology in the Galisteo Dam and Reservoir Area, New Mexico.* Laboratory of Anthropology Note 101. Museum of New Mexico, Santa Fe.

Keeley, Lawrence H.
    1996   *War Before Civilization.* Oxford University Press, New York.

Kelly, Raymond
    2000   *Warless Societies and the Origins of War.* University of Michigan Press, Ann Arbor.

Keyser, James D.
    2001   Relative dating methods. In *Handbook of Rock Art Research*, edited by D. S. Whitley, pp. 116–138. AltaMira, Walnut Creek, California.

Kidder, Alfred Vincent
    1924   *An Introduction to the Study of Southwestern Archaeology.* Yale University Press, New Haven.
    1958   *Pecos, New Mexico: Archaeological Notes.* Papers of the Robert S. Peabody Foundation for Archaeology No. 5. Andover, Massachusetts.

Kidder, Alfred V., and Charles A. Amsden
    1931   *The Pottery of Pecos, Vol. 1, The Dull-Paint Wares.* Papers of the Phillips Academy Southwestern Expedition No. 5. Yale University Press, New Haven.

Kidder, Alfred V., and Anna O. Shepard
    1936   *The Pottery of Pecos, Vol. 2, Glaze-Paint, Culinary, and Other Wares.* Papers of the Phillips Academy Southwestern Expedition No. 7. Yale University Press, New Haven.

Kivett, Marvin F., and Richard E. Jensen
    1976   *The Crow Creek Site (39 BF 11).* Publications in Anthropology No. 7. Nebraska State Historical Society, Lincoln.

Kohler, Timothy A.
    1993   Shohakka Pueblo (LA 3840) and the Early Classic Period in the Northern Rio Grande. In *Papers on the Early Classic Prehistory of the Pajarito Plateau, New Mexico*, edited by Timothy A. Kohler and Angela R. Linse, pp. 1–10. Washington State University Department of Anthropology Reports of Investigations No. 65. Washington State University Laboratory of Anthropology, Pullman.

Kohler, Timothy A., and Matthew J. Root
    2004   The Late Coalition and Earliest Classic on the Pajarito Plateau (A.D. 1250–1375). *Archaeology of Bandelier National Monument: Village Formation on the Pajarito Plateau, New Mexico*, edited by Timothy A. Kohler, pp. 173–214. University of New Mexico Press, Albuquerque.

Kohler, Timothy A., Stephanie VanBuskirk, and Samantha Ruscavage-Barz
    2004   Vessels and Villages: Evidence for Conformist Transmission in Early Village Aggregations on the Pajarito Plateau, New Mexico. *Journal of Anthropological Archaeology* 23(1): 100–118.

Kohler, Timothy A., and Kathryn Kramer Turner
    2006   Raiding for Women in the Pre-Hispanic Southwest? *Current Anthropology* 47(6): 1035–1045.

Kuckelman, Kristin A.
    2002   Thirteenth-Century Warfare in the Central Mesa Verde Region. In *Seeking the Center Place: Archaeology and Ancient Communities in the Mesa Verde Region*, edited by Mark D. Varien and Richard H. Wilshusen, pp. 233–253. University of Utah Press, Salt Lake City.

Kuckelman, Kristin A., Ricky R. Lightfoot, and Debra L. Martin
    2000   Changing Patterns of Violence in the Northern San Juan Region. *Kiva* 66(1): 147–167.
    2002   The Bioarchaeology and Taphonomy of Violence at Castle Rock and Sand Canyon Pueblos, Southwestern Colorado. *American Antiquity* 67(3): 486–513.

Kurota, Alexander
    2006   *Class III Cultural Resources Inventory of 435 Acres in Pueblo Blanco Country, Galisteo Basin, New Mexico.* OCA/UNM Report No. OCA–185-880.

Office of Contract Archaeology, University of New Mexico, Albuquerque.

Kvamme, Kenneth L.
1993   Computer Methods: Geographic Information Systems. In *Stress and Warfare among the Kayenta Anasazi of the Thirteenth Century A.D.*, edited by Jonathan Haas and Winifred Creamer, pp. 171–180. Fieldiana Anthropology No. 21. Field Museum of Natural History, Chicago.

Lambert, Patricia M.
2002   The Archaeology of War: A North American Perspective. *Journal of Archaeological Research* 10(3): 207–242.

Lang, Richard W.
1976   An Archaeological Survey of Certain Lands Adjacent to the Galisteo Dam, New Mexico. Manuscript on file, School of Advanced Research, Santa Fe, New Mexico.

1977a   *Archaeological Survey of the Upper San Cristobal Drainage, Galisteo Basin, Santa Fe County*. Manuscript on file, School of Advanced Research, Santa Fe, New Mexico.

1977b   *An Archaeological Survey of the Galisteo Dam Boundary Line, Santa Fe County, New Mexico*. School of American Research Contract Archaeology Program, Santa Fe, Report 32. Prepared for the U.S. Army Corps of Engineers, Albuquerque District.

1982   Transformation in White Ware Pottery of the Northern Rio Grande. In *Southwestern Ceramics: A Comparative View*, edited by Albert H. Schroeder, pp. 153–200. The Arizona Archaeologist 15. Arizona Archaeological Society, Phoenix.

1993   Analysis and Seriation of Stratigraphic Ceramic Samples from Arroyo Hondo Pueblo. In *The Pottery from Arroyo Hondo, New Mexico: Tribalization and Trade in the Northern Rio Grande*, edited by Judith Habicht-Mauche, pp. 166–181. School of American Research Press, Santa Fe.

1995   The Fields of San Marcos: Agriculture at a Great Town of the Galisteo Basin, Northern New Mexico. In *Soil, Water, Biology and Belief in Prehistoric and Traditional Southwestern Agriculture*, edited by H. Wolcott Toll, pp. 41–76. Special Publication 2. New Mexico Archaeological Council, Albuquerque.

Lange, Charles H., and Carroll L. Riley (editors)
1966   *The Southwestern Journals of Adolph F. Bandelier*. University of New Mexico Press, Albuquerque.

Lang, Richard W., and Cherie Scheick
1991   A Second Look at LA2, the Agua Fria Schoolhouse Site: Recognition of a Coalition Phase Occupation. In *Puebloan Past and Present: Papers in Honor of Stewart Peckham*, edited by Meliha S. Duran and David T. Kirkpatrick,

pp. 87–111. Papers of the Archaeological Society of New Mexico 17. Archaeological Society of New Mexico, Albuquerque.

LeBlanc, Steven A.
1997   Modeling Warfare in Southwestern Prehistory. *North American Archaeologist* 18(3): 235–276.

1999   *Prehistoric Warfare in the American Southwest*. University of Utah Press, Salt Lake City.

2000   Regional Interaction and Warfare in the Late Prehistoric Southwest. In *The Archaeology of Regional Interaction: Religion, Warfare, and Exchange Across the American Southwest and Beyond*, edited by Michelle Hegmon, pp. 41–70. University Press of Colorado, Boulder.

2001   Warfare and Aggregation in the El Morro Valley, New Mexico. In *Deadly Landscapes: Case Studies in Prehistoric Southwestern Warfare*, edited by Glen E. Rice and Steven A. LeBlanc, pp. 19–49. University of Utah Press, Salt Lake City.

2006   Warfare and the Development of Social Complexity: Some Demographic and Environmental Factors. In *The Archaeology of Warfare: Prehistories of Raiding and Conquest*, edited by Elizabeth N. Arkush and Mark W. Allen, pp. 437–468. University Press of Florida, Gainesville.

Legare, David V.
1994   *Wyndelts Tract Lot Split, Cultural Resources Survey of 51 Acres Near Picture Rock, Santa Fe County, New Mexico*. DSS Consulting Report 47234. DSS Consulting, Los Alamos, New Mexico. Copies available from Archaeological Records Management Section, New Mexico Historic Preservation Division, NMCRIS 47234, Santa Fe.

1995   *Henderson Tract Lot Split, Cultural Resources Survey of 50 Acres near Cerrillos, Santa Fe County, New Mexico*. DSS Consulting Report 1995–022. DSS Consulting, Los Alamos, New Mexico. Copies available from Archaeological Records Management Section, New Mexico Historic Preservation Division, NMCRIS 49626, Santa Fe.

Lekson, Stephen H.
2000   Great! In *Great House Communities across the Chacoan Landscape*" edited by John Kantner and Nancy M. Mahoney, pp. 157–163. Anthropological Papers of the University of Arizona 64. University of Arizona Press, Tucson.

2002   War in the Southwest, War in the World. *American Antiquity* 67(4): 607–624.

Lekson, Stephen H., Curtis P. Nepstad-Thornberry, Brian E. Yunker, Toni S. Laumbach, David P. Cain, and Karl W. Laumbach
2002   Migrations in the Southwest: Pinnacle Ruin, Southwestern New Mexico. *Kiva* 68(2): 73–101.

Lightfoot, Dale R.
1990   *The Prehistoric Pebble-Mulched Fields of the Galisteo Anasazi: Agricultural Innovation and Adaptation to Environment.* Ph.D. dissertation, University of Colorado, Boulder. University Microfilms, Inc., Ann Arbor.

Lightfoot, Dale R., and Frank W. Eddy
1995   The Construction and Configuration of Anasazi Pebble-Mulch Gardens in the Northern Rio Grande. *American Antiquity* 60(3): 459–470.

Lipe, William D.
1995   The Depopulation of the Northern San Juan: Conditions in the Turbulent 1200s. *Journal of Anthropological Archaeology* 14: 143–169.

Lowell, Julie C.
2007   Women and Men in Warfare and Migration: Implications of Gender Imbalance in the Grasshopper Region of Arizona. *American Antiquity* 72(1): 95–124.

Luis, Luis, and Marcos Garcia Diez
2008   Same Tradition, Different Views: The Coa Valley Rock Art and Social Identity. In *Archaeologies of Art: Time, Place, and Identity*, edited by Ines Domingo Sanz, Danae Fiore and Sally K. May, pp. 151–170. Left Coast Press, Walnut Creek, CA.

Lycett, Mark T.
1995   *Archaeological Implications of European Contact: Demography, Settlement, and Land Use in the Middle Rio Grande Valley, New Mexico.* Ph.D. dissertation, University of New Mexico, Albuquerque. University Microfilms, Ann Arbor.
2001   Report of Archaeological Investigations at LA 162, Bernalillo County, New Mexico, Conducted by the University of Chicago Archaeological Field Studies Program, between 21 June and August 17, 2000, under permit SE-156. Report to the Historic Preservation Division, State of New Mexico, Santa Fe. Copies available from Archaeological Records Management Section, New Mexico Historic Preservation Division, NMCRIS 74951, Santa Fe.
2002   Transformations of Place: Occupational History and Differential Persistence in Seventeenth-Century New Mexico. In *Archaeologies of the Pueblo Revolt: Identity, Meaning, and Renewal in the Pueblo World*, edited by Robert W. Preucel, pp. 61–76. University of New Mexico Press, Albuquerque.

Lyons, Patrick D.
2003   *Ancestral Hopi Migrations.* Anthropological Papers of the University of Arizona 68. University of Arizona Press, Tucson.

Mackey, James, and Roger C. Green
1979   Largo-Gallina Towers: An Explanation. *American Antiquity* 44(1): 144–154.

Malotki, Ekkehart (editor)
2002   *Hopi Tales of Destruction.* University of Nebraska Press, Lincoln.

Martin, Debra L.
1997   Violence Against Women in the La Plata River Valley (A.D. 1000–1300). In *Troubled Times: Violence and Warfare in the Past*, edited by Debra L. Martin and David W. Frayer, pp. 45–75. War and Society 6. Gordon and Breach Publishers, Amsterdam.

Martin, Debra L., and David W. Frayer (editors)
1997   *Troubled Times: Violence and Warfare in the Past.* War and Society 6. Gordon and Breach Publishers, Amsterdam.

Mathien, Frances Joan
2001   The Organization of Turquoise Production and Consumption by the Prehistoric Chacoans. *American Antiquity* 66(1): 103–118.

Matthews, W., C. A .I. French, T. Lawrence, D. F. Cutler, and M. K. Jones
1997   Microstratigraphic Traces of Site Formation Processes and Human Activities. *World Archaeology* 29(2): 281–308.

McGraw, Thomas H.
1998   *Beverly Finn Property, Cultural Resource Survey.* Feliz Colibri Archaeological Contract Services, Santa Fe, New Mexico. Copies available from Archaeological Records Management Section, New Mexico Historic Preservation Division, NMCRIS 62128, Santa Fe.

McKenna, Peter J., and Judith Miles
1987   Ceramic Manual for the Bandelier Archaeological Survey. Manuscript on file, Division of Anthropology, National Park Service, Santa Fe.

McNutt, Charles H.
1969   *Early Puebloan Occupations at Tesuque Bypass and in the Upper Rio Grande Valley.* Museum of Anthropology Anthropological Papers 40. University of Michigan, Ann Arbor.

Meggit, Mervyn J.
1977   *Blood is Their Argument.* Mayfield, Palo Alto.

Mera, Harry P.
1935   *Ceramic Clues to the Prehistory of North Central Mexico.* Laboratory of Anthropology Technical Series Bulletin 8. Santa Fe.
1940   *Population Changes in the Rio Grande Glaze-Paint Area.* Laboratory of Anthropology Technical Series Bulletin 9. Santa Fe.

Mich, Kerri
2000   A Spatial Analysis of Petroglyph Locations at Petroglyph National Monument. Unpublished

Masters thesis, Departtment of Geography, University of New Mexico, Albuquerque.

Milner, George E.
1999 Warfare in Prehistoric and Early Historic Eastern North America. *Journal of Archaeological Research* 7(2): 105–151.

Moore, Jerry D.
1996 *Architecture and Power in the Ancient Andes: The Archaeology of Public Buildings.* Cambridge University Press, Cambridge.

Moore, Roger A., Jr.
1994 The Lithic Assemblage from a Pueblo Petroglyph Site. In *Artifacts, Shrines, and Pueblos: Papers in Honor of Gordon Page*, edited by Meliha S. Duran and David T. Kirkpatrick, pp. 167–182. Papers of the Archaeological Society of New Mexico 20. Archaeological Society of New Mexico, Albuquerque.

Munson, Marit K.
2002 On Boundaries and Beliefs: Rock Art and Identity on the Pajarito Plateau. Unpublished Ph.D. dissertation, Department of Anthropology, University of New Mexico, Albuquerque.

2005a *Petroglyph Hill Site Survey and Documentation: A Report of the 2004 Field Season of the Galisteo Rock Art Project.* Trent University, Peterborough, Ontario, Canada. Submitted to the Cultural Properties Review Committee of the Historic Preservation Division, Santa Fe, New Mexico.

2005b Historic Rock Art, Vandalism, and Graffiti at Petroglyph Hill, New Mexico. Poster presented at the 70th Annual Meeting of the Society for American Archaeology. Salt Lake City, Utah.

2007 Structured Space, Restricted Use: Examining the Social Aspects of Rock Art Production in the Rio Grande Valley, AD 1325-1580. Paper presented at the 72nd Annual Meeting of the Society for American Archaeology. Austin, Texas.

2011 Iconography, space, and practice: Rio Grande rock art, AD 1150–1600. In *Gathering Ancestors: Religious Transformation in the Pueblo World*, edited by Donna M. Glowacki and Scott Van Keuren, University of Arizona Press, Tucson, in press.

Naranjo, Tessie
1995 Thoughts on Migration by Santa Clara Pueblo. *Journal of Anthropological Archaeology* 14: 247–250.

Nelson, Nels C.
1914 *Pueblo Ruins of the Galisteo Basin, New Mexico.* Anthropological Papers Vol. 15, Pt 1. American Museum of Natural History, New York.

1915 Small Pueblo Ruins Near Lamy. Manuscript on file, Museum of Indian Arts and Culture, Museum of New Mexico, Santa Fe. Copies available from Archaeological Records Management Section, New Mexico Historic Preservation Division, NMCRIS 42654. Santa Fe.

1916 Chronology of the Tano Ruins, New Mexico. *American Anthropologist* 18(2): 159–180.

1919 The Archaeology of the Southwest: A Preliminary Report. *Proceedings of the National Academy of Sciences* 5(4): 114–120.

Ortiz, Alfonso
1969 *The Tewa World: Space, Time, Being, and Becoming in a Pueblo Society.* University of Chicago Press, Chicago.

1979 San Juan Pueblo. In *Southwest*, edited by Alfonso Ortiz, pp. 278–295. Handbook of North American Indians, Vol. 9, William C. Sturtevant, general editor. Smithsonian Institution, Washington, D.C.

Otterbein, Keith F. (ed.).
1994 *Feuding and Warfare: Selected Works of Keith F. Otterbein.* Gordon and Breach, Amsterdam.

2004 *How War Began.* Texas A&M University Anthropology Series 10. Texas A&M University Press, College Station.

Parsons, Elsie Clews
1994 *Tewa Tales.* University of Arizona Press, Tucson. Originally published 1926, The American Folk-Lore Society, G. E. Stechert and Co., New York.

1996 *Pueblo Indian Religion.* University of Nebraska Press, Lincoln. Originally published 1939, University of Chicago Press, Chicago.

Peck, Jay
1999 The Mapping and Recording of Burnt Corn Pueblo, LA 359. Elderhostel Service Project #31130. Manuscript on file, Bureau of Land Management.Northeast District, Taos, New Mexico.

Phillips, David A., Jr., and Deni J. Seymour
1982 *An Archaeological Survey of the Galisteo Dam and Reservoir Area, Santa Fe County, New Mexico.* New World Research Reports of Investigations 77. New World Research, Inc., Tucson. Prepared for the U.S. Army Corps of Engineers, Albuquerque District. Copies available from Archaeological Records Management Section, New Mexico Historic Preservation Division, NMCRIS 3601, Santa Fe.

Plog, Fred
1983 Political and Economic Alliances on the Colorado Plateaus, A.D. 400-1450. In *Advances in World Archaeology* Vol. 2, edited by Fred Wendorf and Angela E. Close, pp. 289–330. Academic Press, New York.

Powell, Melissa
2002 Ceramics. In *From Folsom to Fogelson: The Cultural Resources Inventory Survey of Pecos National*

Powell, Melissa (*continued*)
    Historical Park, edited by Genevieve N. Head and Janet D. Orcutt, pp. 237–303. Intermountain Cultural Resources Management Professional Paper 66. Intermountain Region, National Park Service, Santa Fe.

Powers, Robert P., and Janet D. Orcutt (editors)
1999   *The Bandelier Archaeological Survey*. Intermountain Cultural Resources Management Professional Paper 57. Intermountain Region, National Park Service, Santa Fe.

Ramenofsky, Ann F.
2001   Summary Report of the 2000 Season of Archaeology Research at San Marcos Pueblo (LA 98) by the University of New Mexico. Manuscript on file, New Mexico Historic Preservation Division, Santa Fe.

Ramenofsky, Ann F., Fraser Neiman, and Christopher D. Pierce
2009   Measuring Time, Population, and Residential Mobility from the Surface at San Marcos Pueblo, North Central New Mexico. *American Antiquity* 74 (3): 505–530.

Reed, Erik K.
1943   The Southern Tewa in the Historic Period. *El Palacio* 50(11): 254–264, 276–289.
1954   A Test Excavation at San Marcos. *El Palacio* 61(10): 323–343.

Reed, Paul
1988   A Spatial Analysis of the Northern Rio Grande Region, New Mexico: Implications for Sociopolitical and Economic Development from AD 1325–1540. Unpublished Master's thesis, New Mexico State University, Las Cruces.

Rice Glen E., and Steven A. LeBlanc (editors)
2001   *Deadly Landscapes: Case Studies in Prehistoric Southwestern Warfare*. University of Utah Press, Salt Lake City.

Rice, Glen E., and Steven A. LeBlanc
2001b   Southwestern Warfare: The Value of Case Studies. *Deadly Landscapes: Case Studies in Prehistoric Southwestern Warfare*, edited by Glen E. Rice and Steven A. LeBlanc, pp. 1–18. University of Utah Press, Salt Lake City.

Riley, Carroll L.
1952   San Juan Anasazi and the Galisteo Basin. *El Palacio* 59(3): 77–82.

Robinson, William J., John W. Hannah, and Bruce G. Harrill
1972   *Tree-Ring Dates From New Mexico I, O, U Central Rio Grande Area*. Laboratory of Tree-Ring Research, University of Arizona, Tucson.

Robinson, William J., Bruce G. Harrill, and Richard L. Warren
1973   *Tree-Ring Dates From New Mexico J-K, P, V Santa Fe-Pecos-Lincoln Area*. Laboratory of Tree-Ring Research, University of Arizona, Tucson.

Roney, John R.
1995   Mesa Verdean Manifestations South of the San Juan River. *Journal of Anthropological Archaeology* 14(2): 170–183.

Roscoe, Paul B.
2008   Settlement Fortification in Village and 'Tribal' Society: Evidence from Contact-era New Guinea. *Journal of Anthropological Archaeology*, 27: 507–519.
2009   Social Signaling and the Organization of Small-Scale Society: The Case of Contact-Era New Guinea. *Journal of Archaeological Method and Theory* 16: 69–116.

Rothschild, Nan A., Barbara J. Mills, T. J. Ferguson, and Susan Dublin
1993   Abandonment at Zuni Farming Villages. *Abandonment of Settlements and Regions,* edited by Catherine M. Cameron and Steve A. Tomka, pp. 123–137. Cambridge University Press, Cambridge.

Ruscavage-Barz, Samantha
1999   *Knowing Your Neighbor: Coalition-Period Community Dynamics on the Pajarito Plateau, New Mexico*. Ph.D. dissertation, Washington State University, Pullman. University Microfilms, Ann Arbor.
2002   Understanding Santa Fe Black-on-white Style and Technology: An Example from the Pajarito Plateau, New Mexico. *Kiva* 67(3): 249–268.

Sauer, Carl O.
1925   The Morphology of Landscape. *University of California Publications in Geography* 2: 19–53.

Saville, Dara
2001   Regional Variations of Kachina Iconography in Eastern Pueblo Rock Art. Uunpublished Masters thesis, Department of Geography, University of New Mexico, Albuquerque.

Schaafsma, Curtis F.
1969   The Pottery of Las Madres. Manuscript on file, Laboratory of Anthropology, Museum of New Mexico, Santa Fe.
1993   The Chronology of Las Madres Pueblo (LA 25). In *Of Pots and Rocks: Papers in Honor of A. Helene Warren*, edited by Meliha S. Duran and David T. Kirkpatrick, pp. 155–165. Papers of the Archaeological Society of New Mexico 21. Archaeological Society of New Mexico, Albuquerque.
1995   The Chronology of Las Madres Pueblo (LA 25), In *Of Pots and Rocks: Papers in Honor of A. Helene*

Warren, edited by Meliha S. Duran and David T. Kirkpatrick, pp. 155–165. Papers of the Archaeological Society of New Mexico 21. Archaeological Society of New Mexico, Albuquerque.

Schaafsma, Polly

1990 The Pine Tree Site: A Galisteo Basin Pueblo IV Shrine. In *Clues to the Past: Papers in Honor of William M. Sundt*, edited by Meliha S. Duran and David T. Kirkpatrick, pp. 239–257. Papers of the Archaeological Society of New Mexico 16. Archaeological Society of New Mexico, Albuquerque.

1992a *Rock Art in New Mexico*. Museum of New Mexico Press, Santa Fe, NM.

1992b Imagery and Magic: Petroglyphs at Comanche Gap, Galisteo Basin, New Mexico. In *Archaeology, Art, and Anthropology: Papers in Honor of J. J. Brody*, edited by Meliha S. Duran and David T. Kirkpatrick, pp. 157–174. Papers of the Archaeological Society of New Mexico 18. Archaeological Society of New Mexico, Albuquerque.

2000 *Warrior, Shield and Star: Imagery and Ideology of Pueblo Warfare*. Western Edge Press, Santa Fe.

Schaafsma, Polly, and Curtis F. Schaafsma

1974 Evidence for the Origins of the Pueblo Katchina Cult as Suggested by Southwestern Rock Art. *American Antiquity* 39(4): 535–545.

Schlanger, Sara H., and Richard H. Wilshusen

1993 Local Abandonment and Regional Conditions in the North American Southwest. In *Abandonment of Settlements and Regions,* edited by Catherine M. Cameron and Steve A. Tomka, pp. 85–98. Cambridge University Press, Cambridge.

Schmidt, Kari M.

2006 *Excavations at a Coalition Period Pueblo (LA 4618) on Mesita Del Buey, Los Alamos National Laboratory*. Los Alamos National Laboratory Cultural Resources Report 260, Survey No. 289. Los Alamos, New Mexico.

Schroeder, Albert H.

1979 Pueblos Abandoned in Historic Times. In *Southwest, edited by Alfonso Ortiz*, pp. 236–254. Handbook of North American Indians, Vol. 9, William C. Sturtevant, general editor. Smithsonian Institution, Washington, D.C.

Smiley, Terah L., Stanley A. Stubbs, and Bryant Bannister

1953 *A Foundation for the Dating of Some Late Archaeological Sites in the Rio Grande Area, New Mexico: Based on Studies in Tree-ring Methods and Pottery Analyses*. University of Arizona Bulletin 24(3), Laboratory of Tree-Ring Research Bulletin 6. Tucson.

Smith, Monica L.

2005 LA 359 (Burnt Corn Pueblo): Excavation Field Report. Submitted to the Bureau of Land Management, Northeast District, Taos, New Mexico. Manuscript in possession of the authors.

Snead, James E.

2001a *Ruins and Rivals: The Making of Southwest Archaeology*. University of Arizona Press, Tucson.

2001b Archaeological Survey in the Canada de la Cueva, Santa Fe County, New Mexico: Report of the 2000 Field Season. Submitted to the Bureau of Land Management, Northeast District, Taos, New Mexico. Manuscript in possession of the authors.

2004 Ancestral Pueblo Settlement Dynamics: Landscape, Scale, and Context in the Burnt Corn Community. *Kiva* 69(3): 243–269.

2005a Ancestral Pueblo Warfare and Migration in the Galisteo Basin, New Mexico: Report of the Tano Origins Project, 2004 Season. Submitted to the National Science Foundation, BCS No. 352702. Washington, D.C. Manuscript in possession of the authors.

2005b Archaeological Research at the Lodestar Sites, Santa Fe County, New Mexico. A Proposal for Data Collection Submitted to the Archaeological Conservancy, Albuquerque, NM May 31, 2005. Manuscript in possession of the authors.

2006 Ancestral Pueblo Warfare and Migration in the Galisteo Basin, New Mexico: Report of the Tano Origins Project, 2005 Season. Submitted to the National Science Foundation, BCS No. 352702. Washington, DC. Manuscript in possession of the authors.

2007 Cycles of Conflict in the Galisteo Basin. Paper presented at the New Mexico Archaeological Council Annual Symposium, Albuquerque.

2008a *Ancestral Landscapes of the Pueblo World*. University of Arizona Press, Tucson.

2008b History, Place, and Social Power in the Galisteo Basin, A.D. 1250–1325. In *The Social Construction of Communities in the Ancient Southwest,* edited by Mark Varien and Jim Potter, pp. 155–167. Altamira Books, Walnut Creek.

Snead, James E., Winifred Creamer, and Tineke Van Zandt

2004 'Ruins of our Forefathers': Large Sites and Site Clusters in the Northern Rio Grande. In *The Pueblo IV Period in the American Southwest*, edited by Charles Adams and Andrew Duff, pp. 26–34. The University of Arizona Press, Tucson.

Snead, James E., and Robert W. Preucel

1999 The Ideology of Settlement: Ancestral Keres Landscapes in the Northern Rio Grande. In *Archaeologies of Landscape: Contemporary Perspectives,*

Snead, James E., and Robert W. Preucel (*continued*)
    edited by Wendy Ashmore and Bernard Knapp,
    pp. 169–197. Blackwell, London.

Snow, David H.
    1974   *The Excavation of Saltbush Pueblo, Bandelier
        National Monument, 1971.* Laboratory of Anthro-
        pology Notes 75. Museum of New Mexico, Santa Fe.

Solometo, Julie
    2006   The Dimensions of War: Conflict and Culture
        Change in Central Arizona. In *Archaeological
        Perspectives on the Transformation of War*, edited
        by Elizabeth Arkush and Mark Allen, pp. 23–65.
        University Press of Florida, Gainesville.

Spielmann, Katherine A.
    1994   Clustered Confederacies: Sociopolitical Organiza-
        tion in the Protohistoric Rio Grande. *The Ancient
        Southwestern Community: Models and Meth-
        ods for the Study of Prehistoric Social Organiza-
        tion*, edited by W. H. Wills and Robert D. Leon-
        ard, pp. 45–54. University of New Mexico Press,
        Albuquerque.
    1996   Impressions of Pueblo III Settlement Trends
        among the Rio Abajo and Eastern Border Pueblos.
        In *The Prehistoric Pueblo World, A.D. 1150–1350*,
        edited by Michael A. Adler, pp. 177–187. Univer-
        sity of Arizona Press, Tucson.

Stallings, W. S., Jr.
    1937   Southwestern Dated Ruins: I. *Tree-Ring Bulletin*
        4(2): 3–5.

Steed, Paul P.
    1976   Rock art at La Cienega Mesa. *American Indian
        Rock Art* 3: 115–119.

Steen, Charlie R.
    1977   *Pajarito Plateau Archaeological Survey and
        Excavations.* Los Alamos Scientific Laboratory,
        Los Alamos.
    1980   LA 10607: The Manzanares Site. In *Collected
        Papers in Honor of Helen Greene Blumenschien*,
        edited by Albert H. Schroeder, pp. 129–140.
        Papers of the Archaeological Society of New
        Mexico 5. Archaeological Society of New Mexico,
        Albuquerque.

Stevanovic, Mirjana
    1997   The Age of Clay: The Social Dynamics of House
        Destruction. *Journal of Anthropological Archae-
        ology* 16(4): 334–395.

Stone, Tammy
    2001   Prehistoric Community Integration in the Point of
        Pines Region of Arizona. *Journal of Field Archae-
        ology* 27(2): 197–208.

Stubbs, Stanley A., and W. S. Stallings, Jr.
    1953   *Excavation of Pindi Pueblo, New Mexico.* Mono-
        graphs of the School of American Research and
        the Laboratory of Anthropology Number 18.
        Museum of New Mexico Press, Santa Fe.

Swanson, Steven
    2003   Documenting Prehistoric Communication Net-
        works: A Case Study in the Paquime Polity. *Amer-
        ican Antiquity* 68(4): 753–767.

Thomas, David Hurst
    2001   Excavations at Mission San Marcos, New Mexico,
        1998–2000. Copies available from Archaeologi-
        cal Records Management Section, New Mexico
        Historic Preservation Division, NMCRIS 75343,
        Santa Fe.

Tilley, Christopher
    1994   *A Phenomenology of Landscape.* Berg, Oxford.

Tobler, W.
    1993   *Three Presentations on Geographical Analysis
        and Modeling.* Technical Report 93–1. National
        Center for Geographic Information and Analysis,
        University of California, Santa Barbara.

Traylor, D. E., L. Hubbell, N. Wood, and B. Fiedler
    1990   *The 1977 La Mesa Fire Study: An Investigation
        of Fire and Fire Suppression Impact on Cul-
        tural Resources in Bandelier National Monu-
        ment.* Southwest Cultural Resources Center
        Professional Paper No. 28. Branch of Cultural
        Resources Management, Division of Anthro-
        pology, National Park Service, Santa Fe, New
        Mexico.

Turner, Christy G. II, and Jacqueline A. Turner
    1999   *Man Corn: Cannibalism and Violence in the Pre-
        historic American Southwest.* University of Utah
        Press, Salt Lake City.

Upham, Steadman, and Lori Stephens Reed
    1989   Regional Systems in the Central and North-
        ern Southwest: Demography, Economy, and
        Socio-politics Preceding Contact. *Columbian
        Consequences, Volume I: Archaeological and
        Historical Perspectives on the Spanish Bor-
        derlands West*, edited by David Hurst Thomas,
        pp. 57–76. Smithsonian Institution Press,
        Washington.

Van Zandt, Tineke
    1999   Architecture and Site Structure. In *The Bandelier
        Archaeological Survey*, edited by Robert P. Powers
        and Janet D. Orcutt, pp. 309–388. Intermountain
        Cultural Resources Management Professional
        Paper 57. Intermountain Region, National Park
        Service, Santa Fe.
    2006   *Shaping Stones, Shaping Pueblos: Architecture
        and Site Layout in Bandelier National Monument,
        A.D. 1150 to 1600.* Ph.D. dissertation, University
        of Michigan, Ann Arbor. University Microfilms,
        Ann Arbor.

Vencl, S.
1984 War and Warfare in Archaeology. *Journal of Anthropological Archaeology* 3: 116–132.

Vierra, Bradley J.
2002 Lithics. In *Excavations at a Coalition Period Pueblo (LA 4624) on Mesita del Buey, Los Alamos National Laboratory,* by Bradley J. Vierra, Jennifer E. Nisengard, Brian C. Harmon, Beverly M. Larson, Diane C. Curewitz, Kari M. Schmidt, Pamela J. McBride, Susan J. Smith, and Timothy L. Binzen. Cultural Resources Report No. 213. Los Alamos National Laboratory, Los Alamos, New Mexico.

Vierra, Bradley J., J. Nisengard, B. C. Harmon,
B. M. Larson, D. C. Curewitz, K. M. Schmidt,
P. J. McBride, S. J. Smith, and T. L. Binzen
2002 *Excavations at a Coalition Period Pueblo (LA 4624) on Mesita del Buey, Los Alamos National Laboratory.* Cultural Resources Report No. 213. Los Alamos National Laboratory, Los Alamos, New Mexico.

Wallace, Henry D., and William H. Doelle
2001 Classic Period Warfare in Southern Arizona. In *Deadly Landscapes: Case Studies in Prehistoric Southwestern Warfare,* edited by Glen E. Rice and Steven A. LeBlanc, pp. 239–287. The University of Utah Press, Salt Lake City.

Walker, William H., and Lisa J. Lucero
2000 The Depositional History of Ritual and Power. In *Agency and Archaeology,* edited by Marcia-Anne Dobres and John E. Robb, pp. 130–147. Routledge, London.

Walsh, Michael R.
1998 Lines in the Sand: Competition and Stone Selection on the Pajarito Plateau, New Mexico. *American Antiquity* 63(4): 573–593.

Warren, A. Helene
1971 Forked Lightning (LA 672): An Examination of the Tempering Materials of the B/W Sherds. Manuscript on file, Archaeological Records Management Section, New Mexico State Historic Preservation Office, Santa Fe.
1974 Notes on Santa Fe Black-on-white. *Pottery Southwest* 1(2): 5–6.
1979 The Glaze Paint Wares of the Upper Rio Grande. In *Archaeological Investigations in Cochiti Reservoir, New Mexico, V. 4: Adaptive Change in the Northern Rio Grande Valley,* edited by Jan V. Biella and Richard C. Chapman, pp. 187–217. Office of Contract Archaeology, Department of Anthropology, University of New Mexico

Warren, A. Helene, and Frances Joan Mathien
1985 Prehistoric and Historic Turquoise Mining in the Cerrillos District: Time and Place. In *Southwestern Culture History: Collected Papers in Honor of Albert H. Schroeder,* edited by Charles H. Lange, pp. 93–128. Papers of the Archaeological Society of New Mexico 10. Archaeological Society of New Mexico, Albuquerque.

Watson, Patty Jo, Steven A. LeBlanc, and Charles L. Redman
1980 Aspects of Zuni Prehistory: Preliminary Report on Excavations and Survey in the El Morro Valley of New Mexico. *Journal of Field Archaeology* 7: 210–218.

Webster, David
2000 The Not So Peaceful Civilization: A Review of Maya War. *Journal of World Prehistory* 14(1): 65–119.

Welch, John R., and Todd W. Bostwick (editors)
2001 *The Archaeology of Ancient Tactical Sites.* The Arizona Archaeologist 32. Arizona Archaeological Society, Phoenix.

Welker, Eden A.
1995 Pueblo San Marcos Pottery. In *Of Pots and Rocks: Papers in Honor of A. Helene Warren,* edited by Meliha S. Duran and David T. Kirkpatrick, pp. 175–187. Papers of the Archaeological Society of New Mexico 21. Archaeological Society of New Mexico, Albuquerque.

Wendorf, Fred, and Eric.K. Reed
1955 An Alternative Reconstruction of Northern Rio Grande Prehistory. *El Palacio* 62(5–6): 131–173.

White, Tim D.
1992 *Prehistoric Cannibalism at Mancos 5MTUMR-2346.* Princeton University Press, Princeton.

Whittlesey, Stephanie M.
1998 Archaeological Landscapes: A Methodological and Theoretical Discussion. In *Vanishing River: Landscapes and Lives of the Lower Verde Valley. The Lower Verde Valley Archaeological Project: Overview, Synthesis, and Conclusions,* edited by Stephanie M. Whittlesey, Richard Ciorek-Torello and Jeffrey H. Altschul, pp. 17–28. SRI Press, Tucson.

Wilcox, David R.
1979 Warfare Implications of Dry-laid Masonry Walls on Tumamoc Hill. *The Kiva* 45(1): 15–38.
1981 Changing Perspectives on the Protohistoric Pueblos, A.D. 1450–1700. In *The Protohistoric Period in the North American Southwest, A.D. 1450–1700,* edited by David R. Wilcox and Bruce Masse, pp. 378–409. Anthropological Research Paper 24. Arizona State University, Tempe.
1984 Multi-ethnic Division of Labor in the Protohistoric Southwest. In *Collected Papers in Honor of Harry L. Hadlock,* edited by Nancy Fox, pp. 141–156. Papers of the Archaeological Society of

Wilcox, David R. (*continued*)
New Mexico 9. Archaeological Society of New Mexico, Albuquerque.

1991   Changing Contexts of Pueblo Adaptations, A.D. 1250–1600. *Farmers, Hunters, and Colonists: Interaction Between the Southwest and the Southern Plains*, edited by Katherine A. Spielmann, pp. 128–154. University of Arizona Press, Tucson.

1996   Pueblo III People and Polity in Relational Context. In *The Prehistoric Pueblo World, A.D. 1150–1300*, edited by Michael A. Adler, pp. 241–254. University of Arizona Press, Tucson.

Wilcox, David R., and Jonathan Haas
1994   The Scream of the Butterfly: Competition and Conflict in the Prehistoric Southwest. In *Themes in Southwest Prehistory*, edited by George J. Gumerman, pp. 211–238. School of American Research Press, Santa Fe.

Wilcox, David R., David A. Gregory, J. Brett Hill, and Gary Funkhouser
2006   The Changing Contexts of Warfare in the North American Southwest, A.D. 1200–1700. In *Southwest Interludes: Papers in Honor of Charlotte J. and Theodore R. Frisbie*, edited by Regge Wiseman, Thomas C. O'Laughlin, and Cordelia Snow, pp. 203–232. Papers of the Archaeological Society of New Mexico 32. Archaeological Society of New Mexico, Albuquerque.

Wilcox, David R., and Jim Holmlund
2007   *The Archaeology of Perry Mesa and its World*. Bilby Research Center Occasional Papers No. 3. Northern Arizona University, Flagstaff.

Wilcox, David R., Gerald Robertson Jr., and J. Scott Wood
2001   Organized for War: The Perry Mesa Settlement System and Its Central Arizona Neighbors. In *Deadly Landscapes: Case Studies in Prehistoric Southwestern Warfare*, edited by Glen E. Rice and Steven A. LeBlanc, pp. 141–194. University of Utah Press, Salt Lake City.

Willey, Gordon R.
1953   *Prehistoric Settlement Patterns in the Viru Valley, Peru*. Bureau of American Ethnology Bulletin 155, Smithsonian Institution. U.S. Government Printing Office, Washington, D.C.

Wilshusen, Richard H.
1986   The Relationship between Abandonment Mode and Ritual Use in the Pueblo I Anasazi Protokiva. *Journal of Field Archaeology* 13: 245–254.

Wilson, C. Dean
2008a   Ceramic Analysis for the Land Conveyance and Transfer Project, Los Alamos National Laboratory. In *The Land Conveyance and Transfer Data Recovery Project: 7000 Years of Land Use on the Pajarito Plateau*, edited by Bradley J. Vierra and Kari Schmidt, pp. 125–255. Cultural Resources Report 23. Los Alamos National Laboratory, Los Alamos, New Mexico.

2008b   Examination of Trends for Galisteo Black-on-white. In *Chasing Chaco and the Southwest: Papers in Honor of Frances Joan Mathien*, edited by Thomas C. O'Laughlin, Regge N. Wiseman, Cordelia T. Snow, and Cathy Travis, pp. 207–215. Papers of the Archaeological Society of New Mexico 34. Archaeological Society of New Mexico, Albuquerque.

Wilson, Gordon P.
2007   *Guide to Ceramic Identification: Northern Rio Grande Valley and Galisteo Basin to AD 1700*. 2nd ed. Laboratory of Anthropology, Technical Series, Bulletin 12. Museum of New Mexico, Santa Fe.

Windes, Thomas C.
2002   Appendix E: 1,100 Years of Construction Wood Use in the Upper Pecos Valley. In *From Folsom to Fogelson: The Cultural Resources Inventory Survey of Pecos National Historical Park*, edited by Genevieve N. Head and Janet D. Orcutt, pp. 501–644. Intermountain Cultural Resources Management Professional Paper 66. National Park Service. Santa Fe.

Wiseman, Regge N.
1999   Tracking the Traffic: Plains Artifacts from a 13th-Century Pueblo near Santa Fe, New Mexico. In *La Frontera: Papers in Honor of Patrick H. Beckett*, edited by Meliha S. Duran and Dave Kirkpatrick, pp. 231–240. Archaeological Society of New Mexico Publication 25. Archaeological Society of New Mexico, Albuquerque.

2004   Old Data, New Possibilities: Exploring Activity Synchrony among Late Prehistoric Villages in the Galisteo Basin of North-Central New Mexico. In *Ever Westward: Papers in Honor of Elizabeth Kelley*, edited by Regge N. Wiseman, Thomas C. O'Laughlin, and Cordelia T. Snow, pp. 159–165. Papers of the Archaeological Society of New Mexico 30. Archaeological Society of New Mexico, Albuquerque.

Wiseman Regge N., and J. Andrew Darling
1986   The Bronze Trail Site Group: More Evidence for a Cerrillos-Chaco Turquoise Connection. In *By Hands Unknown: Papers on Rock Art and Archaeology in Honor of James Bain*, edited by Anne Poore, pp. 115–143. Papers of the Archaeological Society of New Mexico 12. Archaeological Society of New Mexico, Albuquerque.

Woodbury, Richard
  1959   A Reconsideration of Pueblo Warfare in the South-
          western United States. *Actas del XXXIII Congreso
          Internacional de Americanistas*, vol. 21: 124–133.
          Editorial Lehmann, Costa Rica.
Worman, Frederick C. V.
  1959   1957 Archaeological Salvage Excavations at Los
          Alamos, New Mexico: A Preliminary Report. *El
          Palacio* 66(1): 10–15.
Young, M. Jane
  1988   *Signs From the Ancestors: Zuni Cultural*

Symbolism and Perceptions of Rock Art. University of New Mexico Press, Albuquerque.
Zimmerman, L. J., and R. G. Whitten
  1980   Prehistoric Bones Tell a Grim Tale of Indian v.
          Indian. *Smithsonian Magazine* September, pp.
          100–107.
Zuckerman, Sharon
  2007   Anatomy of a Destruction: Crisis Architecture,
          Termination Rituals and the Fall of Canaanite
          Hazor. *Journal of Mediterranean Archaeology*
          20(1): 3–32.

Index

Abstract

The Galisteo Basin of northern New Mexico is one of the most celebrated archaeological districts of the American Southwest. A region only 300 square kilometers in size contains the remains of several large villages of the late Precolumbian era set within an intricate ancestral Pueblo landscape marked by petroglyphs, agricultural fields, and farmsteads. One of the most distinctive aspects of Galisteo Basin settlement is that it largely began in the thirteenth century A.D., an era of turmoil and population movement in the Southwest in general. Thus it has long been seen as an ideal place to study issues of central importance to the archaeology of the Pueblo people, in particular migration and conflict.

Burnt Corn Pueblo, a community founded in the western Galisteo Basin in the A.D. 1280s, provides a window into this critical time. Among the particularly compelling aspects of this settlement is evidence that it was occupied for less than a generation, entirely destroyed by fire, and never substantively reoccupied. Of limited accessibility and relatively remote from the more famous and later Galisteo Pueblos, the large residential site of Burnt Corn Pueblo and its surrounding landscape have received limited archaeological attention.

The Tano Origins Project is a research effort focused on Burnt Corn Pueblo and its surroundings in an effort to better understand the dynamics of conflict and population movement in the thirteenth-century Southwest. Support from the National Science Foundation, Bureau of Land Management, Santa Fe County, the Archaeological Conservancy and many local partners allowed for five field seasons between 2000 and 2006. Investigation of several locations in the vicinity of Burnt Corn Pueblo, including the Lodestar Sites and Petroglyph Hill, were incorporated into the study. Excavation, survey and laboratory analysis provided substantial empirical information to address migration and conflict, and to establish the most detailed characterization of an archaeological landscape in the Galisteo Basin to date.

Our results indicate that the Galisteo Basin in the late thirteenth century was a competitive environment. Settlers built communities with an eye towards assuring access to farmland while maintaining vigilance against threats. Considerable effort was employed to root local

Resumen

La Cuenca Galisteo del norte de Nuevo México es unos de los más celebrados distritos arqueológicos del suroeste Americano (American Southwest). Una región de un tamaño de tan solo 300 km contiene los restos de bastantes sitios grandes de la época del precolombiano tardío situados dentro de un paisaje Pueblo ancestral complejo marcado con petroglifos, campos de agricultura y alquerías. Uno de los más distintos aspectos de poblado de la Cuenca Galisteo es que comenzaron en gran medida en siglo XIII A.D., [que] en general fue una época de tumulto y movimiento de población en el Suroeste. En consecuencia, por un largo tiempo se ha considerado un lugar ideal para la investigación de temas de importancia central para la arqueología de la gente Pueblo, en particular [los temas de] conflicto y migración.

El sitio llamado Pueblo de Maíz Quemado (Burnt Corn Pueblo), una comunidad establecida en la área occidental de la Cuenca Galisteo en los A.D. 1280s, proporciona una ventana en este periodo critico. Entre uno de los convincentes aspectos de este poblado es la evidencia que fue habitado por menos de una generación, destruido enteramente con fuego y nunca reocupado sustantivamente. Con limitada accesibilidad y relativamente remota del mas famoso y los tardíos pueblos Galisteo, el grande sitio residencial de Burnt Corn Pueblo y paisaje a su alrededor han recibido limitada atención arqueológica.

El Proyecto Orígenes de los Tano (Tano Origins Project) es un esfuerzo de investigación enfocado en Burnt Corn Pueblo y sus alredededores con la meta de obtener mejor conocimiento de las dinámicas de conflicto y movimiento de población en el siglo XIII del Suroeste. Apoyo departe de la Fundación Nacional de Ciencias (National Science Foundation), la agencia de administración de tierra (Bureau of Land Management), el condado de Santa Fe, la conservación de arqueología (Archaeological Conservancy) y muchos socios locales permitidos por cinco temporadas entre [los años] 2000 y 2006. Las investigaciones de varios sitios en los contornos de Burnt Corn Pueblo, incluyendo los sitios Lodestar y Petroglyph Hill, fueron incorporados al estudio. Excavación, recorrido de superficie y análisis de laboratorio roveyeron sustantiva información empírica para dirigirse al tema de migración y conflicto, y para establecer

identity into a landscape through the use of shrines, petroglyphs and related markers that reflect competitive conditions. At Burnt Corn Pueblo such efforts were ultimately unsuccessful, and the village was destroyed in an episode of violence. Even in this competitive context, however, considerable effort was expended to establish social ties that were maintained between communities at a large scale. This produced a web of relationships that spanned the Galisteo Basin and beyond.

la suma caracterización detallada de un paisaje arqueológico en la Cuenca Galisteo hasta la fecha.

Nuestros resultados indican que en el siglo XIII tardío la Cuenca Galisteo fue un medioambiente competitivo. Pobladores establecieron comunidades con la intención de asegurar acceso a tierras de cultivo mientras que mantenían vigilancia contra amenazas. Considerable esfuerzo fue empleado para fijar identidad local dentro de un paisaje por medio del uso de altares, petroglifos y marcadores relacionados que reflejan condiciones competitivas. En Burnt Corn Pueblo tales esfuerzos fueron ultimadamente infructuosos, y la aldea fue destruida en un episodio de violencia. Hasta en este contexto competitivo, [un] esfuerzo considerable fue expendido para establecer lazos que fueron mantenidos entre comunidades a una grande escala. Esto produjo una red de relaciones que alcanzaron la Cuenca Galisteo y más allá.

ANTHROPOLOGICAL PAPERS OF THE UNIVERSITY OF ARIZONA

Anthropological Papers listed as O.P., D are available as Docutech reproductions (high quality xerox) printed on demand. They are tape or spiral bound and nonreturnable.